Fatherless

by

A.M. Andino Rochon

Available at Amazon.com. Contact the author at a.m.rochon@aol.com to request that Fatherless be made available through your favorite bookstore, organization, library or other group.

Table of Contents: FATHERLESS

Chapter 1

Call Your Cousin

The Fourth of July 2007

I sure wasn't thinking about the murderer in the family when our phone rang.

Born fatherless in 1912, haunted by the memory of hunger, Angelo M. Andino became a man of means. He sheltered a killer in his youth but built a church in adulthood. Ordered out of his Youngstown, Ohio city, our village of Algonac, Michigan embraced him. His death made us fatherless children, rejected by his family.

The back door banged behind Marc, our astonished son. He ran toward me and thrust the phone into my hand.

By answering our telephone, Marc became the first to hear the message soon to take all of us by surprise. Marc came outdoors, holding the telephone as if cradling the caller gently, recognizing her contact as a fragile gift. As I took the phone it was obvious that he knew something that I was about to learn.

All I said was "hello" and she replied in a rush.

She said that speaking with my son had convinced her that she had the right phone number for Angela Andino of Algonac. She'd identified herself as Cousin Sandy from my father's family. She explained to Marc that her father was my Godfather. Sandy said that she was calling to right the wrong. She wanted to make it clear how shocked she was to learn that our family had rejected me. Sandy feared I might refuse to talk to her.

"Angela, you're probably really angry with me, my dad, and our aunt Lizzie. You've got to be disgusted with our family. I'd understand why. I wouldn't blame you one bit. I'd be furious. You probably don't ever want to hear from any of us again. Please don't hang up. Just let me apologize for all of us here in Youngstown."

In the mere moments of this exchange, her voice took me to my past. It had been such a long time since anyone had called me by my birth name. And there was something else. Stunned into silent attention, I attempted to sort out this sensation.

There it was…the key that cleared up my confusion! What came to me through my cousin's voice was Dad's—Youngstown, the cadence, the timber, the intonation of my late father's voice. In the same regional Ohio inflection, Dad whispered his arrival by telephone.

Certainly, her voice was memorable; she was family! But I excused myself for being disoriented. The last time we talked she was fourteen and I was fifteen. My dad died shortly after, and that was 1962.

A lifetime of politeness gave me a pattern to follow when confusion had me in its grip. I had never hung up on anyone. The thought never crossed my muddled mind.

"Sandy! It's really you? Why would I be angry with you? Gee whiz! I'm so happy to hear your voice. Just stay with me. I'm walking over where I'll hear you better. Let's hope this phone doesn't conk out."

Scant minutes before, I was grounded in the present, delighted to be with the children. The sudden sound of the phone ringing and the voice inflection of Youngstown transported me to the past. Talking with Sandy and walking away from the sounds of my grandchildren at play I headed for the quiet street corner of our front yard. And yet, part of me recognized that the children became quiet on their own. No one told them to stop running amok. Had they sensed that something significant was happening? Maybe some of them had noticed their daddy's tears. When I saw him, I too began to cry. How often had I seen my adult son tear up?

Marc was coming to the corner with a lawn chair for me, his brown eyes glistening despite his wide smile. Our identical eyes locked, matching the exact hue and pigment of my father's eyes as well.

5

"Oh, Angela, thank God you're not mad at me! If your phone crashes, I'll call right back. Oh boy! Oh boy! I'm seeing you walking to the corner of your family's home. I'm remembering all the fun vacations on that little corner of Fruit and Michigan Street in your pretty village."

"Sandy, my childhood home is gone now." I informed my cousin that it was razed when our village decided to destroy the old and build new. Urban Renewal was the plan. I told her that mine is now another house on a corner a mile north of the home that she remembered.

"So sorry to hear your beautiful home is gone. We all loved your house. Remember when our dads and our Uncle Pat poured the concrete steps? We'd walk up these steps, knock on your door, and wait on the wide porch. I see the huge door right now. I remember the heavy oak with its brass knocker."

It felt good that she loved my childhood home. I'm glad she remembered it well. But her voice sounded pressured. She already said she was nervous and worried about how I would respond. Therefore, I knew I must be patient. Surely, she would get to her message soon.

As Sandy rattled on, I half listened, eager to know why she called. It certainly would not be to exchange pleasantries, not after forty-some years had passed. My mind drifted.

To come to calmness, I straightened my spine and took a big breath. I rolled my skinny shoulders, hearing my body's clicks. With that, I blew away like a feather gliding into a strange scene in which I was both the star and the observer. I heard the soft score of a movie. The opening shot showed me walking briskly, far faster than any famous athlete. I was traveling by foot from Michigan to Ohio; walking Interstate 94 with ever increasing speed. It felt odd to sprint past autos but, to my amazement, each frame became even stranger; each car appeared shiny and new, but the autos became early models followed by even earlier models. I was trotting back in time. Interstate 94 dissolved at one point leaving me to run on the country roads my parents drove before the interstate system began construction in 1962. I watched myself grow younger as I traversed the present to speed walk into the past.

Spanning to show the whole picture I saw my starting point, that being my yard in my small town, and I saw my destination, the big city home of my father's birth. My teenaged dad, his mom, and his half brothers and sisters were at the finish line cheering as I approached. The soft music score faded, and I heard the familiar voice that was increasingly clear. It was Cousin Sandy still describing my old house on the phone.

"Once inside your beautiful home we'd hang our coats in the vestibule. Then we'd open a French door that led to the front hall. To the side of the hall snaked the polished wood banister for the staircase that took us to your bedrooms upstairs. There were two more French doors that led to the living room on the right and the formal dining room on the left. From the dining room was the swinging door into the kitchen. Your dining room was special because of the dark wood tea cup rack high up on every wall. Your mom's bone China tea cups were on display."

"You're taking me back in time, Sandy. I'm enjoying the trip."

But I was just being polite. In truth, I was flummoxed by all the time tripping.

Because I was confounded by her call, my thoughts returned to the present. It was the Fourth of July 2007. The summer sun warmed us and smiled on our grandchildren's curls. The little ones ran, stumbled, and giggled in the yard where their parents once played. Watching in wonder, I saw generations in each small face.

Before Sandy phoned I was barefoot at our backyard clothesline. I drip dried in the sunshine, rivulets running from my bathing suit. I hung towels and swimwear, a succession of sizes covering my entire family, convinced I could never be happier. Our clothesline stretched between our backyard oaks. I marveled as our grandchildren stuck their tiny noses through the chain links forming the fence we share with the good folks next door. I smiled when I heard the little ones softly call the names of the big dogs who roamed our neighbor's yard. The children loved the neighbor's gentle giants.

Elastic. That is one word which describes our house. When we brought each baby home three years in succession, this little house hugged them, wrapping three small cribs in warmth and shelter. As our children grew, so did our home, making room for their playmates as well. When our last child left, our house seemed to shrink, creating a snug shelter for my husband and me. We cleared out clutter, making room for the people we love and the objects we enjoy. Now when our children come home with their children our house stretches wide in welcome. The walls do not shift. We fill every corner including the green niches outdoors.

Again, my cousin drew me to the past. Sandy was still describing my old home.

And then I heard her deep sigh.

"You need to know the reason for my call. Our dad had a heart attack last month. From his hospital bed he asked my sister, our brother, and me to go through his desk for his insurance documents. In doing so we found the letter you sent him. He'd attached a copy he made of the horrible note he wrote you in reply along with a copy of his sister Lizzie's scathing letter rebuffing you. Our mutual Aunt Lizzie brutally rejected you. She wrote, 'You are no longer an Andino.' What gave her the right to decide?

"When we showed him your letter and their replies Dad looked very sad. We feel that he was very ashamed. He knew that he couldn't take back what he did to you. In his heart, he knew that he disgraced himself by dishonoring his oldest brother's daughter. You reached out and he cast you out. Dad often told us how much he loved your father. As we grew up he repeated the story of how his oldest brother once saved his life."

Sandy and I talked a bit about the time my dad insisted that their impoverished mother take his youngest half-brother to the doctor. Father paid the bill with his savings as a paper boy.

Then she returned to the subject of her call. "Our dad shocked us again and again. First there was our discovery of your beautiful letter and then Dad's terse note and then the heinous letter Dad knew that our Aunt Lizzie sent you. Then, for the first time, we saw him cry. We waited in silence. Dad was inconsolable. We had only seen Father as the strong, fit, retired big city fireman who never expressed his emotions.

"Finally, my brother, Patsy, softly stated that he, our sister, or I would soon call you. Pat said that when dad recovered and came home from the hospital he would visit you.

"'No, I won't be coming home,' Dad said. He was right.

"Patsy took us into the hospice room hallway. He said, 'We know Dad is dying. We should wait until it's all over, the funeral and the family hysterics that always follow. We know that Angela would come, and Aunt Lizzie would reject her, in person this time.'

"And that's why I'm calling you, Angela. That's why we are doing what our father would want us to do. We know he'd want us to call you. You need to know that he was very sorry."

At this point the tears were streaming down my face. I was grateful for the chair our son brought. I felt weak with joy, drained by emotion.

Through blurry eyes I glanced at our picture window that faced the street where I sat. My husband's big smile shone through the glass. Our adult children stood beside their father. They were crying and somehow smiling too. The little ones were still, eyes fixed on their parents. Curious? Bewildered?

When my next-in-line-of-age cousin finally had no more to say, she closed with a promise. Others would soon contact me. I am their oldest cousin. What I didn't know then was that cousin Pat would tell me all about killer in our family. Patsy would be the first to visit me.

The now silent telephone still seemed like a magical instrument. Like my son earlier, I cradled it tenderly.

Again, I looked at our large window. It had become a living picture, framed and mounted on the front of our home. For a fleeting moment, I saw another among them, a man nearly fifty years old when I last saw him smile forty-five years ago. His was the familiar face that I love but his expression was one I had never witnessed. Now his joy was otherworldly. No one seemed to notice him slipping silently among my other family members. I reminded myself that none of them had ever met him. I loved him in life until he died in my childhood. Because I longed for him all the days of my adult life, I sensed that my face now mirrored Father's peace.

All of us were happy. Even the children seemed content. But Father and I were the most elated. The last time I sensed this ecstatic connection with Dad was when our son named his newborn Andino.

Chapter 2

How Andino Got His Name

In every school he has attended, in every sport in which he participated, in all the locations his family travels have taken, in short, in all the thirteen years of his life, our grandson Andino Rochon has never met another person with his first name. To address any confusion that this unusual name might bring we told him, early on, that he was named after his great-grandfather.

This explanation, while concise, is not entirely accurate. In fact, his maternal great-grandfather's first name was Angelo. His last name was Andino, which was the last name of his stepfather. This is not exactly correct either. It is so confusing.

Is that why we have failed to tell Andino the full story of his name? Families give us the gifts of our names. Our names help define us. Doesn't Andino deserve the whole, long, convoluted, tempestuous tale?

At the time when Christians almost universally gave saints' names to their infants, family often educated their children in the lives of the saints. Growing up, some took on the saint whose names they shared as their role models.

Saints are, after all, imperfect human beings. Unlike the rest of us, saints are people who attained religious perfection. Perhaps one reason I left nursing school and became a teacher was because I studied the life of Saint Angela de Merici. She rejected nursing and founded what became the first teaching order of women. Of course, my theory breaks down when I left teaching to become a clinical therapist. Later I became an Emergency Center Behavioral Health specialist in a hospital with a psychiatric inpatient floor. The point is that our son deviated from our family's pattern of choosing names of saints.

Why did we simply tell Andino he was my father's namesake when the whole truth is complex? Perhaps we withheld the details because it is such a sad story. Maybe we considered the explanation too long. Certainly the story is gut-wrenching in light of lost opportunities. Family, over so many years in multigenerational circumstances, could have done the right thing. Instead the consistent choice was contention over compassion, rejection over rejoicing, isolation over embracing.

Without exaggeration, I report one hundred years of family conflict. A family member became a murderer. Andino's birth marks the beginning of thirteen years of peace.

15

My father's mother is dead. His father died before his birth. His stepfather was killed during Father's youth. Most of his siblings and all their spouses are dead. His wife (my mother) died. In Mom's family, her contemporaries have memory loss challenges. Now only my sister, Camille, and I are left to bear witness. I am the oldest. She was thirteen when Father suddenly died.

Now it's time to tell our grandson how he got his name. Andino deserves to know. He's old enough to understand the history of his unique name. Then again, I don't really understand my family history. How could so many relatives over so many years cause so much pain? On the other hand, by naming their son Andino, his parents began the long overdue process of family healing. Do they know how much they gave with the precious gift of their firstborn's name?

When he went into the Navy during World War II, my father learned some shocking news. He'd been called Angelo M. Andino all his life. Now he discovered that this was not his name. He knew he was the son of his mother's first marriage, but he learned that the only father figure he'd known had not adopted him. The military insisted that his induction papers reflect his birth name or that he legally change his name.

Andino was the name that identified him. It appeared on his high school diploma, social security card, life insurance, etc. As a young man soon to ship off, he did the expedient thing. Time was off the essence. He legally changed his name to the one he always thought was his. In this way he avoided the name changes required on his lifetime of paperwork.

It must have been a traumatic time for Father as he prepared to leave the only city he'd ever known, to face whatever wartime would require. Sadly, the name associated began an unresolved family feud.

Conflict connected to the Andino name when my parents were a few years married. They traveled from Michigan to Ohio to visit Father's family, bringing me, their baby, Angela M. Andino. After a lovely visit with his mother and half siblings my parents decided to look up the Marcheoma name in the telephone book of the same city. The Marcheoma family, surprised and delighted, immediately invited us to their home.

Years later my parents described this visit as a joyful reunion with the family of his birth father. There'd been no contact with the Marcheomas following the funeral of my pregnant grandmother's first husband. All were overjoyed to meet Father and his family. The Marcheomas

17

spoke lovingly of Dad's long deceased father. They regaled Dad with stories of the father he never knew.

Their long visit ended, everyone resolved to visit each other often and make up for the lost years. They asked for the information with which to keep in contact. Mother wrote our names, address and phone number. Upon reading the requested information the Marcheomas flew into a rage.

They saw the name Andino.

Dad's uncle said, "What happened to the Marcheoma name? Why are you an Andino now? You changed your name and dishonored our family."

The Marcheomas withdrew their welcome. My parents made many attempts to connect with the Marcheomas. They were ignored.

Today I talked to my father.

"Dad," I said, "your father's parents really hurt you."

At first, he just sighed.

"I felt awful at first. Then I tried to see their side of it. They were the ones who lost the man I never got to know. They knew I wouldn't keep his family name alive in my children.

"And then there's the fact that they immigrated from Calabria, the 'toe' of the Italian 'boot.' Theirs was one of the poorest areas of Italy. Mountainous. The soil was eroded. Just think, honey, they were peasants, tenant farmers. They were at the mercy of the rich who had large, landed estates. My father and his people made it to America. They came with nothing but their names. How could they accept that I'd given up their name?"

"Ya, but Mom thought they should've been kind to you out of respect for your father."

Dad laughed mirthlessly.

"Your mother didn't grow up among Calabrians. I did. They're contentious. It was a rough neighborhood and they were the toughest of all. We called 'em 'hard heads' and they were proud of the name. Guys were vengeful. There were blood feuds even among the boys in my high school.

"And, thinking about my ancestors, I know that only the strong survived. It's one thing to be dirt poor. It's another to be isolated. Calabria is one of the few areas of southern Italy where Italians are in the minority. Albanians settled there. My Marcheoma grandparents' elders no doubt remembered Guiseppe Garibaldi's 1860 expedition. That's when Calabria became part of Italy."

Dad's family stayed in our Algonac home for weeks each summer of my childhood. We crossed Ohio's rural

19

routes each year to stay with Grandmother Julia and celebrate Easter with Dad's large, extended family. Travel was taxing. In 1962 our interstate highway system was under construction. Dad predicted it would open our world. It did just that, but not in time for him to see it.

In addition to the traditional summer vacations and Easter celebrations our Ohio and Michigan families spent together, we shared special occasions such as family baptisms, first communions, and weddings. There was also the fact that Grandma Julia lived with us for approximately six months of every year. After Father's funeral, Cam and I never saw Grandmother again.

The last and most vivid image I have of Grandma Julia is bizarre. She suddenly began dancing at the funeral parlor. Stunned silence ensued as all of us stared at this little, gray haired, black clad Italian. Lifting her long skirts above her tiny feet, she danced the tarantella. Her whole life marked by sudden sorrow, she was again deep in grief. My heart broke to see her so. Many years later I was to learn that she was never the same after Father died. She died a few years after his death.

This is a long and complicated chronicle.

One might think that families who ignore their grieving relatives have a history of rare contact. This was not true of Mom's selfish, cruel relative who declared at Dad's death scene his refusal of money. No one had even asked for his money! This wealthy relative lived out his long life in the same small town in which we lived. We were often in his company.

Rejection appeared regularly in my father's short life. It dominated when Father died. A relative arrived at our home after the doctor left and the undertaker was pulling away. In his immigrant English, he was among the few to call Mother by her given name. Many called her Vera. In front of the rest of our family, he said, "Venera, be strong. Take care of yourself and your daughters. Do not ask me for money. You should not have married a man ten years older than you."

Abandonment from Father's family took only slightly longer. His mother and half siblings came from Ohio for Dad's funeral and drove back home. With one exception, this was their last visit. My Godfather came for my high school graduation, six months after Father's death. I never saw my Godfather again. Dad's family never acknowledged invitations to Cam's graduation and to our weddings. I was sad. We were never invited to Father's family's occasions.

Seven years after Dad died, a relative was driving Mom to visit her New York City relatives and stopped to visit one of my uncles in nearby Youngstown, Ohio. She said she yelled at him, describing our whole family's shock of losing Dad and then his entire family.

She said, "You used to drive your mother to Algonac each year and come pick her up months later. We put you up. We took you fishing. I cooked for you. We entertained your children."

"Of course, I remember your hospitality," said my uncle. "We have missed seeing all of you."

Together they all acknowledged the long-ago losses, pledging to get together and renew the family bonds.

When she told me she'd upbraided my uncle, I asked myself why she thought I'd be as refreshed as she was by venting her feelings. I suspected that she'd closed the door on Dad's family without thinking that her sense of satisfaction might mean I'd never see them again. What about me? I was young and still lived at home. I held back out of respect for my mother.

Just as I'd feared, she and my uncle never reunited our family.

Fourteen years ago, longing for contact with my lost cousins, I wrote my Godfather. Now a grandmother myself, I reflected on the great times I shared with my many cousins in Grandma Julia's home. I was curious about my long-ago playmates.

Although I didn't mention it, I felt fear as well as curiosity. What if my cousins were criminals or addicts or dead? I am the oldest. I well remember those closest in age to me. They were decent young people born to working class parents, just as I was. But Dad and all their parents were raised in abject poverty in a rough urban neighborhood. Had all my relatives raised law abiding children? Did they still live in this near lawless environment?

Filling a large manila envelope with photos of my husband and me, our children, and our grandchild, I inserted my heartfelt letter. I expressed my confidence that surely, we could share our family stories after all these lost years. Within days I received a response.

I recall my excitement when this stuffed envelope arrived. I see myself in the chair by the picture window where I opened the letter, eager for photos of my dad's family. I loved my cousins and missed them. I felt a dull ache in my heart when I slowly realized that my uncle had simply returned my own photos. His response was terse. "Do not contact me again."

Sharing my disappointment with Mother I expected her support. Instead I got her ire. Rather than mellowing with age, I witnessed her pent-up anger. The long-ago disappointment she felt in her husband's people had festered into a pernicious infection. Eyes ablaze she directed the purulence at me. Mother reinjured me, tearing open my own wounds from Dad's death and family abandonment. She didn't care that I'd lost my cousins. Now she was elderly and ill. I had my hands full just trying to convince her to follow doctor's orders.

Finding neither my mother nor my Godfather open to my reconciliatory gesture I wrote to Father's oldest sister, Lizzie. Again, I enclosed my family photos. Again, I received a quick response and another stuffed envelope. This time my eagerness was somewhat tempered by experience. I was cautiously hopeful. Sadly, the only photos I received were my own, returned.

Aunt Lizzie wrote a letter unlike anything I'd ever read before or since. She sent her eldest brother's oldest daughter a heinous message. In her handwriting reminiscent of calligraphy, she clearly and coldly stated that I'm not a member of her family. She said that I'm not an Andino.

She declared, "Now and forever I have no interest in you or in your family. I return your album photos without wasting time to look at them. Do you understand?"

Aunt Lizzie never actually spoke to me. If she had, what I would've wanted to say to her was, "Yes, I understand. I know that you are using the name Andino as a weapon to hurt me."

She and I belonged to the same family. That fact seemed to have escaped her. She sent an incomprehensible response to my heartfelt outreach. While I'd like to report that I shrugged off this maniacal venom, I must admit that I did not. Instead, I let her hurt me. I cried long and hard. In fact, I sobbed.

Aunt Lizzie's letter arrived when we were planning our oldest daughter's wedding. Our son, younger daughter and their spouses met us, along with our oldest daughter and her fiancé, at the hotel where the wedding reception was to be held. We tasted the dishes to be served at the reception.

These details complete, we relaxed in each other's welcome company. Our wonderful, only daughter-in-law was pregnant. We celebrated the upcoming birth. Then our son looked long and hard at me and asked, "Are you okay, Mom? You seem a little sad."

Instantly, I burst into tears. Then I read aloud my Godfather's terse note and Aunt Lizzie's scathing letter. Embarrassed by my racking sobs, pressing my eyelids to dam the flow of tears, I tried without success to compose myself in front of our astonished children. They had seldom seen me cry. They had never heard me sob. In calm, measured tones our son said, "It is not possible for your aunt to banish you from the family. You are family. You are blood. With her words, she cannot change the fact that you are an Andino."

Locking his eyes with mine and listening intently, I wanted to say that technically neither I nor my late father were Andinos. We had the Marcheoma bloodline. But this was an emotional issue, not a technical one. Then I slowly realized that her letter did not matter at all. Her vicious words were not rational. Nor was it in her power to define who I am. What made her think that she could? I had reached out. She had rejected. This was about her, not about me.

The logic in our son's words, the love in his voice eased my pain. I realized I had the love I needed from those who've always loved me unconditionally. I never cried again over these long-ago injuries. However, I did wonder about my intense response to the irrational rejections by my Godfather and Aunt Lizzie. Eventually I recognized that I still struggled with unresolved grief.

Having recognized the problem, I put my early family issues behind me. I stopped looking to some older members of my family for the love they would not give. At that pre- wedding dinner I began concentrating on the fine husband and wonderful family I have today. I counted myself fortunate in my sister Camille's family. In turn, she is blessed in mine.

Perhaps it was at that dinner when Marc and his wife, Mindy, began to consider naming their first-born baby Andino. I don't know. But I do know how Andino got his name. He was not named for my father, who was a man my husband and children never met. Our son and daughter-in-law named him Andino out of love for me.

Although Mother died shortly before Andino was born, she experienced the joy of knowing that he would be named Andino.

This long, sad story had a happy ending. The fact is, there is no end to the happiness. From the trauma of written rejection came the joy of a gift in the form of a name. Our family has a living, breathing, loving boy named Andino.

27

Our son and daughter-in-law countered contempt with compassion for my pain. They gave me a gift of love in the form of the beautiful name of our first grandson. They made sure there would always be an Andino in our family.

Now I realize that I should have taken my father's long view of this sorry situation. Today I imagine our thoughtful conversation.

"You know, Dad, your oldest sister and your youngest brother rejected me when I reached out to them. They really hurt me."

"I know, honey. Families should be gentle with each other. But remember, my dad's people were tough Calabrians. One, they were outsiders in their own country. * And two, my mother and step father immigrated from Abruzzi, where their people were shepherds with mountain pastures. ** They also raised pigs. Maybe we shouldn't expect a great deal of sensitivity."

Dad's twinkling eyes and his gentle laughter would meld with my guffaws.

*Albanians invaded Calabria, an area of 5,823 square miles. Albanians fled the Turkish conquest of their homeland in the 15th and 16th centuries, settled there, becoming the majority of the population. They retained their use of the Albanian language, the Greek Orthodox rite in their churches, and, on occasion, their colorful national costumes. https://www.britannica.com/place/Calabria-region-Italy.

**Abrussi (also called Abruzzo) fronts the Adriatic Sea. Their homeland varies from hilly to mountainous. The Apennines now, as then, dominate the region, three mountain chains trending northwest-southeast. There are a few small coastal harbors, but they have little economic importance for fishing or commerce.

Abruzzi's rugged terrain hindered its economic development then and it continues as a permanent impediment to prosperity. Agriculture is important, but only locally. Wheat, grapes, fruit, and olives are the most widespread crops. Tobacco, sugar beets, and saffron represent the meager cash crops. Livestock has always been the mainstay of the region. In 2006, an area of 4,168 square miles housed a population of 1,305,307.

Source https://www.britannica.com/place/Abruzzi

Chapter 3

I Alone Can Tell

At the funeral of my elderly friend, Doris, I contemplated making public my private musings on fatherlessness. I sat quietly in the place of worship that is so special to our family. I was married in the same parish in which my father and mother, all her siblings, all our children, my sibling, and my husband's siblings were wed. Grandchildren were baptized here. Grandchildren might choose this church when they marry. Dad chaired the building committee, raising funds to replace the tiny, white, wooden chapel in our Algonac village with this modern church, the newest in our City of Algonac to this day.

Thick, white, smoky incense assaulted my nose, lungs, and gut making me lightheaded and queasy. The pungent smell and Requiem hymns took me back to my youth when I last sang in Latin. The long-ago liturgy and the familiar patterns and colors of the priests' vestments swept me out of the everyday. A sobering thought snapped me from further reflection on my physical and emotional reactions to scent and song. Creeping through my consciousness was the thought that I have grown too old to die young.

Using a walker, our ancient priest carefully made his way up to the altar. I saw him not as the frail figure he is today, but as the man he was, a newly ordained, robust, young clergyman teaching the art of altar serving to the boy, Louis, who grew up to be my husband. Louis grew old with me.

"Concentrate!" I commanded myself. "You're here to pay respects to ninety-one-year-old Doris and her daughter, Lyn. You made it a practice to honor Dad and Mothers' friends. Do it right. Honor Doris and Lyn with your full attention. Lyn's been your friend forever. Sympathize. It's never easy when a parent dies, even when old and sick."

Slipping back into the solemn celebration of the funeral mass honoring a long life lived in our hometown, I had a dishonorable thought. I confess that I envied Lyn.

All my adult life my first reaction to any intact family is to covet their connection. After Dad's death, whenever I saw a family enjoying a restaurant meal, I resented their blessing. They no doubt failed to fully appreciate the simple joy of togetherness. Fatherless, I ached for what I once took for granted.

Even today, part of me is the girl who aches for her father. Attending the funeral of my parents' old friend, I wished that Father had lived to be old. And I confess to an emotion even more ignoble than my envy of my grieving friend. I felt relieved. I was grateful.

Father's sudden death meant that I never had to take care of him. Father took care of me. I didn't witness his decline. He did not have a slow, debilitating illness. We mourned Doris, but she spent years in deterioration. This once strong woman railed against her sickness. She became a shadow of herself. Her daughter retired early, sold her home, and moved in to care for her mother.

In contrast, I never became the parent to Father. I am ashamed to report that I am glad that I never had to assume this role. Dad told us that he prayed for a quick death. His answered prayer meant that we never became his caregivers. But this bittersweet blessing meant that we never said goodbye.

On the other hand, Doris was a relatively recent widow. She and her husband lived to be old. They looked after each other for sixty of the sixty-five years they were married. In his final years she took care of him. He experienced a late in life, rapidly progressive memory loss. She cared for him kindly and without complaint. Doris requested "You Are My Sunshine" sung at the funeral home. I was touched. Even when he no longer remembered her, she still saw him as her sunshine. They were companions for most of their lives. They supported each other physically, emotionally, and financially. She did not rely on their daughter until the last two years of her life.

It was a different story when Father died young, catapulting my sister Cam and me into instant adulthood. In some ways Mother relied on us physically and emotionally. I spent the rest of her long life worrying about her. Envy raises its head every time I see old couples devoted to each other. Their togetherness gives their children freedom.

The weight of their children's worry and responsibility pales in comparison to their surviving parent's grief and longing. I had only to observe an elderly couple in the pew ahead for a shining example. Long gray hair flowed over her shoulders. He sported a hat over his bald head. She laid her hand on his. He put his arm around her. She leaned her head on his shoulder. Here was love. And it was not new love. Young love is sweet. Long love is tender. My dear mother and father did not have a long marriage. Not the least among my parents' losses was that neither got to say goodbye. Who could anticipate his sudden death in his sleep? She lived another thirty-eight years after his death. He wasn't with her in her chronic illness, her devastating decline, her death.

Fiorenza, my ninety-three-year-old friend and former colleague, had a long marriage that ended with the death of her ninety-six-year-old husband. I told her that I prayed to die before my Louis. I would not want to live without him. Her response was both immediate and emphatic.

"Don't pray that Louis sees you out," she said. "Ask for the privilege of being there for him in his final days."

Her words taught me an important lesson. Her actions taught me even more. When her husband fell sick at ninety-five, Fiorenza was his caregiver. I assumed that looking after him was hard on her. She assured me she was honored to help. He was not a burden. He was her lifelong love.

Gathering my free-floating thoughts I returned my attention to the woman to be buried today. Lyn told me that her mother and all her plainspoken people anticipated her death. Doris calmly pre-purchased her casket.

Noticing the gleaming wood of the handsome casket I remarked on this unique piece. Lyn said her mother chose this handcrafted casket from a monastery catalog.

"Did the pre-purchase of the casket upset your brothers or you?"

"Not at all," she said. "All of us knew Mother was dying."

The solemn songs began to work their magic. I felt the peace that comes from accepting that life is finite. There is an end and that is as it should be. But before long, a dark realization disturbed the still waters of acceptance. Someday there'll be no more funerals for my parents' friends. Someday, maybe even soon, it will be my contemporaries who will die in ever increasing numbers. That is, if they haven't already attended my own wake.

That sobering thought compels me to write the story I alone can tell. Father cannot speak for himself. I am the oldest capable family member left. Details die with me. I must speak the truth, sharing our dark history as well as our good times. From the beginning, early and repeated loss marred many of our family relationships. Deprivation and insecurity spawned contentiousness. Like my father, I learned what it meant to be a fatherless child.

Chapter 4

In the Beginning
1912

The saga of my dad's parents began with humble backgrounds. Father's mom arrived as a three-year-old with her impoverished parents. Their Bartolomeo family of three endured the maelstrom of Ellis Island, even more challenging because my great-grandmother was pregnant with the first of their two sons. In the lean years to come in America, their boys would complete their family.

The conditions on their voyage were rough. Food was scarce. Communal toilets often overflowed. This little family, sleeping on deck, was well acquainted with challenging settings, however, having lived in Abruzzi in central Italy where floods and landslides occur frequently.

Just out of their teen years, Mr. and Mrs. Bartolomeo trudged down the ship's plank exhausted and sea sick. Neither could keep their meager rations down as their ship sailed to America. Stinking buckets surrounded them. No matter. They had reached the New World together. Brave beyond description, the young parents left their families, friends, neighbors, and familiar surroundings. Their hardy toddler, Guilianna, brought smiles to her parents' wan, exhausted faces. They watched in wonder as their beloved daughter pointed to the statue of the big, green lady in the harbor.

"Let's call our Guilianna by her American name now."

"Right. It is as Julia that she'll grow up in this new land."

My great-grandparents undertook this voyage saying goodbye to their loved ones, fully aware that they were never to return and that their families would never afford the fare.

The Bartolomeo family sailed away from abject poverty and into the same crushing poverty in America. They had nothing, had never had anything, and might remain poor forever, but there was a chance that they might prosper in the land of opportunity. That is why their parents and siblings saved to pay their passage. The young couple were excited and sad. They knew they were soon to be without the emotional and physical support of their families, friends, and neighbors. Nevertheless, they were joyous. They had what was most important. They had each other, their youth, faith, and hope.

They gave these gifts to their little one. Julia, extending her tiny fingers to clutch the hand of each of her parents, was completely unaware of what it meant to walk out the massive doors of the Ellis Island processing center that cold and windy day. But the child who would one day become my grandmother inherited from stalwart parents all that she would draw from in her long and difficult life to come. She was resilient and healthy. She was learning to be brave.

From Ellis Island, they moved directly to Youngstown, Ohio, where their earlier immigrant extended families established homes. Every potential immigrant had to specify on the ship manifest the name of a sponsor willing to support them as they acclimated in the USA.

Meanwhile, Dad's father immigrated as a little boy from Calabria, Italy with his parents. That is what led Guilianna and Angelo to grow up together in their sponsors' neighborhood in Youngstown.

Just like her mother, Julia was in her early teens when she fell in love with another teen in her community. Angelo Marcheoma fell in love with her also. Soon the youth were betrothed. Life was good for the sweethearts who were to become my grandparents.

Julia and her mother (affectionately named Mamouche) joyfully sewed Julia's trousseau. To brides today not only is the word *trousseau* foreign, but also the concept of creating a collection of bridal goods is unfamiliar. In the early 1900s, however, most Sicilian girls spent childhood anticipating their weddings and creating the linens their marital home would require. Families and daughters saw marriage and motherhood as the basic definition of women's lives.

For this reason, Mamouche, assisted by all the other willing women in their extended family and neighborhood, taught her daughter to sew. Training in this womanly art began as soon as Julia's tiny fingers could grasp an embroidery needle, as soon as she could focus her eyes well enough to thread the colorful strands through the practice potholder fabric. She was awkward with little blunt scissors. But Mamouche encouraged her daughter. Julia slowly progressed. By the time she could handle her mother's prized sharp scissors Julia was learning to darn her family's rough clothes. Only when she had shown enough skill was she allowed to practice her fledgling cutting, basting, and hand stitching to create plain cotton pillowcases used in her parents' home. She hand sewed simple shirts and trousers, first for her brothers and later for her father. As soon as her legs were long enough to reach the treadle of her mother's Singer Sewing machine, she created the men's clothing of a more finished design. Then she sewed her mother's clothes and her own.

In early childhood Julia began embroidering the family's rough pillow cases that she'd created. As she grew more able she perfected embroidery and tatting. Soon she learned to knit and crochet. When evening approached and families had been fed, Julia was the smallest seamstress to sit with her mother and her mother's friends. On the wide porch of her family's humble home, their fingers flew over fabric as they shared the neighborhood news.

By the first of her teen years Julia began embroidering the fine bed linens and creating the intricate cutwork tablecloths for her formal settings in the home she'd someday set up for her husband. By now she was a skilled seamstress. She wove her bridal shawl, fashioned some good dresses, sewed simple housedresses, aprons, and long white cotton nightgowns and stored them in her Hope Chest. Her goods lay lined in cedar in this fine finished wood box awaiting her wedding. She had resolutely practiced the skills that women taught her. Like all the girls she knew she readied her trousseau long before she would marry. Once betrothed, she fashioned fine shirts and slacks to fit her handsome bridegroom-to-be.

When my grandparents married, they had neither money nor education, but this was true of everyone else in their crowded, noisy neighborhood. They were strong, healthy, and happy. They shared their faith, their nationality, their work ethic, their dream, and their love. With his wages, her homemaking skills, and their shared thrift, they saved enough to buy a house among those of their immigrant Italian, Polish, and Irish neighbors.

Her parents lived a block away where Julia gardened with her father and brothers. Her efforts provided fresh produce for her own table. On her mother's kitchen table, she and Mamouche rolled the dough and cut the noodles for the homemade pasta to serve in their homes. They worked together slicing the strips of dough which they'd rolled across the long kitchen tabletop. They waited for the strips to dry and stiffen. Then they gingerly lifted the stiff pasta noodles to place them in their boiling pots.

Julia and her brothers helped their mother bake bread and pizza in her parents' brick oven. As soon as her young groom had the time and energy he constructed just such an oven in their own backyard. The arresting aroma of fresh baked bread permeated their neighborhood.

41

Grandmother worked with her mother on the family's foot treadle sewing machine. It pleases me to think of the pretty cotton dresses they created with pride. She would only wear brilliantly colored clothing for a short time in her long life. However, before loss leached her life's color, Grandma and Mamouche were again at the sewing machine producing brightly colored, fully cut clothes she would wear with joy. Julia and Angelo had become expectant parents.

The neighborhood midwife delivered their baby and then washed up and walked down the wooden steps of my grandparents' home. Neighbors in their close-knit community sat on their steps awaiting the word on the baby's birth. Family and friends prayed for the young parents as they watched the progress of my Grandma Julia's pregnancy. This was an era when many mothers and babies died during birth. Pregnancy was a perilous state. The midwife was delighted to spread the good news. She announced the newborn's arrival as she ambled to her own nearby house. Little Luigi was born!

All the community celebrated in relief, welcoming a new life to the neighborhood. There was limitless joy. The new father and grandparents began pouring their homemade wine. First the family was grateful that mother and baby were healthy. Then they were thrilled that the baby was a boy.

Luigi's birth began the four best years of my grandparents' married lives. They were very happy. Their baby was strong. He grew to be a lively toddler with a sweet personality. Their boy had boundless energy and an infectious smile.

And then Luigi got sick.

Chapter 5

When the Bad Times Began
1907

One night Luigi was sleepless. He fussed in his little bed.
Angelo laid his big ear on his boy's tiny chest. He told Julia
he heard a hiss like a cat in a corner. Should they spend
their sparse savings on a doctor's visit?

By morning their son's chest heaved as he struggled
to breathe. It was as though a tire within his little chest was
leaking air. Luigi shivered despite his high fever. Angelo
stripped off his shirt to hug his near naked son, his wide
chest warming his beloved boy. Julia ran for the doctor
who pulled out his bag and they quickly returned.

Within minutes their neighborhood doctor had the
diagnosis. Luigi's cough had quickly become pneumonia.
In those days there were no antibiotics with which to treat
this dreaded disease. That night the kindly, sad doctor
arrived again. In the days that followed, the doctor was
often in their home, listening to Luigi's lungs, treating their
four-year-old who lay listless in his baby bed beneath their
wooden crucifix.

My grandparents witnessed the withering, the draining away of his energy. They prayed by his bedside, holding his little hands. They rotated the steaming pots of boiling water intended to help him breathe. Julia and Angelo laid cool rags on his tiny forehead. They said a rosary, the sound of the repeated prayers calming themselves and soothing their boy. From under his clothing Angelo removed the blessed scapular he always wore. The scapular consisted of small cloth squares joined by shoulder tapes to hang on his chest and back. Julia sewed her husband's precious scapular to their son's nightshirt. They lit tall candles in St. Anne's Church. The flame inside the candle holders' red glass softly glowed in silent petition, "God save our son!"

When Luigi died, they grieved deeply.

Angelo wore the black armband, as did every man who visited their home to view the small, white casket. Julia dressed all in black. Her wide hat with its full veil distinguished her from all the other women in black. Luigi, who was their joy, now became their shared sorrow.

The funeral was awash in blackness. The black cloth that encircled the arm of each man was strikingly visible. There were other black circles, unseen but still present. One surrounded the neighborhood. Others girdled each grieving heart.

Chapter 6

Death Follows Death
1912

Emerging from the traditional mourning period, anguishing over the death of their boy, my grandparents were again expecting. Pregnancy was the answer to their prayers. They announced the glad news to all who loved them. They celebrated in joy and gratitude. Again the homemade wine flowed as their community rejoiced. In months Julia and Angelo would have a new baby, "God willing," the automatic Italian cautionary phrase. They asked Mother Mary and their patron saints to pray for God's blessings. They lit tall candles at St. Anne's Church. Thrilled by this pregnancy, hopeful for the future, Angelo decided to make a pilgrimage.

A pilgrimage is much more than a long, rugged hike. It is a religious retreat in motion, affording a change from the daily routine, an opportunity for mindfulness, a window into the eternal. Some talk quietly together. Others choose private prayer. Some do both. Angelo Marcheoma chose silence.

Walking through woods, fields, and valleys, Angelo connected with God. Fresh scents and quiet drew him inward. Nature contributed to his peace. He compared the sunshine and breezes to the intense heat, smoke, cinders, and booming blasts in the hellish steel mills where he worked ten hours daily, six days minimum. Angelo paused at each grotto, concentrated on the religious statuary, and prayed from the depth of his soul. A young, devout pilgrim, Angelo walked with his hands clasped behind his strong back, his mother's rosary entwined in the huge fingers of his muscular hands.

Walking alone, distracted by his grief, absorbed by gratitude in anticipation of their next baby's birth, Angelo stumbled among the weeds and rocks along the rough path. He fell beside a railroad track, broke his leg, and was unable to move his twisted body from the rails of the oncoming train. With an odd sense of detachment, Angelo wondered if he had broken his back. In any event, he knew that tragedy had come again. He saw the train round the bend. He heard the conductor blowing the whistle. He knew he would soon die. And he felt no fear.

Angelo experienced a strange splintering of time. He was fully in the present, seeing the train, hearing the whistle, smelling the smoke, feeling the stickiness of his own spreading blood. But he was simultaneously in the past, gazing at his smiling Julia in her wedding gown, smelling the scent of her baking bread, welcoming their newborn Luigi, experiencing the exhilaration of their boy's brief life. Angelo also thought of his wife in the future, acutely aware that Julia would soon grieve. He sent her his love and he smiled. He sent his love to their baby within her womb. He vowed to watch over them always. He promised to be waiting when they faced their deaths. And that's why when Julia died, many decades later, on her lips was Angelo Marcheoma's name.

He exulted, anticipating the sight of the baby they awaited. Angelo knew that soon he would be the first in the family to greet their unborn infant.

Serene, he returned to the moment. He asked God to forgive his sins. He turned his face to the sky, away from the view of the train fast approaching. In awe, Angelo felt a peace beyond measure. He saw his Luigi waiting.

Chapter 7

Widowed While in Mourning
1912

In the instant when my grandfather was killed, life as she had known it ended for my grandmother too. The outward change was in the clothing that she and her mother now sewed. Grandmother would wear black yet again, this time the color of her maternity dresses. The inward alteration was just as obvious, striking her soul, and stealing her joy. First a teen bride, she became a devoted mother, then a bereaved parent, and soon after, suddenly, a pregnant widow.

She appeared to be living while dead. When the train struck her husband, it was as if it hit her too, smashing her spirit. She appeared doubled over, deflated. Grief stole her strength and she became gaunt. The depth disappeared from the big pools of her dark eyes. Her wide-mouthed smile shone no more. She yearned for her young, loving husband. He would never return.

Grandma worried that there was something terribly wrong in her pregnancy. When walking she had an overwhelming sense of heaviness in her legs. It felt as if

she were plodding through gigantic snow drifts or as
though she were walking in waist-deep water. But this was
not true. She was in step with everyone else. She greeted
the mourners who came to their parlor to view Angelo, then
guided them to her dining table that her mother filled with
food. She set herself to the task of gathering her late
husband's clothes. She strode from room to room quickly
while packing them up for the poor. But she could not
shake the sense that she was walking extremely slowly. Her
legs appeared to be of their normal size. Yet they seemed as
heavy as giant logs, and they felt stiff. It was an effort to
move through each day.

Her unborn was active. That was a comfort. Yet
Grandma was haunted by fear. Did this overwhelming
heaviness signal a problem within? It was awful enough
that sweet Luigi would never be a brother. She prayed to
God for her newborn to come. Her dear Angelo could never
give her another baby to love.

In addition to her pervasive, slogging sensation,
Grandma Julia also experienced an instant economic
adjustment. Grandma and grandpa were born into poverty
in Sicily. In Youngstown, Ohio, with his job in the steel
mill and her homemaking skills, my grandparents felt that
they had achieved the American Dream. They helped their

aging parents. He walked proudly to the mills with his neighbors each day. She and her next-door friends talked on their porches as they watched their children play.

In their neighborhood, my grandparents' income was average. Their lifestyle was the norm. Everyone they knew worked hard to earn a meager wage, save money, grow and preserve food, and take care of their family. Everyone was poor. But there is a big difference between a low income and no income. Scarcity is difficult. Destitution is horrendous. Now her income was gone. In every aspect, she was bereft.

Plunged into poverty, grandmother gave birth to their only living child months later. So it was that my father was born fatherless.

Chapter 8

Childhood's End

Imagine an infant swaddled in sorrow. It was as if he was a newborn wrapped in a black blanket, his mother deep in mourning. Consider that baby, who would become my father. Loved ones died young in his family. His father had already been killed suddenly. Within twelve years his stepfather was also killed without warning. His family secret remains an unsolved murder on the court records. And yet, death did not define my father's life. Despair did not dominate. Hope prevailed. Perhaps Dad's resiliency was rooted in the immigrant optimism of his father, mother, grandparents, uncles, and neighbors. All my great-grandparents and grandparents were born in Italy. They left a legacy of hope over a century ago.

When does childhood end? Our family album has pictures of Grandma Julia, her arms enfolding her month-old infant. Mother and baby Angelo share the same solemn expression. He would grow up one day and become my father but, in this photo, mother and baby both seem to be grown-ups. It is as though mother and infant are the same age.

Grandmother stares at the camera, her face ravaged by the grief that stole her youth. She bears little resemblance to the smiling teenaged bride next to her handsome young husband in their wedding portrait taken scant years before. She looks nothing like the radiant mother pictured cradling their first-born Luigi. When her beloved husband was killed, she was still mourning Luigi.

In his baby photo, Father and his mother share the same solemn look. Did he inherit her grief? My infant father peers out of his baby blanket with a miniature old man face. All the youthful photos which followed this somber snapshot of Grandma and infant Angelo support the bizarre theory that in childhood Father was a little old man because he was born fatherless.

Fortunately, solemn baby Angelo had a good Godfather. Italians have a special bond between parents and their babies' Godparents. This was especially true for my parents' families. As immigrants they were vulnerable and relied on each other. Many did not trust governments, police, or even Italians from other regions. There are responsibilities involved in becoming a Godparent, particularly when my father was a toddler.

By extending the invitation and accepting the honor, parents and Godparents become cummaris and cumparis. Cummaris and cumparis help each other in whatever way assistance is needed. Sicilians value family over all others. Many value Godparents over family. By forging a strong bond with Godparents they extend their family, adding those they chose to those to whom they were born. Potential Godparents consider carefully before entering this special relationship.

With the honor of this role came strongly suggested duties. Godparents accepted responsibilities for the religious training of their Godchildren upon their parents' deaths. They formed a spiritual bond. When Dad was very young, the custom was to extend the spiritual upbringing duty to include actual parenting. This was a social welfare component. Tradition urged Godparents to care for widows and orphans. Unmarried Godfathers who were not blood relatives often married the widows out of a sense of duty.

Grandma Julia's cumpari, Pasquale Andino, was unmarried. He told Julia that it would be his honor if she became his wife. She accepted his hand because he promised to take care of her and provide for her little boy.

While her first marriage was a love match, her second wedding was purely practical. Grandma's situation was grave. She was young and penniless. She had a baby. Her parents and brothers helped but they also lived a hand to mouth existence. Neighboring families extended themselves but poverty was the norm in this ethnic community. The government provided no safety net such as social security.

Although her elderly parents were willing to take her in, their small home was cramped. Their childrearing years had long ago ended, along with their patience with clutter and noise. Her two bachelor brothers remained home, as was the custom for Italian unmarried adult children. They loved their sister and her tiny son but babies mystified them. She was ready and willing to work any job, no matter how menial, to support her son. But she knew she could not ask her aged parents or her clueless brothers to help care for her baby. Destitute, she was in danger of losing the house that she and Angelo bought.

Therefore, Julia Marcheoma married Pasquale Andino in a solemn ceremony in the rectory of St. Anne's church.

Julia and Pasquale Andino had five children in quick succession. She was able to keep her house. Pasquale's labor coupled with her thrift and hard work returned her to a lifestyle comparable to that of her neighbors.

Despite the security the hardworking Mr. Andino provided for the family, Father has the same serious expression in the photos which ritually mark passages in Italian early childhood. There is my grave father in his First Communion portrait. His cheerless face appears at his Confirmation. Of course, these are formal portraits. The photographer may have called for a solemn likeness in keeping with the sacred sacraments my dad received. Perhaps I am seeing a sadness that Father did not then have. Nevertheless, I get the impression of a sad baby who skipped childhood.

And then, tragedy struck again and again.

Mr. Andino was killed. Shortly thereafter, the man who killed him was murdered. The sensational details come in pages to follow. For now, however, I concentrate on the impact on grave little Angelo, born fatherless, now fatherless again. Death upon death upon death had an effect on the little boy who would someday be my dad.

Angelo and his mother bore the brunt of loss after loss. They were instantly impoverished again, their situation now even more grave because there were five more Andinos to feed. Later in his youth there was also the international issue of the Great Depression and the threat of war. Certainly his poignant photos must reflect these turbulent times. In his high school graduation picture and in his photo upon completion of the US Navy Great Lakes School, my dad is a somber young man who appears elderly, having just trained to serve in World War II.

In vain I scrutinized my father's early photos for any sign of whimsy, any indication of joy, any hint of happiness. Saddened by my search I fell into bed last night, depleted. In the moments just between wakefulness and sleep, Grandma Julia came to me. We talked at length about the sadness I saw in Angelo in her photos.

Grandma and I locked our identical brown eyes. She rubbed my back with hands grown strong from kneading bread dough. She sadly admitted that my dad's early deprivation was so dire that it was capable of robbing him of a childhood. She said she understood why my father never spoke of his youth. However, she softly suggested that which I had not noticed. What I saw as his sadness, she felt was his seriousness. Surely I should understand that their dire circumstances required a serious attitude toward survival.

She said slowly, "It is true that Angelo was never playful, never full of fun or mischief. But from birth he was a person, not just an infant. He was unlike anyone I had ever known before or since. Angelo was deep. He was unfailingly kind."

Grandma went on to say that baby Angelo was born not only as her "little man," but also as a wise old man. She said that everyone was drawn to his obvious goodness. His half siblings, his classmates, his teachers, their neighbors, family, and friends saw something exceptional in Angelo.

Grandma Julia said that Mamouche adored Angelo because he was good to her when her husband died. Angelo filled in for his grandfather, who used to plant her favorite vegetables in their garden. He also ran errands for Mamouche, who was often ailing.

According to Grandma, not only was Angelo good to his Mamouche, but also his grandmother was good to him. Grandma smiled when she said to me, "You know. You're a grandmother now. You realize that grandparents can be very special, particularly to the children who need more attention."

Grandmother also stated that her bachelor brothers grew to cherish her child. As an infant he baffled them but as a little boy they adored him. He was content in their company. The uncles never worked for others. They spent their time assiduously managing their investments. Daily they donned suits and visited the city's stock exchange. They met often with their Customers' Man as they considered which stocks to trade. They read the city paper, both morning and evening editions. They read every outside newspaper available. By "playing the market" they supported themselves and Mamouche. They analyzed international, national, and local events; discussed how the daily news affected trade. They introduced the concept of "futures" to their special nephew. Little Angelo listened and learned.

Grandma said that Mamouche questioned her. "Julia, why did you banish your son to the upper room? Why couldn't he sleep with his brothers?"

Grandma stated she told her mother that no one banished Angelo to an attic (as I had long suspected). She said he chose the quiet, sparse upper room, separated from the rest of the rowdy family by a steep staircase and a door he kept closed. He chose quiet over chaos.

Then a heartrending look crossed her face. "I must tell you that my Angelo may have kept himself apart from the other children because he might've felt he was not really one of them."

While Pasquale provided for her and took care of her son, as he said he would, he favored his own children.

Grandma also admitted that, although she loved all of her children, she loved her Angelo the most.

"I spent my lifetime feeling guilty about that but now I've been forgiven, and I think God forgave Pasquale also. We did the best we could for the children. We worked as hard as we were able. I honored my vow as wife to Pasquale and as the mother of his children. He honored his duty as cumpari after my beloved Angelo Marcheoma was killed. I wish I could have lived to old age with my first love. I'm sure my second husband wished he could've married for love and not duty. Nevertheless, we cared for each other out of mutual respect and we grew into a deep affection. Our children brought us closer as we looked after them together. Had he lived a long life I know that a greater love would have come.

"When, ten years later, Pasquale was killed, it was my Angelo who helped me raise the other children. It was so hard. I worked as a scrub woman. Angelo watched over the others. I wish I hadn't needed his help, but I did. He was the oldest and he'd always been the most helpful. Pasquale and I should've loved each of our little ones equally. But we thank God that each of our little ones grew up to be a good person, decent and honest. In bad times we raised good children."

Grandma returned to describing her conversation with Mamouche. She said, "I thanked my mother and my brothers for all their help."

She said to Mamouche, "Angelo might have enjoyed his private room because he was an early artist. He loved to draw. One of the reasons he like his solitary space was because he didn't want his little brothers and sisters to mess up his cartoons. His early doodles led to the comics he created for his elementary and high school newspapers. Angelo's art remains in the huge neighboring Rayen High School where he graduated. His murals line all the long walls of the top floor."

I couldn't tell Gramma that today filmmakers might choose Rayen High School as the location for monster movies. Its cavernous interior is exposed, not just through the shot-out windows, but also deprived of large sections of exterior walls due to rot or vandals. In the summer of 2009, my cousin Patrick Colucci, our spouses, and I stared at the highest walls with vestiges of Dad's murals.

"I'm so glad we drove the few blocks from Gramma's house to this school," I said to Pat. "Rayen High School is important to all of our family. Teachers there must have inspired our parents. And even though schooling was not an option for her as a youth, Gramma worked hard to keep her children in school. She was proud that all graduated high school. She and the other immigrants living here saw education as the way out of the neighborhood's poverty and crime."

Pat said, "I sure wish our grandmother could know that all her kids sent their own children to college. Most of us went on to graduate school as did most of her great-grandchildren and their spouses. She would be so proud of the lot...teachers, nurses, librarian, engineers, accountants, professors, authors, attorneys, artist, therapist, an orthopedic surgeon and another doctor (who is also a pharmacist).

"My wife, Denise, and your husband, Louis, probably just see the filth and sense only the danger in the old neighborhood. But you and I see the streets our parents walked to school. We remember Gramma's backyard where we cousins played. I can name the neighbors who once lived in these homes. I remember the small bakery and candy shop and drug store."

"You're right," I said.

Patrick smiled. "Look at this, Angela. See my dad's initials and our Uncle Sam's? Remember they poured cement for Gramma's steps. Their marks remain."

Pat left my mind then and our grandmother slipped back in.

Grandma smiled her rare smile, a brighter smile than I had ever seen when she lived. She shocked me from sleepiness. She passed some signature features to her son who gave them to me. There's the prominent nose, the bottomless pools of eyes, and the full mouth fit to frame the large, straight, white teeth. I see the three of us in every morning's mirror.

Our shared smile shone on a maternal memory of my own. Our son is an artist and, as such, Marc is often otherworldly. Sometimes he is absent even when present. He gazes at scenes and seems to slip away. As a boy he frequently spent long hours in his room painting or drawing. Marc would emerge, share his work, go back to his bedroom, and return to his efforts. Did my father pass to my son his talents and his disposition? Had I given Marc a version of Dad's Marcheoma name along with my father's art talent? With that thought in mind I slipped off into sleep.

When I awoke this morning Grandma Julia was gone. She left me the potential answer to the question I had asked. When does childhood end? Possibly Father was born with a childlike goodness. Maybe his serious approach to life simply set him apart. His pure love for those he knew as a child and those he met as an adult made Dad unique. Poverty in youth might have made him generous in his relatively affluent adulthood. His devotion to family, country, and faith never wavered. Maybe he was born who he was and he never grew up and apart from that person. Perhaps Father's childhood never did end.

Chapter 9

Murder as Justice
1925

Imagine a vintage movie. The year is 1925. Settle in a small maroon-colored seat, plush upholstery covering horsehair cushions. The lights dim. The projector hums, its beam illuminating the smoke emanating from the audience. The men, having politely removed their hats, relax with their cigars and cigarettes in the darkening theatre. The thick red curtains part and the newsreel rolls. The credits then come. Clara Bow stars in Capital Punishment. *The black and white silent film requires outsized action to tell the story of murder and intrigue. The cinematography contrasts gradations of black, using shadows and shades. In the orchestra pit the musicians underscore the drama about to unfold. The action begins on a dark, rainy night.*

Sharp rapping on their paint-peeled door roused a young mother from her half empty bed. It was long past midnight and she was short on sleep. Pushing aside the curtain to look through the glass, she saw a face much like that of her husband. But he was killed the week before!

Was this rain-soaked man born of her dream? No, he was not the ghost of her husband. Sleep-slowed she struggled to open the heavy wood door, failing to notice her oldest child in a dark corner, acting as her silent sentinel. Her boy's stepfather died last week. He was there to make sure his mother made it safely through the night.

The shivering caller stared empty-eyed. He shoved the big door. He rushed into the house.

"It's done," her husband's brother said bluntly. "I butchered the man who killed your husband."

Cut! Enough with the motion picture images! Did I confuse you with the mention of Clara Bow *starring in* Capital Punishment? *You and I know that the scene I just described was not in that movie. Did you think we simply slipped into an unnamed double feature? But no. I was setting the scene for a far more important story, one we need not imagine. It's a true story. There was a capital crime. The cops caught the criminal but the law could never punish this killer. Return with me to a truly dark night in 1925 in my family history of a heinous crime.*

Grandmother Julia was the grieving widow. Shocked, she was silent and numb, flinching as he approached her. Her thoughts, blind like bats, crashed into the bones that cradled her brain. Was this wild-eyed man her brother-in-law? Why was he here in her home? What was in his duffel bag? Was he trying to give it to her?

Impatient with her confusion, the man I shall call Vito quickly reverted to brute. "I've no time to waste here, Julia. The cops are gonna be on my tail." He forced his stuffed satchel into her hands.

Vito's use of the word "cops" immediately seized Grandma's attention. She was no longer confused or curious. She felt raw fear.

Fear was not foreign to Vito. Fear was his stock and trade.

He shot off an explanation. "I sold everything I could sell. I gotta travel light. You and I know that you're gonna need cash. Here's all my money. I gotta go fast. As soon as they know I skipped bail they'll be after me all over the city. Tell our family goodbye. I'll never be home again. Tell 'em I'm proud I did it. The bum had it coming."

He swore Grandmother to the code of silence. He slipped silently back into the rain. He walked house to house, engaging the entire neighborhood in the same code.

Locking the front door, she headed back to her bedroom. Then she saw her twelve-year-old son, witness to the scene that shocked them both. But she need never worry. She knew her oldest child would not reveal what he heard or saw.

In the turbulent years to follow, this twice fatherless boy would become my dad. He never told me what I have just described. I was a grandmother by the time I learned the whole story but I had some hints as a kid. Ignored by the grown-ups, I was delighted to play with the cousins close to my age. We were in our adolescent-centered universe anyway. However, my ears picked up traces of talk among the adults in our family.

Grandma's huge wooden table was reserved for the adults. My parents, all of Dad's brothers and sisters, their spouses, and Grandma talked at this round table when dinner was done. Later they would spend hours there, playing cards. Listening in, I sometimes sensed a change in the conversation. I was thirteen in 1958 when I first heard hints of a fugitive.

Vito's name surfaced on other visits to our grandmother's home over the years but, knowing no one by this name, I paid little attention. As I got older I wondered why they spoke of Vito in hushed voices.

Gradually I connected Vito to other times when I overheard our grandmother whisper about the police searching house to house "years ago." She named the streets the officers canvassed in their search for a killer who slashed a man's throat. When she first described the police combing the area I didn't distinguish street names. Once I was old enough to drive I paid attention to street signs. I realized that cops searched Grandmother's neighborhood for the fugitive.

Intrigued, I made it my mission to eavesdrop after family dinners. I found many reasons to slip away from the children's table and slide surreptitiously among the adults. In time, I picked up plenty. It seems that Vito had been arrested for murder. Who was this man? Why were they sad and ashamed when they spoke of him?

The time came when I was no longer able to listen to the adults at their table. The Easter of 1962 was my last visit to Grandma's home. Easter is very important to Catholic Italians and our family celebrated this holiday with my father's people each year. But Father's death that winter changed the relationship between Mother and his family. The last time I saw all Dad's people was when they drove through a rough snowstorm to Michigan for his funeral. They didn't return Mom's calls. The bond between Mother and her mother-in-law had always been strained. Father was the link between them. With his passing there was no further connection.

We no longer drove to Grandmother's home and I stopped hearing about Vito. It's hard to believe that his vague but violent story slipped my mind. Many years have passed since I was a teen in Grandma's home. Although all except Dad lived long lives, the adults around her table are dead.

What brought this unsolved murder to mind? I thought of Vito's early 1900's crime when I recently read the following from Joseph Eisen's, *Murder: A History* (1949):

"That murder might be any business of the state is a relatively modern idea. For most of human history, homicide has been a purely private affair. In traditional societies, a killing was simply the occasion for a dispute between two clans. The killer's family or tribe was expected to resolve the dispute equitably by some sort of offering to the victim's family or tribe. The restitution varied from society to society. It might involve anything from a fine to the death of the murderer (or a stand in). If the victim's kin was unsatisfied, a blood feud might ensue. This pattern endured across many centuries and many societies…Current practice notwithstanding, by long tradition murder has been strictly a family matter."

Refusing to cooperate with the police in a murder investigation was in keeping with my family's time, circumstances, neighborhood and larger community. Theirs was a mix of many ethnic groups. Some recently immigrated from what history defines as police states. For some of them, the very countries of their births were no longer countries. The Hapsburg Empire destroyed, they lived in lands where the rule of law was in flux. They came as strangers to an unfamiliar land where they had to learn life anew. By the force of will and wits they managed to make it to America where they expected to find streets paved with gold. Instead they quickly learned that they were expected to pave those streets.

These were strong people, surviving in a tough neighborhood. Some had seen the horrors of two world wars. They were engaged in their own daily struggles with poverty. Having lived with fear and witnessed retribution, they never confided in police. They trusted no one. Many felt that the only ones they could depend on were in their own families. They shared a code of silence.

In 2009 cousin Patsy told me the whole shameful story. He shocked me with the secret Father took to his grave. Dad's stepfather was killed in a hit and run accident. Dad's stepfather had a brother I call Vito. Vito drank himself senseless with his friends. The friends said it was his duty to avenge his brother.

Still intoxicated, Vito paid a visit to the drunk driver, who was always inebriated. When Vito judged the man insufficiently sorry for killing his brother, he slit his throat. Then he returned to drinking with his pals, bragging about getting justice. The police arrested him for murder. Vito disappeared. Everyone in the neighborhood and every member of the family chose to aid and abet his disappearance. Vito was never found, never convicted, not once seen again. Technically this remains an open case. There is no statute of limitation on murder.

How could this sordid tale be true? No one I knew in Dad's family was ever anything but ordinary. Born of immigrants who were born of immigrants they were humble people who raised good families. A postman, fireman, barber, housewife, landlord, and nurse were the roles Father and his half siblings played throughout their lives. They took care of their mother. They cared for their spouses and children, paid their bills, and kept up their homes. I'm related to working class people who labored daily, doing the right things. These were our young parents gathered around Grandma's table. And yet there was Vito. He killed a man without remorse.

When cousin Patsy finally told me the whole story I felt physically ill. Learning the truth made me wretched, heartsick to know there are those who murder, that they live in our midst, and that they belong to our families.

But is it really a leap to become brutal when raised in a lawless land? In the muck and the crime that was Youngstown, who would rise from the cesspool? Instead, I am amazed by the goodness that emerged from this sludge.

Grandmother raised her family in a city where the air reeked of soot. The sky flamed like hell from the blast furnaces illuminating scenes of crime everywhere. And yet all of Grandma's fatherless children growing up in this inferno chose to be decent, respectable, and moral despite others modeling choices that were always open to them.

The word on the street was that Vito moved to another country. Maybe he married there and established a new family. Perhaps I have people somewhere, strangers who bear my family name.

Chapter 10

An Odd Encounter
2015

Pasquale Andino visited today. It was an odd encounter because he is long dead. Also, he and I had never met. Apparently, these factors did not prevent my step-grandfather from suddenly showing up at my desk and formally introducing himself. He was deferential in that turn of the century attitude of an older man toward a young woman.

He was initially indignant but spoke with controlled calmness. He asked if he might share some thoughts of his own, seeing that I deemed myself capable of describing his young family's home life.

Mustering all the graciousness and respect ingrained by my Italian upbringing, I thanked him for coming and asked for his insight. He had long ago earned my respect because he helped raise the fine young boy who would one day become the finest of fathers.

"Certainly," I said with a smile. "You know much better than I the conditions which colored your home life from 1913 through 1925. Please sit down."

He relaxed a bit then, took off his hat, and sat.

"Your grandmother is right when she says we should have loved each of the children the same," he said sadly. "I favored my own and that was not fair. I worked, ate, and slept and did that over and over each day. I was always tired. I never thought much about how my preference for my own blood might hurt Julia's son. But I want you to know that I came to love Julia's child too. I quickly saw that he was a good boy. Angelo was kind. He made life easier for Julia and Mamouche. He helped his half-brothers and half-sisters. Angelo worked hard at school and at home. He was always respectful to his mother and me."

He said, "Julia is also right when she says we raised good kids. She worked very hard every day. My wife kept our home in order and she kept the children clean. She showed all the children how to work her parents' garden. She made good meals from what they grew. She bartered vegetables for eggs, butter, some sausage, and a rare chicken. Her pasta and her bread were the best in our neighborhood. Her meals were plain but plentiful and all our food was for health. She made sure that our children were always well behaved.

"I thought I was proud of Julia's son as a boy. But after my death he took on the job of helping raise the other children. That was when I became even more aware of his strength and kindness and I felt even prouder for Julia's boy. From the beginning it was an honor to wed my cumpari's widow and help her to raise their son. My cumpari was my best friend and he was a magnificent man. I witnessed magnificence in my cumpari's boy. I want you to know that he was exceptionally good. I want you to be proud of him too."

When he praised the child, who became my father, I felt very happy. He seemed to relax when he realized how much his visit meant to me.

As he picked up his hat and turned to go I wondered if I could make him comfortable enough to stay a while longer. Perhaps he would share more of my family's early life.

"Must you leave so quickly? I am just getting to know you."

"Of course, I can stay. Time is not an issue. Thank you for asking." He again sat.

Surprisingly comfortable, we continued to chat. I asked about work and he seemed glad to talk.

"What did grandma pack for the lunch that you carried?"

"A couple of thick slices of her homemade bread came with scamorza cheese. I loved the small sausage she sometimes packed in my lunch. In winter she would add some olives. In summer and autumn there were garden fresh tomatoes, green peppers, and hot peppers too. I drank from the glass bottle of milk wrapped in a rag and stuck in my big jacket pocket."

"How long was your workday? How far away did you work?"

"My shift was twelve hours. I walked a half hour to the mill. I left home in the dark, worked in the light of the blast furnaces, and walked home in the dark. I worked six, sometimes seven days a week.

"The steel mills were worlds within themselves. The noise hurt my ears. The heat sapped my strength but still I worked hard. The stench made me gag. It was dirty and gritty. I worked like a bull and got filthy as a pig. But I was grateful for the pay that came steady each week. When I was a boy in Sicily I saw how hard my poor father worked. Despite his back-breaking labor, the weather could wipe us out. He farmed on the hillside and rains made it muddy. Land was scarce. We raised lots of chickens.

Chickens are mean. We raised sheep, pigs and goats. We gardened with mother, but the soil wasn't rich. Our little house had a gravel dirt floor.

"That's why I was glad to be in America. My Julia and me...we gave our children a good life. We worked hard to do it. We were proud. We loved our big house. We came to love each other."

Then I teased him. "So," I said with a smile, "Youngstown felt like heaven to you. Mom, Dad, and I lived there awhile when I was four years old. I had a different impression of your community. This huge city made me imagine hell. Sometimes red-orange balls of fire burst from steel mill furnaces. Later we moved back to Michigan but would visit each Easter. Arriving at night I'd see the sky on fire. We'd drive into your grungy city from our pretty village, edged by a big, blue river."

"Well," he said, smiling back at me, "Sicily was beautiful too: the mountains, the olive groves, the sun shining on the farmers' fields, the blue of the sea. But I was lucky we could leave the old country and come to America. Youngstown was my city of opportunity. I ignored all the grime. Julia and I, we loved our home. And she always kept it scrubbed."

"I remember Grandma's clean house. It was hard to keep anything spotless in her grimy city. I saw her wash the same laundry over again when ash suddenly fell from the soot-filled sky, soiling the sheets she'd hung fresh on the clothesline."

By now we were deeply engaged in our unusual encounter, having overcome our initial and mutual wariness. We enjoyed an amiability that was remarkable considering our differences in both experience and status. Who could be more dissimilar than the living and the dead?

When he again reached for his hat, I decided that he may be my only ancestor capable of clearing up the yet open case of murder in our family. I hated to dispel our quiet camaraderie, but I just had to know more. I took a deep breath and dove into the murky waters of this event.

Softly, I approached the subject of our family secret. "I often think about the man who murdered the drunk driver who crashed into you," I said. "No one ever told me that there was an honor killing. After fifty years, Patsy told me that your brother murdered your killer."

The change in our conversation was as subtle as it was immediate. It was as if a dark scrim slid swiftly over a previously pleasant scene on our stage.

He was silent.

I was silent.

He locked his brown eyes on my equally dark eyes. In the uncomfortable quiet I noticed the pulsing at his temples. Fury seemed his first reaction. Silence continued to be my response.

I waited.

Finally, in a clearly visible shift of emotion, shadows of sadness overcame the anger and enveloped my visitor. I started to share his misery. I began to regret my inquiry. I knew full well that I'd introduced a sensitive subject which was bound to cause him pain. But I reminded myself that this was the moment to shine some light into the darkest corner of my family history.

Putting aside his wretchedness, he chose to be helpful.

"First of all, I never use the term 'honor killing.' There never was and never can be any honor in murder," he said. "Since you seem to persist in telling our family story, please get the words right. You must know that word choice matters. If you decide to speak of the unspeakable, watch your language. Honor is a sacred word.

"This is a matter long offensive to me. My brother deluded himself at the time and our fiery debate continues still. He has never convinced me that he acted out of honor.

Anger, yes. He was a hothead whose misguided sense of justice dishonored us all. Of course, he had hell to pay. He shamed our family name. We were never people of means. In fact, we had very little. But we were honorable.

"Think how hard it was on Julia. She had to lie to authorities who came through the neighborhood. Consider what it meant to her Angelo, hearing his mother lie. The police did not question our children because they were too young. Julia's boy, however, must have carried the burden of protecting his stupid uncle. But what else could Julia and Angelo do? Family is family after all.

"Two years older than me, my brother was a lazy, rash man who fell in with bad company. He drank himself senseless when he heard I had been killed by a drunk driver. His worthless friends told him it was his duty to avenge my death.

"He went to the home of the man who struck me as I crossed a street. What followed was a shouting match between two angry drunks. The driver, who was rarely sober, said I should have watched where I walked. My brother was furious. He took justice into his own hands. He slit this man's throat.

"What did he accomplish by killing a man? What good could come from anger and ignorance?

"When he and I were young he said I was foolish to work so hard when there was 'easy money' to be made. But once the thugs he ran with shipped him out of the USA his life became anything but easy. For one thing, I'm sure my brother missed family. He could never again contact us. For another thing, he soon learned that his 'friends' just used him as an enforcer. Sometimes I feel bad for him. But he made his own decision."

Together we sat in silence and sadness. Then he slowly turned to leave, and I watched him go.

Chapter 11

Stranger in a Small Village

1943

Suddenly, Father became a stranger in a small village. Maybe those in his new home could sense goodness, seriousness, and loyalty in his nature. Perhaps the local citizens were drawn to this quiet, serious outsider. Many in the village helped him adjust to his new surroundings. He certainly needed all the help he could get. It was as though someone fished him from the ocean and dropped him into a pond.

Why had he come to Algonac?

Father never chose our community. Dad was well rooted in his big, booming city.

Why would he decide to leave his city and state, family and friends, career and security?

He had no choice.

Dad came to a village which did not appear on most maps. He arrived in Algonac because he was literally commanded to do so. In 1943 the world was at war. He entered the US Navy.

Dad was stationed in our secluded village to work in a factory essential to our war efforts. The Chris Craft factory manufactured wooden speed boats. Chris Smith converted much of his Chris Craft operations to build landing craft for military use at Normandy beach. Father calibrated compasses for the craft.

World War II not only brought Father as a stranger to our village, but war prompted a strange event as well.

Militarily, even though our tiny village was both remote and somewhat bucolic, we weren't above suspicion. This was wartime. All actions were scrutinized.

Michigan long led the manufacture and sailing of small boats. Algonac is located on the largest freshwater delta in the world. There were many businesses that supported the needs of small craft boating. Among them was a small business that manufactured and distributed boat parts. Their family name was D'Eath and they also operated a marina.

One day a federal agency contacted the officers in charge of the wooden boat factory, Father among them. United States officials commanded an immediate shutdown of operations. They ordered a lockdown of all personnel. All deliveries into the plant and all shipping out of the factory were suspended with notice given to the railroad officials who scheduled both transports.

The company commander was astounded by this sudden suspension of operations. All personnel at this little base were flabbergasted. They awaited the arrival of the federal representatives.

Immediately upon arrival, federal officials placed all persons under armed guard. Then they scrutinized all the railroad shipping cars. After a thorough inspection, they were completely satisfied that the incoming boxcars contained only manufactured boat parts and the outgoing boxcars contained only landing craft components.

It was only then that they revealed the nature of their inspection. A visitor in the village observed a boxcar clearly labeled on the exterior. That label was "Death." He alerted the War Department, reporting that he'd seen a boxcar labeled "Death" arriving by railroad in the Village of Algonac. Officials immediately suspected sabotage, treason, or enemy action.

The small contingent of Navy men under armed guard responded to this information with immediate and shared relief. Dad and the other officers explained to the federal inspectors that boxcars from the D'Eath boat parts business were labeled with this family's name. The letters spelled D'Eath, not Death!

Dad's duty station, while it was in the US, in a state among those bordering his home state of Ohio, was worlds away from the city where he grew up.

Father spent his whole life in the behemoth of fire-belching Youngstown. He was lonely for his family. He ached for other Italians and he said so to everyone he met. An older villager befriended him. She knew the only Italian family in the village. She asked the Italians if she could bring a lonely, young Italian GI to their daughter's wedding. They immediately extended an invitation, doing their part to honor a military man during the war.

That is how Father and Mother found each other in Algonac. She was the maid of honor at her sister's wedding. He looked at the young, beautiful woman standing next to the bride. She gazed at the serviceman she had never seen before. It was love.

Love can be rash. War was raging. He could be shipped out at any time. A local courted Mom for years. Both his and her families wanted them to marry. She declined.

My serious-minded, responsible, intelligent parents astounded themselves, their families, and their friends.

They fell in love immediately. In two months they were married. Theirs was a lifetime love.

Chapter 12

Rationing World War II
1944

The war affected everybody everywhere. My parents
were forever grateful that our military sent my dad to
Algonac. How else would they have met? However, their
immediate decision to marry during wartime presented
some challenges.

When two Italians marry, food is always a factor.
Both Mom and Dad had big families. Big Italian
weddings call for huge platters of delicious dishes. In
ordinary times Mother's family would easily handle the
required quantity of cooking and baking recipes. Mom's
parents owned and operated the Knife and Fork restaurant
in our village for years. But these were no ordinary times.

The war made many everyday items either scarce
or entirely unavailable. To spread the commodities,
rationing in our country took effect in 1943. Dad and
Mom married in 1944. Friends shared their food rations
and their larder, enabling my parents to serve wedding
meals in her parents' home. Friends and family
contributed gas, oil, and automotive parts rations so Dad's

family could drive to Michigan from Ohio. At great sacrifice, friends helped both sides of their family and their other loved ones get together.

Rationing was based on family size and dependent on availability. Possession of a Sugar Buying Card, for instance, did not guarantee that the family would be able to get its share of sugar because it was a scarce commodity. Many recipes require sugar, especially for those dishes often seen as wedding fare. A wedding cake comes to mind.

Mother asked for help from her young Aunt Leonardi (Nardi for short). Neigh Dee is the phonetic spelling of her husband Antonino's Italian accented pronunciation. She said, "Nardi, please bake your famous cucidati cookies. We missed them at Christmas." These are the traditional cookies, but figs, pecans, raisins, dates, and honey were too scarce at the holiday.

Aunt Nardi said, "I'm glad to do it but how am I gonna find the ingredients? Of course, I'd use sugar instead of honey if need be. But I might not get sugar, or honey. If I had to, I'd substitute almonds, apricots, or hazelnuts for some batches if I run low on the other stuff."

This is a success story. Everyone pooled their rations so that the family could serve my great aunt Nardi's cucidati at my parents' February wedding.

Her famous cucidati cookies were sweet. When Aunt Nardi and Uncle Antonino had their first baby daughter they named her Stella, in honor of his late mother. But they found their baby so sweet that they nicknamed her after the cookie. Soon everyone called her Cuchi.

There were also the anise cookies. Our family recipe calls for a stick of margarine, four eggs, two thirds of a cup of sugar, two and a fourth cups of flour, two and a fourth teaspoon of baking powder, one half teaspoon of salt, a teaspoon of anise extract and/or a tablespoon of anise seed, and a teaspoon of vanilla. The anise extract and/or anise seed and the vanilla extract in the recipe came from the treasured items purchased prior to the war.

J.R. Watkins salesmen sold baking and cooking products to homemakers door to door. Years later I heard Mom refer to the friendly fellow who long delivered to her mother's home as the Watkins man. He added my parents' address to his route and mother came to rely on his products for her recipes. As I grew up, my mother and all her girlfriends took pride in their homemaking skills including the fact that they used the very best spices available.

J. R. Watkins founded his business in 1868. His company won gold medals at the 1925 Paris International Exposition for its vanilla extract, cinnamon and black pepper. These medals are prominent on their packaging to this day.

To support the Allied war effort, Watkins devoted ninety percent of its production capacity to fill government contracts. During World War II, Watkins produced dried eggs, powdered juice packets, vitamin tablets, hospital germicide, DDT and insecticide powder.

Nevertheless, my mother and her family were determined to serve their best-loved anise cookies for her wedding. Her friends were equally eager to learn how to bake the cookies they learned to love for years when visiting my mother and her family. The unique scent of anise marked the dessert tables. These cookies crunched but they softened when dunked into coffee, milk, cocoa, or tea.

Perhaps that is one of the reasons why women willingly shared some of their wonderful Watkins products, not knowing when these extracts would again become available. Family and friends pooled the contents of their cupboards for the ingredients for these traditional cookies, farmers proudly contributing their fresh eggs. Many gathered in grandmother's large kitchen to mix the batter, shape it into three long logs, bake the logs on cookie sheets for twenty minutes at 350 degrees, and cut the long logs diagonally before toasting these slices an additional ten minutes on the sides of the cookies.

This was an arduous process, but a labor of love for the bride-to-be, her family, and their friends. They shared the joy of communal preparation for a celebration, the work of the wedding becoming a bit of respite from the worry of the war.

Most of the guests could not afford traditional wedding presents. They shared their food, their skills, and their rations. These were welcome gifts indeed.

Our government used rationing to guarantee each family its fair share of goods made scarce due to the war. When friends gave my parents their ration cards they did so knowing that their upcoming meals would reflect the consequences of their generosity until it was time for them to again collect their own family's weekly distribution.

Nor was sugar the only commodity rationed. All meats, butter, fat, oils, and most cheeses were in limited supply. Fruits and vegetables, canned, bottled, or frozen were rationed too. So were juices and dry beans, and such processed foods as soups, ketchup and baby food.

Picture the steaming platters of spaghetti and meatballs my grandparents and their older children served at the wedding. Reflect on the requirements for that recipe. Think of the farmer who sold sides of beef to our family at reduced rates. Imagine the butcher friend whose skills insured that there would be ground beef for those meatballs. Consider the homemakers who contributed the garden tomatoes that they'd canned. Think of the farm families who gathered their eggs and gave them.

The wedding dinner wasn't the only meal. In 1944, the Catholic Church had yet to begin offering afternoon or evening masses. Therefore, after the wedding mass my grandparents served a lunch. Their out-of-town guests enjoyed this meal and some of the local guests also accepted their invitation to lunch. Then there was the light meal near the late-night conclusion of the long wedding reception. My grandfather served his homemade wine at his daughter's wedding. The thought was that food might help to decrease drunkenness. Also, my mother's family did not want guests to go home hungry. In short, hosting a large wedding called for lots of food and plenty of effort.

Rationing included shoes, coffee, gasoline, tires, and fuel oil in specific quantities. People had to use their ration cards within the designated timeframes or the deadlines would expire. Friends gave my family gas and tire rations. Without these gifts my father's family couldn't make the out-of-state drive to his wedding. Because rationing of gas and tires strongly depended on the distance to one's job, those who gave some of their gas rations had to calculate how they could drive to work with their reduced rations. Some shared rides by accommodating each other's work schedules. Most were already used to cautiously calculating mileage and gas prices for their job-related driving. In this way, they could amass a small amount of gas remaining at the end of the month to visit nearby relatives and friends. Some who gave gas rations to my family had to forgo their cherished monthly social visits.

For the wedding wardrobes, my mother ordered a simple satin gown from the Sears Roebuck Catalog. Her mother and sisters wore an assortment of party gowns they'd worn for past occasions. Dad and his groomsmen were all in the dress uniforms of their varying military branches.

There was also the matter of putting up the wedding guests. Mom's parents' house slept as many relatives as possible, in every bed, on each sofa, and rolled in blankets covering the hardwood floors. Family members moved quickly upon awakening, converting their sleep spaces into entertainment areas for the home wedding reception. The family sleepover of sorts created congestion and chaos and still failed to provide sleeping space for all the guests.

The only inn our village offered quickly filled. The tiny hotel had a great view of the river but only four guest rooms. Family friends lodged visitors with hometown hospitality. For years to come their big city guests remarked about small town graciousness. Long distance travel was rare in 1944 not only because gas and tires were rationed, but also because the interstate highway system we take for granted today was still twenty years in the future.

Fast food restaurants did not exist for travelers in the 1940s. People packed food in wicker baskets, hot coffee in Thermos jugs, and cold sandwiches in bulky, boxlike coolers, heavy with blocks of ice. Country roads called for caution, especially in the icy month of February, my parents' pick for their wedding. Young and in love, my parents wanted to marry quickly because of the ever-present possibility that Dad might be shipped overseas to the war.

Travelers were weary. Therefore, the friends and neighbors who graciously opened their homes to the out-of-state strangers in town for the wedding gave my parents a special gift. Likewise, locals received gifts in return. Many who hosted and numerous travelers who lodged bonded quickly, sharing the stories of their differing hometowns. Travel experiences quickly became shared adventures, each person's world becoming a bit bigger.

Chapter 13

Love Came Quick; Marriage Took Work
1944–1954

World War II ended in Europe on May 8, 1945. Apart from the exuberant celebrations all over the world, Mom was also quietly celebrating her birthday. What a gift! Pregnant with me and working in a Detroit factory for the war effort, she began to anticipate peace. Her husband might not be shipped off to battle after all.

Formal victory over Japan was signed September 2, 1945. The Navy disbanded their Algonac base. The men were honorably discharged. The Chris Craft boat factory returned exclusively to commercial operations. The war was over.

Dad and Mom had lost one baby and were expectant parents by VE Day 1945.

"Well, sweetheart," Dad said, "now I gotta get a job."

"Don't worry, Angelo," said Mom. "You can find work. You've worked your whole life."

They thought about Dad starting as a teen bussing tables at the Ohio Club. He was *maître de* there when the

Navy called him up. He'd learned how to deal with people in the private club, social skills that came in handy when managing squirrely young sailors in the Navy. As Chief Petty Officer, he kept production going. They discussed his experiences; first he had to learn how to compensate compasses, then he trained the men.

Mom said, "You learn quickly, honey. I saw that when you worked with Dad and my brother building our house. It's a shame we couldn't live in that house but I can accept that you found country life lacking. I didn't mind the peace and quiet and darkness but you sure did. Oh well, we sold it fast and made a profit."

"Ya but," Dad said, "as far as home building, I was just the helper to your skilled father and brother. I'm not in my big city anymore. There's no job in your village. Sure Detroit has its big clubs and high-class restaurants but I'd hafta commute almost two hours from Algonac to Detroit. You know how busy that main drag can be. Gratiot Avenue gets congested. Besides I kinda liked the Navy daytime hours. I don't mind restaurant and bar work but it means most nights and every weekend."

Dad found a nearby job in a small factory that produced small craft marine supplies. Boat businesses thrived in Mom's village of canals, bays, channels, and rivers. Within six months, he said, "I just can't do it, Vee. I'm sorry. The work is a grind. Cutting and sanding the same size piece over and over for eight hours is driving me crazy. I'm losing my mind in boredom."

Father left factory work. It was the first and only job he ever quit. He was skilled at mixing drinks and quickly became a bartender at a family-owned restaurant named Henry's. He'd hand a customer a martini or a Manhattan with a bit of a flourish. Dad worked long hours but liked the job. He was much more comfortable working with people than with machines.

Many women, my mother and mother-in-law among them, did what was then traditionally men's work. They held the jobs millions of men vacated when they served in the military. "Rosie the Riveters" * became the generic term for women who answered the call: America Needs You. Recognition for their contributions was etched into the World War II monument in Washington DC. The American Rosie the Riveter Association was founded in 1998. There are terms for their offspring. Louis is a "rivet" and I am a "rosebud." In peacetime, Mom no longer worked in a factory. My mother-in-law also gave up her lucrative factory work, driving a fork lift in Detroit. Our country needed jobs for the returning GIs.

Both Mom and my mother-in-law became expectant mothers. In the same year, I was born in October and Louis came in November. Born in the same hospital, Louis and I might have been roommates in the nursery bassinets if I hadn't been six weeks older. I expect his deference due to all the wisdom I acquired prior to his birth but Lou simply shakes his head and smiles.

When I was born, my parents bought a home in Algonac. As a new mother, Mom was glad to live down the street from her parents and siblings. She helped her sister by watching her little one, six months older than me.

Then the couple who employed Dad as a bartender offered to sell him their landmark bar and grill.

"No, Angelo," said Mother. "I'd hate the bar business."

Mom reminded Dad that she was only seven years old when she worked at her family's business. "I stood on a wooden box making change at their cash register, helping out at their Detroit convenience store. My parents and I worked long days but we didn't work half the night. I've seen enough of bar businesses. I remember corner taverns down the street. I heard my parents talk about their bar owner friends. Mom got pretty graphic about a friend she called Mrs. Tega having to clean the toilets late at night. Closing up, she dealt with the mess of drunks who got sick!

"As if that wasn't bad enough," Mom said, "Mr. Tega became a drunk himself. My dad told me, 'Whata ya think happens when you got a bar? Everybody drinks.' No siree, Angelo, no bar business. And working late hours! It's bad enough that you work lots of nights and weekends bartending. If we owned the bar we'd both be working every afternoon and night. How could we be good parents?"

"Okay, so let's just move back to Ohio. I'll get back to my old job at the Ohio Club. We can stay with Momma."

Mother was a dutiful 1940s wife. She handled the details of selling their home. She packed up my toddler-sized clothes. And so, we settled in Youngstown, Ohio.

One of my earliest memories is the Michigan Christmas visit with Mom's family when I was three and a half years old. I heard Mother crying as she sat at the wooden table in her mother's tiny kitchen. Grandmother Jennie gave me a cookie and I played with my baby doll on her kitchen floor.

Grandmother said, "It's not that your mother-in-law doesn't like you personally. She wouldn't like anyone who married her son. She never thought he'd marry. She sorta thought he was already married to her. After all, he was her favorite, her confidant, her partner in raising her children."

Mom and Grandmother Jennie discussed the background. Grandma Julia's two brothers were bachelors and content to take care of their mother. She might have considered her Angelo well past marrying age. He'd never brought a girlfriend home.

"Bear in mind your bridegroom was closer to my age than to yours," said Grandmother. "She must have been in shock when her Angelo announced he'd met a woman twelve years younger than himself and that you two scheduled your wedding within two months of meeting."

Four years later, at age seven I became Mother's reluctant, clueless confidant. Grandmother Jennie died. I became the stand in. Clearly this was a role for which I never auditioned. Maybe I remember this well because it was the second time I saw my vivacious mother cry.

"I knew I had to do something," Mom said. "Here's why. I overheard Grandma Julia and your aunts' gossip. The neighbor's boy grew up, married a girl from Kentucky, and they had a son. She missed her family and begged him to move. When he refused she took their child and went back to her hometown."

Mother told me that my Grandma Julia and my aunts figured that their neighbor's family was well rid of this "runaway" wife and their little son/grandson as well; they weren't worried about how that young husband could be a good father now. By extension, Mom got the impression that Dad's mother and sisters could also lop their own daughter-in-law and me off the family tree.

"Want to know how we got back to my hometown? I figured I was living in enemy territory, that my in-laws might be glad if I was gone—and the four-year-old you also. Grandma never did like me anyway.

"I told your father I was leaving him, keeping you, and taking all the money," said Mom. "He was shocked. I showed him I'd already drawn all our funds out of the bank. I figured, it's a man's world. He could earn money. I'd have to learn how to make a living, and quick. I knew that my father would never give me any cash."

Mom said, "It wasn't that I didn't love your father. And I knew he loved me too. Sure, we argued. It was mostly about money but I understood his thrifty nature just by looking around his impoverished neighborhood. The big issue was that your Dad missed his family and wanted to live near them. I loved my family too and didn't want to move away from them.

'We had you, our religion, and nationality in common. That meant that both of us loved you, honored our parents, and craved our Italian families. Our biggest difference of opinion was where we'd live. I didn't want to leave him, but I couldn't stay in Youngstown.

"We compromised. I told him his mother was always welcome, that our home was her home, that his mother's neighborhood was dangerous and depressing.

"Momma's never going to sell her home," he said. "She and Father bought it; the house she and my stepfather shared; the bedroom where she gave birth to all her children; the home parlor where loved ones viewed her two dead husbands and her little Luigi. I thought maybe she'd move after Mamouche died and her brothers sold their mother's home. But she stayed, even as the neighborhood got worse."

"Well, honey," said Mom, "let's invite her for the summers. She'll learn to love our little village, just as you do."

Having worked through their differences, my parents decided to return to Mom's hometown once Gramma accepted their invitation to live with us for up to six months of each year, returning to Youngstown when Michigan laid a snow blanket over our sleepy village. Eventually Gramma spent a month or two with her other children, but she never sold her home.

The conundrum resurfaced. How would Dad make a living? They considered their family members' jobs. Dad realized he was too old to qualify for training as a fireman. Besides, he never felt the passion his brother had for this job.

Father and Mother decided that a post office government job might take too much time, what with applying, taking the civil service exam, waiting for an opening. One brother-in-law liked his post office work but Dad had misgivings because he worried that some tasks might be as repetitive and mind numbing as the factory job he quit.

Mom's only brother was a carpenter who learned from their contractor father. Unluckily, Dad had no skills in the trades and, sadly, never had a father long enough to learn manual trades from him.

Yet another brother-in-law was a teacher. Father saw teaching as a noble profession. Colleges and universities were bursting with men returning from the war. Unfortunately, the years of study, even with the help of the GI Bill, eliminated this field from Dad's consideration.

Dad said, "I think I'm gonna be a barber. I like barber shops. The GI Bill will pay for barber school. I'll be done with the course real soon." That was all Mom had to hear.

"Great idea," said Mom. "I'll bet Uncle Eduardo would take you on as an apprentice. I'll ask Aunt Leonardi if we can stay with her and Uncle Antonino while you go to school in Detroit. Their little Cuchi is our Angela's age. Remember?"

As soon as Dad got his barber's license, my parents made a new start in her village. They took on a big adventure. They bought the jail.

*http://rosietheriveter.net

Chapter 14

I Grew Up in a Jail
Early 1950s

I grew up in a jail. Friends, cousins, classmates came to play with me there. Okay, I exaggerate. I didn't spend my entire childhood locked in a jail. But I lived in a jail.

Mom's contractor father and her carpenter brother urged my young parents to buy the old jail. Mother and Dad bid highest at our village auction. Old John Short was the only other bidder.

"Hah," John said as he shrugged off defeat. "You'll rue the day you bought the slammer. I'd have torn it down...built new. Good location it is, right in the middle of everything. But you fools figure you can make something of the jail. You'll work like slaves to do it."

Given her father's mercurial temper, Mom attempted to hurry him out of the auction. Grandpa wasn't budging. He let loose a torrent of curses, his voice louder than that of the auctioneer. Dad guided Grandpa by one elbow, Uncle Calogero gripped the other. The family group lock stepped out in a blast of Italian obscenities sure to cause a fist fight if John knew the language.

With Grandfather securely stashed in the big Packard, taciturn Uncle Calogero spoke as he drove. His voice was rusty from lack of use, the direct result of growing up in a home filled with a bellicose father, a subservient mother, and four strong willed sisters.

"The jail's structurally sound. We'll get er gutted and divide er up. We'll make the jail a money machine."

In the roomy backseat Dad moved closer to Mother, impressed by the calm efficiency with which she and her brother dispatched their furious father from the scene.

"Good job, honey," Dad said.

"We've had lots of practice."

Over the continuing harangue erupting from his red-faced father, Uncle Calogero spoke twice in one day. "We'll rip down the walls, knock a big window hole in the cinder block, split the first floor… a barber shop in front… a meeting hall behind."

Influenced by Uncle Calogero's soliloquy Dad also tried on a new personality trait. He interrupted the ticker tape ever rolling in his mind to make room for the building reconstruction details he'd never entertained before, seeing himself as the skilled tradesman he was not.

"Yes," Father said, "we'll divide the upstairs, our apartment with the jail yard view—an office rental facing the street. We'll need money. It'll take me time to build a clientele. Cripe, this village already has five barber shops!"

And so it was.

Mom and Dad leased the office to various dentists over time. Fraternal orders met in our hall and other groups rented it for receptions and the like.

Friends played with me in this back room. Mom served us snacks and juice. On rare occasions, she'd give us soda pop. When she returned to the kitchen, we held burping contests. At nine and ten years, we were skilled contenders.

The jail yard view featured the rock piles our family removed over time. Modern incarceration includes exercise plans and well-equipped gyms. Those locked in our slammer must have waited their turn to pace around the grassy yard. If a prisoner wanted a cardiovascular workout or a bodybuilding experience, village police lent a sledge hammer for the rock pile and supervised. Perhaps mindless activity distracted offenders from the stress of being jailed.

My parents loved the big home on the corner two doors down, but they couldn't buy it. Besides the fact that it was not for sale, they didn't have enough money. What they had was a goal.

They bought the shoe repair shop next door, converting it to a rental. A florist leased, so the building became a flower shop. I was in third grade before I realized that Mom, Cam and I were the only ones wearing corsages for every occasion. We supported the florist who backed us.

Rentals, savings, investments, and barbering helped my parents qualify for a mortgage when the shoe shopkeeper put his home up for sale.

While the old jail made money, it also took what money could never buy back. Dad, Grandfather, and Uncle Calogero angled the plate glass while installing the picture window. An edge caught Dad's face. It knocked out his front teeth.

Dad's teeth were magnificent in shape, whiteness, and strength! Mine are the exact replica of my father's. I love them. I look for bargains in the grocery and in the shops but I spend whatever it takes on my teeth. I take meticulous care of them. I rarely bother with makeup. I give my curly hair a wash and shake. I don't care about the latest fashions. My teeth, Dad's legacy, are my vanity. They make my smile; they make me grin.

Poor Dad! He lost his perfect feature. Sure, he bought good dentures but he grieved for the best of teeth.

He never smiled quite as broadly again. He was already self-conscious about being a prematurely balding barber. I didn't help. At age four I said, "I want a different daddy. I want one with lots of curly hair like Uncle Antonino."

With a ready tenant for our apartment, we moved into their dream home. Dad relied on his family for home improvement. His half-brother and brother-in-law drove from Ohio to remove rotting wooden steps and pour cement stairs and walkways.

The old jail building not only paid for itself, but also became a family bonus. When the hall wasn't rented, my parents hosted everyone in my school class and Cam's for our birthday parties.

At my fiftieth high school reunion, a classmate recalled a birthday party in our hall.

"We were in fifth grade," he said, misty eyed.

Never witness to much emotion on his face, I thought he must have been drinking. But I was wrong.

"You asked me to dance," he said. "I'd never danced with a girl before. I've never forgotten it."

I smiled as sincerely as possible, given that I couldn't remember much about fifth grade, or my birthday. I recalled nothing of our dance together.

New York City, Detroit, and Youngstown cousins recall Sunday dinners in our grandparents' main street restaurant until they closed it, effectively moving family gatherings to our hall. Stella, finally called by her beautiful name instead of her nickname of Cuchi, talked about the long drive from Detroit in the pre-interstate era.

Stella smiled. "It was worth the hours squashed in the car's backseat, my two sisters and I balancing baskets on our laps. Dad would stop to buy produce, peanuts, and cheeses at Detroit's Eastern Market. Mom clutched our bouquets from Cusamano's Florist, placing the Bommarito cookie boxes on the front middle seat. Your gramma served the best homemade pasta and meat sauce and taught your mom to do the same."

A cousin complained, "Ma, can we eat the scamorze yet? Why'd I have ta hold off? I've been dying for this cheese since we left Youngstown."

His stern dad's immediate glare stopped his whining. He knew better than to upset his father.

In my case, it was Mother I had to please. "Geez, Mom? How come I've gotta say grace in fronta everybody? Nobody listens anyway. Grandpa gives me his 'Get on with it' look! The other kids just start eating. "

"Do as I say, young lady," Mother said. She pursed bright red lipstick lips.

Grandpa poured his homemade wine. With enough of his "Italian Red" Grandpa could be persuaded to play accordion. Dad's mother slowly sway danced alone. Later she fast danced the Tarantella. With the adults mellowed in each other's company, Cam, our cousins and I ran amok in our meeting hall.

Sunday dinners were always fun but Christmas Eve dinner was festive. The "Cena della Bigilia" (dinner of the vigil) celebrated the wait for Christ's birth in which early Christians fasted on Christmas Eve.

Our traditional Christmas satisfied my every wish. We got to stay up very late, Midnight Mass being our family's choice. The feast began immediately after. And we were hungry! Church Fast and Abstinence rules meant no food for all aged seven and up. Seven-year-old Catholics reached the age of reason and became eligible to take Holy Communion at mass.

Most Italians served a seven-fish dinner. Our family ate as many types of fish as our relatives could bring from their big cities. The New Yorkers checked with the Detroiters' Eastern Market offerings. Between them they contributed triglia (red mullet); seppie (called cuttlefish or ink fish in English and like squid but with a rounder body and thicker flesh); cicale (a relative of shrimp); langostino (a small, spiny lobster); tiny vongole (clams); baby eels; fresh sardines and anchovies. I could've eaten as much as my heart desired, but my eyes spoke to my stomach which twisted in protest. No matter. The sight of this exotic seafood amazed me annually. In addition, we feasted on pasta, vegetables, confections, and fruit. Mother was preoccupied with cooking and serving. Father concentrated on the gambling games. After each long, lazy course, I was free to play with my cousins until, one after another, we crawled onto blankets strewn on the hall floor.

Christmas was the best of times for family celebrations. I'm glad for the good times. They did not last. After Mom's mother suddenly died at forty-nine, fewer relatives traveled long distances. My parents served in our home's dining room instead of the jail's hall.

Times were changing. During Father's last summer, the former jail became less of an economic asset and more of a financial burden.

A pinch-faced, old woman on a limited income lived in our apartment for many years. Orphaned young, she grew up in what was called a Poor House. Without fanfare my parents reduced the apartment rent when Miss

Flan moved in. In addition to her limited budget she had the burden of loneliness; not only were her parents long dead, but she never had siblings, aunts, uncles, and, saddest to me, she had no cousins. Our family became hers. She loved the steaks Dad barbequed in the jail yard pit. She taught me how to eat steak. "Cut each piece and eat it, dear. Then cut the next. That way you enjoy hot, delicious meat with every bite. I learned that growing up. Meat was such a luxury."

Eventually infirm, Miss Flan moved into group living. The last dentist bought his own building.

Dad's barber shop customers began to modify their hairstyles. This was the 1960s; men and boys sported longer hair styles, resulting in fewer haircuts. Later, men went to beauty shops.

Revenue from the big building plummeted. The flower shop closed when the florist died. The Veterans of Foreign Wars and the Fraternal Order of Eagles stopped renting as soon as they raised the funds for their own buildings. Mother tried to keep the floral business going but the rent payments my parents long counted on were gone.

The dark winter my father died, Mother alone faced the prospect of heating and maintaining the near empty, big, old building. She quickly moved the barber shop into the former flower shop as it was much smaller and newer.

A barber who'd worked with Dad rented the shop. Mom listed the big, empty building for sale. There were no takers.

It was a difficult time for Mother, Cam, and me. Sadly, all these events occurred just as I was graduating high school. I had planned to go to a university. I'd earned scholarships.

The stock market continued the slide which stressed my father just prior to his sudden heart attack. Without Dad's investing expertise, we were at a loss.

Our parents valued higher education because their immigrant parents, unable to study beyond elementary school, yearned for education for their children and grandchildren. First generation Americans and high school graduates, they saw education as the way out of poverty.

From the broader perspective than that of our family, there was a national dynamic. I'm forever grateful to President Lyndon B. Johnson's "Great Society." Among other good works, his program helped finance higher education for children of single parents. Also, I thank veteran organizations that assisted the children of deceased veterans with education expenses. Now advanced study, while impacted by Dad's sudden death, was still open. I didn't have to give up my dream of college and my plan for a profession.

Mother's and Grandmother's widowed lives would've been easier had they been professionals. Nursing and teaching were open to women when I graduated high school. Other fields were less than welcoming. The local junior college offered an intense twenty-four month straight study R.N. and I was accepted. Not only could I complete my education quickly, but also I could soon earn a salary. My ill health and Dad's fatal heart attack reminded me that nurses treat and comfort. I figured I'd be a good nurse.

I was wrong. I was emotionally unprepared for the clinical rotation in the emergency room. Distraught young parents carried in their dead infant one evening shift. The next day I switched my major to teaching.

Cam and I earned financial aid and worked on campus; she in the Speech and Communications Department and I in the Job Placement Office while completing undergraduate and graduate degrees.

Mother used her real estate expertise, patience, and perseverance. After maintaining the empty building for many lean years, she convinced a newly graduated chiropractor to buy the structure. Dr. Wick financed his education working in the trades.

"Reconstruct this sturdy building! Use it as your family's apartment, your office and waiting room. I'll finance a land contract seeing as how you can't qualify for a mortgage."

Once again the jail became a bountiful building.

Mom introduced Dr. and Mrs. Wick to everyone she knew. Her sister, Agata, was a teacher. She referred his wife to a teaching job and served as her reference. Dr. Wick hired Mom as his receptionist. Gregarious and well organized, she loved the job. His practice soon thrived. They escaped the usual difficulties in establishing a clientele and relocating their family in a small and somewhat closed community. Over the years our families' friendship flourished.

The federal government wrote the last chapter in the history of my parents' properties. Urban Renewal came to our community, analyzed the acreages, reviewed our city services, and presented a plan to empty the residential properties and the city commercial center which lay on land they designated for development.

Many stores had two entrances, one off the main street and the other off the water. Small boats docked at the waterside doors of various stores along the river. Some shoppers tied off their craft, disembarked and bought their items. Other customers purchased without exiting their boats. They handed the storekeepers their shopping lists. Merchants gathered and bagged the goods and exchanged them for the cash. As the stores became old and the docks rotted out, rats increased both in number and in boldness. This wasn't good for business.

Urban Renewal officials offered to clear the waterfront with its decaying docks atop shaky wooden piles. They promised to build a modern mall, a housing complex for the elderly, and housing for those with low incomes. City council accepted.

Officials entered into financial negotiations with property owners. Some homeowners were delighted to sell old homes and buy new. A few displaced small business owners were pleased. They were ready to retire or relocate. Others were not. Ready or not, happy or sad, all located on the designated acreage had no choice but to sell. Properties were under eminent domain.

Dr. Wick had few ties to our community. He was pleased to sell the big old building at a gain. Federal representatives financed his long distance move in compensation for imposing relocation. His established a practice outstate, near family, and they bought a big home.

Prior to Urban Renewal, citizens could live full lives within our small city. Recreation was diverse: bowling alley, roller rink, movie theater, stores, and fine restaurants. At his shoe store, Mr. Folkerts always pulled a salty pretzel rod from a tall glass jar and gave one to every child. I hoarded my birthday money and the change Dad sometimes gave me to buy comic books. My best friend Kris and I swapped the comics and Mad Magazines we bought from Watts' Drugstore racks. In addition, I treated myself at Babcock's Dairy Soda Shop. I savored cold malts poured from sweating, silver tumblers. Ames Bicycle Shop kept the one bike I've ever owned in top condition.

Unlike Dr. Wick, most of our business and professional people didn't relocate. They had close family, lifetime friends, and generational business connections. Most went out of business. Of the sixty-six small businesses that came and went over the years, eleven remain today. There are no barber shops. The beauty shops are unisex.

Urban Renewal simply hastened the inevitable. Times were changing. Malls, medical complexes, and freeways beckoned. Those who once walked to work earned enough in distant jobs to afford cars for the commute that interstate highways quickened. Our small town life is different now, not better, not worse, simply changed.

City demolition drew spectators. Animated conversations described the implosion of our old jail. Some applauded, "They tore down the lock up." Somebody joked, "They put the hammer to the slammer." But the devastation was not funny to me.

Watching experts implode our family home, barber shop, and the big building, my sister and I were sad. Mother wept. I saw the irony in the implosion. Attempting to lighten the mood I remarked, "Most of our classmates moved out soon after high school. We three stayed. Now our home is leaving us!"

Scenes shifted in the smoke. Dad in the jail yard firing up the brick oven he'd built for his mother to bake bread and pizza. Dad and the barbers who worked with him over the years, white coated, proud sentinels standing by their chairs.

Barber shop views slid through my mind as if projected on a screen. Our classmate boys sat in Dad's barber chair. Cam and I would wave to them as we walked by the picture window.

The little Catholic elementary school, our church, and the big old public high school were a block from our home. We walked the two blocks to our local library. None of these went down with wrecking balls. Librarians employed my mom, me, and one of my daughters as pages as teens. The old high school, where Mom, all her siblings and I graduated, continued to serve our community for many years. I met Louis there when he and I were new teachers.

The implosion of our home and business properties did not destroy my memories. Cam and I played with our out-of-state cousins, our swings and sandbox in the old rock busting jail yard. I climbed the outdoor steps to the storage floor of the shoe store/florist/barber shop. Louis gave me an engagement ring in our family's formal living room. In that living room, we brought our newborn who made Mom a grandmother and Camille an aunt.

"Help!" Cousin Nardi screamed, sitting up straight in bed in the middle of the night. "What's that scary sound?" She awakened me during her one and only sleepover in our village. Long accustomed to the fog horns on freighters or ocean-going vessels, I hardly heard the horns. I reassured her that this was the way boats navigated our river through the murkiness.

The living room in our big home loomed large in Mother's mind. She was gracious. We did a lot of living in that lovely room set off by French doors of leaded glass. The fine wood-framed doors led to the hallway with its polished banister stairway where a tiny table held the little black telephone and another set of French doors opened into the formal dining room. Yet another leaded glass door led from the hallway to the vestibule, where we hung the coats of those we welcomed at our thick, wooden front door.

As she sobbed, Mother was also seeing the dining room with its dark wood cup rail and its polished hardwood floors leading to the kitchen through a swinging wood door. She would miss the kitchen she and Dad had made modern. She would also yearn for the deep cast iron footed bathtub in our pink tiled bathroom.

Our living room showcased Mom's antique desk, called a secretary. It became Cam's treasure when Mother died. In later years as the nieces and grandchildren grew up, my mother gifted each bride with one of her treasured bone china tea cups. In my home, on wooden cup racks are Mother's remaining cups. Drinking tea in our home took on Mom's sort of ceremony. Each guest had the choice of tea cup. I continue that tea tradition.

Our French doors went on to live another life on the stage. Mom gave them to my friends who were community theatre players. It was good to save them from destruction. It was always odd, however, to see them used as props. They seemed out of place to me. They were "away from home."

Recently I mentioned the French doors to one of these community theatre friends. She well remembered their prominence in long-ago theatre productions. She said that an actor bought the French doors when the theatre group ran out of storage space and sold some of their larger props. An architect by day, an amateur actor by night, he installed the doors in his family's home in the nearby city of Port Huron. I'm happy to know that the doors are "at home" again.

Mother's move from our family home was a difficult one. Change is a challenge. For all of us. Always. Even when it is a change we chose. Change is harder when it's thrust upon us. Mother didn't initiate the events that radically impacted her life. Dad's sudden death left her a thirty-nine-year-old widow, unemployed, and with two dependent daughters.

She bought a house in a better location and lived in that lovely house with its beautiful view of the river for many years. But she always longed for our family home. She tried to make her final house more pleasing. She put into this smaller place all the antiques she had in our original home. This made it awkward to get around. Perhaps, however crowded it became, she found comfort from her familiar furnishings.

A piece of property that our government took was always a source of Mother's real estate pride. It was the jail that became a bountiful building.

Chapter 15

Faraway Places

"Faraway places, with strange sounding names, are calling, calling me…" This old song plays on and on in my memory. I close my eyes and see my young parents. I watch them chose among their collection of large, black recordings sized 78, select this album, place it smoothly on the spindle, and ever so gently move the arm with the needle to lay it on the black, shiny disc.

How long ago was that? I had not yet entered school and I began kindergarten when I was four years old. I did not know the words *phonograph*, *album*, *recording*, or even *needle*. Nevertheless, I do remember the somewhat scratchy sound that would magically begin when they put the tiny tip on the big, black, flat, round, spinning thing. And, young as I was, I sensed a change in my parents. They seemed to relax. Were they kind of happy?

Once I had reached second grade I was even more sensitive to my parents' moods. They amazed me. They no longer looked old. They seemed young when they listened to Margaret Whiting sing about faraway places. Mom and Dad appeared to go off to the faraway places that must have been calling them. They grinned at each other. They smiled at my little sister. They beamed at me. Mother appeared to be a person, a pretty woman, in fact. I watched as Father slipped off his barber coat. His rare smile appeared as he asked our mom to dance. I suddenly saw him as a handsome man.

As they danced in our kitchen there was no trace on his face of the worry, responsibility, and tedium of running his barber shop in our village. Mother seemed to shed the yoke of the 1950's housewife. We were all in our kitchen but they were really somewhere else. I knew that. I wondered just where it was that they had gone. Blissfully unaware, however, my beautiful sister was too young to contemplate. She simply joined them in dance. She spun around and around. All by herself she swayed, perfectly in tune with the music.

In their private reverie, were Mom and Dad ever aware that I traveled with them in joint imagination?

Although very young I was apparently old enough to realize that there were indeed other places. I began to sense that our home and our town were just parts of a bigger world.

Raised in Algonac, with its strange sounding name, I have traveled often to faraway places. Maybe our first television, a tiny black and white, planted the love of travel in my malleable childhood mind. An advertisement ditty might have been the means because I can still hear Doris Day urging us to "See the USA in your Chevrolet." Decades later my husband also remembered Doris Day in this ad. Three years ago we drove off in our Chevrolet to see the USA. We traveled Route 66. We saw beautiful sights.

Nevertheless, although faraway places called, I have always lived in the village in which I was born, except for university studies. I chose to live my life in the little place where all my big events took place. I discovered the art of seeing the new in the old places, the strange in the everyday, the surprises among the routine, and the deep dramas that sometimes play out in seemingly simple scenes.

Chapter 16

Wild About a Washer
1954

At age eight I planned a party (a precursor of the events
planning I do as an adult). Unlike most surprise parties, this
one was truly an astonishment. My parents were
dumbfounded when family and friends arrived and I
graciously ushered them to our unfinished, box-filled
basement.

The party scene must have mortified my mother. I,
however, was proud of my decorating achievements,
including the crepe paper streaming over the ceiling pipes,
the pretty comforter flung over the laundry tub, and the
welcome sign I printed, colored, and taped to our gleaming,
new washing machine.

With no floor space for chairs, the guests gamely
stood on the concrete floor with their cookies and juice
which I filched from our kitchen. Short people were fine.
Tall people stooped due to the low ceiling. Grandmother
Jennie, a real sport, navigated with her cane down our
shaky basement steps.

Even today, I consider a washing machine cause for celebration. I'm grateful every time I wash clothes, never taking for granted the privilege of time for other tasks or for simple relaxation at home while laundering.

Dad calculated the cost per load and decided that commercial laundry use was cheaper than the purchase and maintenance of home laundry appliances. Therefore, the early years of my life included trips to the local Laundromat carrying our dirty laundry. When a washing machine close-out sale tipped the fiscal balance, our family acquired the washer I celebrated. We saved money until it made sense to spend money. My father taught me this lesson.

Dryers must have remained pricey, however. I was seventeen when my widowed mother purchased a dryer, splurging on convenience. This eliminated trips to the laundromat with baskets of wet wash. Convenience is sometimes worth the cost. My mother taught me that lesson.

Mindfulness lies in recognizing the extraordinary in the ordinary. Laundry is the case in point. Not only do I thank God for the good fortune of a home washer and dryer, but also for the good parents who taught me life lessons.

With his attention to detail my dad made me aware of money matters. What greater gift could he give than to show me basic financial planning? Money management might help me to avoid ever becoming destitute or dependent. By spending less than what we had, our family always had enough. In time we were blessed with more than enough. Most importantly, we learned to appreciate all we had, in lean times and in plenty.

Building on the foundation of living within our means, I realized that time for pleasure, joy, comfort, and memory-making also belongs in the cost analysis process.

Both parents gave me yet another life lesson, again by example. Both were community minded and devout. Despite our ever-fluctuating family finances they always gave to the less fortunate. They reminded us that we were blessed and therefore obligated to share.

What I learned early is to celebrate what I have. The washing machine party is an example.

Chapter 17

Money Matters
1950–present

Earliest memories include seeing Father counting money.
At times I'd happen upon Dad counting out small stacks of
dollar bills, fives, tens, and twenties. He had a distant look,
concentrating intently. He didn't notice me. I watched as he
counted each stack again and again.

Even as a child I thought this was somewhat strange
behavior. Now, I recognize his need to reassure himself. He
had to touch money, to count it, to remind himself that he
was no longer a poverty stricken child; no longer the
responsible teen whose jobs helped his widowed mother
feed the family; no longer an uneasy adult uncertain of his
financial future; not penniless now.

Breakfast unfailingly reminds me of Dad pampering
us. Whenever we poured milk on our cereal Dad would
smile and say, "Have as much milk as you want." He
would beam as we did so.

"At your age," he said, "we rarely ate breakfast.
When we had cereal there was the cheapest canned
evaporated milk. We'd dribble just enough to moisten the

cereal. Today I hate the strong scent of evaporated milk and its sickly sweet flavor."

Some think of cereal for breakfast as a simple meal. My focus is on abundance. Like Dad, I encouraged our children and theirs to pour as much milk as they want. I told them Father's milk and cereal story. I showed them by example that it's wrong to waste. I always ate as much cereal as I took. I never lingered until dry cereal became soggy. I drank the milk left in the bowl. Our kids and theirs discard food sometimes. The lesson I told them can never have the impact of the lesson Dad lived.

Throwing away soggy cereal or pouring excess milk down the drain feels like a sin, not a sin against God the Father, but an offense against my father. Waste would hurt him to the extent that anything could injure a long dead man. It would hurt me, knowing it would have hurt him.

Other early memories include restaurant scenes. Dad and Mom took Cam and I to dinner at a local restaurant where he tended bar for years. He earned extra money to help finance our car, incidentals for his G.I. Bill-funded Barber College, and the big building for our apartment and barbershop.

At dinner, Mom and Dad assured Cam and me that we could order whatever we wanted. My favorite drink was a Shirley Temple. I loved the look of this soft drink in a fancy glass. I delighted in the bubbles that tickled and the cherry on a swizzle stick. I played with the tiny paper umbrella. I liked the look of the shrimp cocktails and enjoyed the taste and textures of the seafood and sauce.

Dad said, "Thank the waiters politely and often. It's hard work." He remembered bussing prior to waiting tables in a posh dinner club.

Having risen to the ranks of headwaiter and then *maître de*, Father's manners were impeccable. No doubt Dad encountered dinner customers with impolite children. Mom's parents owned and operated a restaurant a block from our home. Mom and Dad saw unruly kids ruin their families' meals. They wanted to raise polite children and felt we'd learn to behave in restaurants by early exposure to table manners and good conduct in public.

But also, I think Father loved the largesse of giving his children experiences that he couldn't have as a child. Dad smiled broadly as Cam and I delighted in our festive drinks and fancy foods. That bountiful feeling was the pleasure of his dining experience. He never ordered extravagantly for himself. Quite the opposite, he always chose the daily special, based solely on the lowest price. He insisted, however, that nothing was too good for his wife and children.

His bigheartedness was all well and good but even as a child I felt there was something amiss. I wished that Dad would be as generous to himself as he was to us. By the time I was a teen, I was dismayed at how stingy he was with himself. His unrelenting self-denial meant that he didn't eat lunch when we were away from home for a day.

Each week my parents drove along the water on Jefferson Ave. to reach Gratiot Ave. and continued our nearly two-hour drive to Detroit. Mom took me to a medical specialist. Dad visited the stock market to confer with his Customers' Man. We'd meet at the end of the day.

He delighted in our accounts of the lovely lunch Mom and I enjoyed in the elegant Kresge Court of the Detroit Institute of Arts, then ceilinged in parachute-like silk. He ate vicariously through descriptions of our delicious meals. Father never even bought himself a cup of coffee. Even I, as self-absorbed as any other youth, realized that Father was treating himself badly.

Early lack prohibited instant gratification, so he developed the habit of anticipating eating and drinking. Perhaps he enjoyed them even more because of the wait.

Simple pleasures such as coffee or lunch would be even more pleasurable after delayed gratification.

Maybe he used logic. Without question, eating the same meal at home, drinking home brewed coffee was less costly than eating and drinking in restaurants. The scent of the roasted coffee beans or home cooking would be a bonus. Then there is the matter of math, perhaps integral to his logic and definitely an asset in his investing. He routinely computed long figures in his head. Debit and credit columns were ever present.

As sad as I was because of his persistent self-denial when Dad was alive, I was devastated by it when he died young. Father had just started spending for his simple enjoyments when his life suddenly ended.

In his last few years he started to golf with the "fellows." Father began to not only golf with Mother, but also to eat out with her.

Two months before dying he made a curious purchase…a very expensive hat. It was a Dobbs hat. An Esquire magazine ad published in 1961 encouraged every businessman to buy a Dobbs. The tongue in cheek message was that the Internal Revenue System should approve this fine hat as a business expense.

All men wore hats at the time but few in our community wore a Dobbs hat. This promo stressed that a Dobbs hat meant business, making it well worth the financial investment. Prices started at $20.00. Father charged $2.00 for a haircut. He must have decided that a Dobbs hat was worth a lot of his time, labor, and money. The advertisement noted that the fedora pictured was available at fine stores everywhere, including Park Avenue at 49th in New York City.

It was in an impressive hat and he wore it with pride. For many years after Dad's death his Dobbs hatbox took lots of space in a cramped closet in the home my husband and I share. Maybe I needed reassurance that Father had finally splurged on an extravagance for himself.

Fifty plus years later, I wonder if his unusual purchase was prompted by the same premonition that may have inspired him to take me for our one and only long drive alone together, to walk and talk in a park. Did he realize that his time was running out?

Father rarely spoke of his early poverty. His childhood neighbor described Dad's family's deprivation. I shall call her Fiorenza Magdalena. She said, "When we had a little extra in our garden or when Giuseppe got a coupla extra hours in the steel mill, we'd drop by and give 'em what we could. One night, they were eating their dinner of saltine crackers and water."

Dad's preference for saving instead of spending stemmed from his early life of lack. If that were a universal given, however, I wonder about people who were born poor and proceed in adulthood to spend every penny, some spending even more. Generations of Magdalena families spent with abandon. My childhood friend's family did the same

Sue said her father grew up impoverished. Her dad worked very hard. Father did the same. He married, had a family, established a business, and made money. Father did the same. Then her dad bought everything he ever wanted, all the time. That's where our fathers differed.

"Dad filled our big home with the latest," she said. "I have irreplaceable memories."

Sue and her husband, Don, work very hard. They also play hard. They don't plan to retire. They often take expensive and exotic vacations. Sometimes she tells me, "I wish Don didn't buy so many toys for himself and our kids! We rent storage for boats, motorcycles, and cars."

By contrast, my frugal husband and I followed our parents' pattern. We enjoy simple, frequent, inexpensive travel with occasional costly vacations. We often buy used cars. Because our greatest value is time, we retired young. We love long walks. We host home dinner parties and enjoy such parties in our friends' homes. We buy few toys for ourselves or for loved ones. Our gifts to our grandchildren contribute to their college funds. We value security over spending. But an aspect of being a saver instead of a spender bothers me very much. Not only do I get little pleasure out of spending large sums of money, but also I feel guilty.

While I value benevolence, both in funds and in service, I wonder why I feel guilty spending money for my pleasure. Certainly I've never spent money that I didn't have. I sometimes regret purchasing a product that doesn't have all the features I could use, because I made expense the more important factor. Other times I lived with outdated or worn out items when upgrading would have increased my daily pleasure. On occasion I delayed purchases so long that they were no longer available when I finally justified the expenditure.

In other words, I sometimes act a little like my father. I must want the little pleasures I could easily afford enough to overrule my reluctance to spend. The same self-denial that I hated to witness in my father influenced my own attitude.

Guilt is a powerful and complex emotion. It is also a factor that I did not consider when mentally berating Father for treating himself badly.

Perhaps the deep deprivation of his youth prohibited Dad's spending. One thought is that he felt unworthy of affluence, having known so many hardworking people who never escaped indigence. Perhaps he saved every penny out of fear he might again become destitute.

His mother reinforced that fear. "Why are you two throwing away money on art museums? Art doesn't feed, clothe, or shelter. You were a poor boy, Angelo!"

The rational man within him must have fought with the penniless, fatherless boy, also inside. He knew there were stock market fluctuations he couldn't control. He established a lifetime of gains and losses. With daily research and by holding a variety of investments, he never came close to losing everything. Wisely he made money work for him instead of simply making money and spending it all.

In addition, my parents were good business partners. Mother was confident in real estate, learning the basics of buying, selling, and renting from her fearless father, Giuseppe. Born in Italy, in the Sicilian city of Palermo, fourteen-year-old Giuseppe Polito came to New

York City with his father to visit friends. During their visit, he and his father met other Italians in their relatives' neighborhood. They met the Guarella family. They learned that Salvatore and Serafina Guarella and their first child, Giovanna, were born in the same Sicilian city of Palermo.

Giuseppe loved New York City. He said, "Poppa, I do not want to go back home. This is the new land and it is an exciting place."

"Son," said his father, "you and I must return to your mother and to our family. Our visit is over. You have to get back to school."

"I can learn all I need to know right here, Poppa. I want to stay."

"This is a decision for a man, not a boy. Are you sure you can say goodbye not knowing when you'll see your family again, accepting that you may never return to your country?"

"I shall miss you, Poppa. Tell Momma I shall miss her, my brother, my sister and friends. But this is the country for me. Your friends here will help me. I cannot be happy anywhere else now that I have seen America. I just can't return to the old country."

His father said, "I can see that you have made up your mind. I'll write to your mother about your decision.

I'll prolong my visit to help you find a friend to sponsor you. However, the rules are clear: I cannot extend my visitor status beyond six months.

"If your mother and I agree, and if, after we have spent more time here you still wish to remain, you'll have to make your way."

As the months passed, convinced of his son's determination, great-grandfather gave his son the money they had saved for his education and future. My great-grandfather, just off the boat and soon to sail back to Italy, may not have been a sophisticate but he knew human nature. He saw the looks between his young teen son and the younger Giovanna, his friends' daughter. He thought perhaps that his son might someday become part of a fine Italian family. Maybe this consideration made saying goodbye a little less heart wrenching.

That is how Giuseppe Polito became the lone member of his family ever to immigrate.

Seven years older than his bride, Giuseppe Polito married Giovanna Guarella. Giovanna, age sixteen, gave birth to their first, my mother. In all they had nine babies, five of whom survived childhood. Giovanna was her mother's first baby. The family pattern of early marriage and young parenthood meant that Giovanna's mother became a grandmother at age thirty-two. Mom married Dad at twenty. They lost their first baby. She gave birth to me at age twenty-one. Knowing my mother's parents and Mom's grandparents as well as my Dad's mother and grandmother enriched my life. Each of these brave immigrants taught me their unique survival skills.

Mom's dad had only a grade school education in Italy but he pored over homework with his children. He improved his English but he especially honed math concepts. He studied high school geometry, algebra, and bookkeeping with his daughters as they did their homework. He learned drafting as his son completed shop class. Figuring he knew enough by then, he decided he was a builder and he built. "Buy land," Grandfather said, "and make sure it's got a good view. Build near the river, lake, or woods."

Grandpa Polito's real estate experience and confidence were assets he shared with his children.

While it is true Dad's signature condition was that of being fatherless, he did have loving uncles. His mother's brothers supported themselves and their mother solely on their investments. They never worked for others. They learned early how to invest and they taught their fatherless nephew. They went to the stock market twice daily, often taking him along.

In the 1920s and 1930s when Father visited the Youngstown stock exchange he got an inside look at our nation's free market economy. From the visitors' viewing arena, they could see trading of pork bellies or other commodities. They could watch the hectic bid and ask activities.

Today the viewing areas of stock exchanges are closed, an aspect of the world impacted by terrorism. Luckily I saw the Chicago Stock Exchange from the observation deck in the 1980s. A fascinating scene unfolded as those wearing various colors of vests rushed about the trading floor.

In Father's time daily news didn't stream into homes with minute-by-minute broadcasts of unfolding events. Newspapers proliferated however. The uncles read them all. In a world digging itself out from the Great Depression, they taught their eager student to make connections between national and international events and the fluctuations in the stock market.

Confident in the lesson in economics he learned young, one would think that Dad could overcome his guilt over spending money. Using a logical approach, one would think I could do the same. I realize I have enough money to treat myself to simple pleasures. I chastise myself for the miserly attitude I criticized in my father. And I'm finding it easier to dispel the twinge of guilt I experience when indulging in a luxury.

It's important to define luxury. I don't mean that I buy luxury cars, extravagant homes, designer clothes, or jewel encrusted baubles in my newfound self-indulgent attitude; nor do I want any of these items.

A luxury is an appealing item of clothing, food, books, art, and music; extravagances because I don't need them. I have nice clothes. I have books, art, music and I can borrow more from the library. I'm allowing myself to not only spend money on these pleasures, but also to fully enjoy them by pushing back guilt.

I treat myself, our kids, their children, with fine dining, sight-seeing, concerts, plays and galleries; luxuries because I can cook at home; extravagances because we can see sights in travel magazines, hear concerts on the radio, enjoy art in fine books, watch plays on television or on film. But live performances, original art, and gourmet meals feed the soul. Louis and I strike a balance, splurging for what we can afford and relaxing in the reasonably priced starter home we purchased forty-five years ago. We like to lie around, watch television shows or movies, and listen to music, walk or read.

Louis and I always saved part of what we earned and because we have been lucky, we've always had an income, sometimes modest but always steady. One would assume I could dispel my guilt over spending. I'm working on my attitude.

Travel is a pleasure we both enjoy. We love visiting our families and friends. We treasure trips we take independent of visiting others. There are thrifty ways to travel. We pack sandwiches to picnic in parks. We switch drivers often. Vacations give us great times in each other's company away from the ordinary. We are good to ourselves. We frequently stop to rest in clean, reasonably priced lodgings. We visit the sites on our way to our destinations. Sometimes those little explorations become the occasions we appreciate most. We love National Parks.

Louis and I have less trouble justifying the expense of travel. Maybe this is because the joy we share in exploring together, and our happiness when including our kids and their children whenever they are available, overrides our mutual reluctance to spend money. Our memories of travel are in themselves pleasures. I indulge more often than Louis, but he is working on his attitude

too. His childhood was marred by money problems.
Perhaps Lou and I recognize that our time together is not
unlimited. Recently recovered, I had a serious illness. Not
long ago, a bee bite plunged Lou into anaphylactic shock.
The next year we were in the same emergency room and
Louis soon had triple bypass surgery. Now we are in
excellent health. Strength and energy don't last forever.

Guilt is complicated. My husband's frugality
bothers me when he won't spend on such a simple pleasure
as a cup of coffee for himself. Yes, he could make coffee at
home, but gee!

Perhaps my friend Sue and I both married men just
like our fathers. Money matters.

Chapter 18

Two Dollar Haircuts

Name the best of gifts. Perhaps you appreciate jewelry, flowers, golf clubs, and haircuts. Haircuts? Haircuts can have great worth!

Growing up in the 1950s, two dollars was the going price for a haircut. Dad took in a modest income in his barber shop. Although haircare prices have risen since then, another factor remains constant. Barbers know everything that goes on in their communities. This is true for beauticians as well. The wise ones know but never tell. This was Dad's ethical code.

In the grocery, Mom heard that a woman I call Mrs. Jones was finally divorcing her drunken, adulterous, abusive, worthless husband. Mom told us. Dad already knew, of course, but he never spread barbershop gossip.

That's the last I thought about Mrs. Jones until she approached me, some fifty years later.

"Aren't you Andy the barber's daughter?" she said.

Touched, I said, "Well, yes I am. It's a pleasure to hear his name after all these years."

"You were a lucky girl to have had him as your father, even though he died so young. He was a truly kind man."

Mrs. Jones said, "Your dad phoned me shortly after my divorce. He asked me to accompany my three boys the next time they came for haircuts. In his barbershop your father taught me how to cut my sons' hair. He bought me a pair of shears and some clippers from his barber supply catalog. He supervised my 'barbering' for months until I felt confident. Like I said, your father was utterly kind."

By cutting her sons' hair, Mrs. Jones saved money. Of course, her savings were his losses. This was a strange strategy. Dad was a frugal man. But my father was more than a businessman; he was also the eldest of the six young children of an impoverished, twice widowed mother. He knew how tough it was for fatherless families.

Dad's good deeds didn't even turn out badly for his business. He didn't lose the two dollars he would have earned for each haircut for each of the three little Jones boys throughout their childhoods. Father died young, shortly after giving their mother the tools and skills to eliminate barbering expenses.

Mrs. Jones told me that every time she cut her sons' and grandsons' hair she blessed the memory of my father. I thanked her for telling me of his long-ago kindnesses. I loved my father. I sorely miss him still.

It was good of Father to help a single mother in need. Likewise, it was kind of that mother to give me the gift of the story of his kindness. Dad's gifts prompted Mrs. Jones' thoughtfulness. Both my late father and the recently deceased Mrs. Jones live on through the magic of her shared memories.

"There are three deaths. The first is when the body ceases to function. The second is when the body is consigned to the grave. The third is that moment, sometime in the future, when your name is spoken for the last time."—David Eagleman, Sum: Forty tales from the Afterlives.

At a recent family reunion, my cousins shared childhood scrapbooks. Cousin Mike pointed out that the photos over his entire childhood show him with the same hairstyle. This is true of his siblings' hairstyles and those of all our cousins in every family's scrapbooks. There's a reason. Dad bought scissors and clippers for all the family. Then Dad taught his half siblings and his in-laws to cut their children's hair. Dad cut Camille's hair and mine. Therefore, like our cousins, we sported the same styles over the years.

Julie, our beautician daughter, inherited her Grandfather's barber scissors. Recently neighbors told me that Julie routinely gives free haircuts to needy community members preparing for job interviews. Years earlier I heard that Julie visits the homebound, giving haircuts without charge.

Goodness endures. Sometimes generosity becomes a legacy.

Haircuts are not humble gifts. They are priceless presents.

Chapter 19

The Bread of Life

1955

By the time my father had his own family, his mother's claim to fame was her amazing ability to bake bread. She engaged my little sister and me in this fascinating process. We watched in wonder as the yeast did its magic. We loved the smell of yeast. Then we helped our grandmother in the decision making. Did the dough rise enough? Was the surface too sticky to knead? Should we form the dough in loaves or make the little buns?

Grandmother Julia honored our work, even when our actions crossed the border between work and play. I close my eyes and see my middle-aged sister as the little girl she once was. Her beautiful blonde hair was in tight ringlets in the Shirley Temple style of the day. She became bored with the time consuming job of breadmaking. She formed bread balls from the risen dough and was supposed to place all of them on the pan to give them time to rise before baking. Instead, she checked to see if Grandma was looking and smiled in knowing Grandma was not. She snatched a bread ball. Soon Cam was happily tossing her bread ball back and forth hand to hand. She was a little juggler.

Getting away with that little caper emboldened her. She scampered out the swinging kitchen door into our dining room. There she rolled her bread ball around and around the hard wood floor. When she finally realized that grandma might notice she was gone, Cam slipped back through the swinging kitchen door. Her little hand reached up to the kitchen counter. She quietly slid her bread ball onto the baking pan.

As the only other member of the team of baker helpers, I had the good grace to neglect to mention this infraction of baking protocol. Later Grandma Julia asked for our help in checking the buns before we put them in the oven. Yes, we agreed with the master baker that the bun dough had risen enough. All the buns were puffy. The unique scent of yeast perfumed our kitchen. No one could fail to notice that the buns were white, with one exception. Cam's covert action had produced a dirt dappled, brown bun.

It was then that I saw something rare. There was a slight smile-like curve of Grandmother Julia's mouth. This was remarkable. Her usual expressions ranged from sad to severe. I saw something I had never seen before and I never saw it since. As she slid the baking pan into the oven Grandma Julia looked from the brown bun to me. And then she winked. I smiled at my grandmother, thus sealing the silence we agreed upon regarding Cam's little sin.

Later the scent of fresh baked bread summoned all of us back to the oven. Then Grandmother just happened to drop a bun as she slid the pan from the oven. It turned out to be the little brown bun. We all had to agree that a bun that fell to the floor could not be eaten. God bless Grandma!

It was my father's mother who made the bread that everyone loved. Maybe that connection formed an association between bread and my father for me. There is something basic about bread. Good bread is the supreme sustenance. Bread is my favorite food. Bread is the stuff of life.

Shopping the fresh food market last week in New York City's Union Square I noticed a huge sign. The Bread Alone Bakery emblazoned on its banner the words of Robert Browning: "If thou tastest a crust of bread thou tastest all the stars and all the heavens."

If a person is admirable, good to others, nurturing, good through and through, that person is good like bread.

The Sicilian expression "Good like bread" truly describes the fine man who was my father.

Chapter 20

Good, Like Bread
1945–present

What is this connection between bread and the men in my life?

As a child I heard family and friends describe my father as "good, like bread." They would murmur these words in Italian as add-ons to expressions of gratitude. I recall an example. An aged immigrant said in accented English, "Thank you for coming to my wife's funeral." He added softly, "You are good, like bread."

Elderly or infirm neighbors appreciated that Dad did their errands, such as delivering their packages when picking up his family's mail or shopping for their groceries while shopping for his mother and young siblings. When he delivered the sturdy brown bags containing their heavy food stuffs they'd conclude their repetitions of gratitude with, "You are good, like bread."

Sometimes I'd walk with Father the few blocks between his mother's home and that of her mother and brothers. Dad affectionately called his widowed grandmother Mamouche. These are vague memories because I was four when we moved from dad's childhood city. Nevertheless, I remember calling on Father's tiny, frail grandmother. When Father and I visited we'd always have something for Great Grandma and her adult sons, Ralph and Antonio. Possibly we'd picked fresh vegetables from his mother's garden. Maybe we'd deliver a pot of steaming soup. Perhaps we'd give Great Grandmother hot bread straight from her daughter's brick oven. Dad's uncles, Ralph and Tony, might get some of the pasta with beans Grandmother knew her brothers loved.

Great-grandmother spoke no English. Her face expressed her emotions. She had the sweetest smile. I figured that the flood of Italian words she uttered spoke of being happy to see us. I picked out words which were by now familiar, words she'd whisper as we left. I asked Dad to translate. He smiled and said, "You are good, like bread."

Dad's snowy-haired Mamouche was a vision of white on white. She pulled to her chin elaborately embroidered, crisply ironed white sheets. Great Grandmother's massive, soft, fluffy, white comforter kept her warm, her frosty home heated by the wood stove in the kitchen. Her bedroom was stark, furnished solely with a black iron bed and a small wooden dresser. The only contrast on the white walls was a large wooden crucifix.

The identical wooden crucifix appeared in every home of my father's and mother's family members and in the homes of most of their friends. I've seen this crucifix all my life. Now it's a legacy that my husband brought from the home of his late parents. The emaciated, barely clothed, nailed to the cross, loin cloth draped, surprisingly calm depiction of Jesus Christ fascinated me as a youth.

It wasn't the nearly naked feature of the Christ figure that mesmerized me. Instead I thought often about the serenity of Jesus as he experienced the slow death characteristic of crucifixion. Why did his face show no sign of the agony of this torture?

In time I understood the significance of the tranquility that the craftsperson molded into the face of Christ. I came to this conclusion in an offhand way.

Dad and my uncles were painting their mother's bedroom walls. By then she had become too shaky to paint. She was still strong, having developed many muscles through the tasks called for in kneading bread and cleaning houses.

Poverty during the Depression meant that most women did their own cleaning. It was only for the most demanding chores that they spent scarce money on help with their households. As a cleaning woman Grandma did the most labor-intensive work. She washed walls, climbing ladders. She scrubbed floors with a wash brush and pail. She rolled up and hung heavy carpets to beat them on the line. Now she was prematurely old.

Dad and his brothers prepared to paint Grandma's bedroom. They removed the large wooden crucifix from her wall. It lay on a dresser in the bedroom where my little sister and I slept when visiting our father's people. I couldn't resist playing with it. I discovered a well within the wood.

What could be more fascinating? This was the familiar crucifix that I'd come to expect in homes. By gently jiggling the inlaid upper piece of wood I not only found a secret section, but also discovered that this curious compartment contained some interesting, strange stuff.

Why did it hold tiny candles and a matchbox? What was the reason for the little piece of white cloth? Why the miniature, empty bottle?

Bingo!!! I unfolded a yellowed sheet of paper. This is exactly what was written on it:

Instructions for use of the Divinity Crucifix-Sick Call Set

On a small table, which is situated so as to be seen by the patient, and covered with fresh linen, place the Divinity Crucifix-Sick Call Set and have the crucifix inserted in the slot at top of base. Place a Sacramental candle in each candle stick holder. Also, have on the table a glass of water, a spoon, the communion cloth, and the bottle, which is supplied, filled with Holy water.

If the Sacrament of Extreme Unction is to be administered, a member of the family should meet the Priest at the door with a lighted candle, and conduct him to the sick room. In addition to the above have a small plate containing crumbs of bread, and make up five small balls with the absorbent cotton furnished in the set.

Maybe the priest used the absorbent cotton to apply the holy oils he would bring. By this age I knew the sacraments of the Roman Catholic Church. I learned a little about Extreme Unction. I didn't know the definition of "Unction" but I knew that this sacrament was for those who were dying. It was also called The Last Rites.

Much has changed in the Roman Catholic Church regarding the Sacrament of Extreme Unction. The name has changed to the Anointing of the Sick. This sacrament is a ritual healing not only for physical, but also for mental and spiritual sickness. When the priest arrives at the bedside, his very presence no longer announces impending death. In the past, I recall expressions of anticipatory grief and soft whispers around the deathbed that it was time to call the priest. Often this was also when the family alerted the undertaker. Now, however, there is less danger in scaring the sick to death.

These days some of the faithful receive this sacrament repeatedly. Perhaps they are chronically ill with a serious ailment. Maybe they are critically ill but on waiting lists for organ transplants that could be their return route to good health. The emphasis is now on comforting and healing. Some things have not changed, however. It is only a priest who can confer this sacrament. While imminent death is not the only impetus for calling for a priest, there is often serious sickness or injury involved.

After all these years, I think I understand why the little statuette affixed to the cross shows Jesus as serene as he experienced the slow death characteristic of crucifixion. His face does not show signs of the extreme agony of this torture because Christ is at peace. Well aware that he is approaching the end of his life on earth, his expression shows acceptance of dying and anticipation of life after death.

The depiction of serenity while in the process of dying gives all of us who are ever ill, and those of us perhaps experiencing physical, emotional, or spiritual pain, a reminder of one of the great virtues. That is the virtue of hope. Indeed, we cannot avoid death. Death comes to each of us. What we should resist is hopelessness. It is despair, not death, which is the danger.

Even in the old days when Extreme Unction was also called The Last Rites, when everyone thought of this as the sacrament for the dying, hope may have been the reason why this particular Divinity Crucifix-Sick Call Set was the only item on my great-grandmother's bedroom wall.

Elderly, uneducated, infirm, and unable to use the language of the country into which she had long-ago immigrated, she was nevertheless wise and courageous. In her youth she left behind all that was familiar. She was impoverished in war torn Sicily. Unfortunately, she was again impoverished in the USA. She found freedom from fear, fascism and political instability, however. Therefore she was happy to be in America. She and her young husband, determined to make a better life for their child, who with her parents braved the rough seas in a ship packed with people. These young parents navigated the

163

labyrinth of entry on Ellis Island without the benefit of the language. Then they raised a fine family of good, strong, and honest children while wars were waged in Europe and during the depths of the greatest Depression in the world.

Perhaps over the years, gazing at the crucifix on her bedroom wall she was not thinking of death. This could be true even though she was not noticeably afraid of death. She looked at the crucifix that would one day be used for The Last Rites. Possibly she focused on the peaceful expression of the face of Jesus Christ. Maybe what she saw was hope.

Like Great Grandmother, I do not have a notable fear of death. This mindset may be somewhat signature for us as Sicilians. Our ancestors came from a rough terrain, where living was hard and life was often short.

Significantly, bread figures in the sacrament of Extreme Unction, just as bread is also integral to the sacrament of Holy Communion. Remember that the instructions in the Divinity Crucifix-Sick Call Set called for "...a small plate containing crumbs of bread..." The bread crumbs would be used as a substitute for the communion wafer. The dying, whose digestive systems had slowed, could still consume a crumb of the bread the priest could consecrate as Holy Communion.

Bread is a staple in the lives of all people. It is the stuff of life for all and the mainstay of those who cannot afford more costly comfort foods. Some types of bread are somewhat short on nutrition. Most bread, however, is a means of feeling full.

Bread is basic. That's why to be "good like bread" is high praise indeed.

Bread is good. It fills us and nourishes us. The scent of fresh baked bread makes us salivate. Every nation has its unique version of this staple. Immigrants yearn for the bread of their country. Bread becomes one of the ways that we are linked to our origins. We speak of "breadwinners" as those who keep their family fed. We refer to vast acres of the USA as the breadbasket, the farmlands that feed us all.

Bread literally kept Father's impoverished family going. His mother baked. The scent of her delicious bread wafted from the brick oven in their backyard throughout their humble neighborhood. Walking home from school her children caught the scent of her fresh bread. Approaching their house, her little ones knew that their mother's fine bread would be on their dinner table. They couldn't be sure that there would be anything else.

Providence placed Father's home next to a busy city fire hall. The scent of his mom's bread never failed to reach the hungry, husky firemen who worked next door. They loved her bread.

During and after the world wars, during the depths of the Depression, there were shortages of many staples. Rationing spread the supplies as equitably as possible and included the bread baking ingredients of flour, sugar, and yeast.

There were different ration rules for those who provided vital services, firemen among them. Rations for firemen were considered critical. In this city of steel mills, firemen were even more essential than elsewhere. Special caution was in place considering the potential for constant combustion. In this filthy metropolis, where blast furnaces from the mills would erupt in flame, ashes would fall from the sky like dirty snow. Fires sprang from the sparks of the massive ovens smelting steel.

Some liked the shooting fires that lit up the night sky, much like fireworks on display. Some found fire fascinating. My childhood reaction was the opposite. I feared fire. The city night sky depicted what I imagined as hell. Perhaps this explains why I've always hated fireworks as well.

Grandmother's neighboring firemen figured large in the well-being of their city. With access to more rations, they had flour, sugar, and yeast. They gave Grandmother large sacks of flour. In turn she baked bread and gave them loaves. They countered by paying her for bread. She responded by refusing their money. They insisted on paying. Thus it was that Grandma Julia ran an open-air bakery with her backyard brick oven. The firemen helped her pay her bills, assisting her to keep her house.

Nor were flour, sugar, and yeast along with money the only assistance these fine men gave. They helped the young widow bring up her family. The son left fatherless at age two became especially dear to them.

Firefighters fascinated Dad's youngest brother, Sammie. He loved their big truck. He found the alarm exciting instead of irritating. He liked the big, strong men who welcomed his frequent visits to their fire hall. He shared the huge meals they prepared and served for themselves. They taught him to cook and bake. They nurtured his spindly body. They reveled in his hero worship.

Not surprisingly, my Uncle Sam chose their career, serving their city as a firefighter for forty-four years. With the cooking and baking expertise he learned as a little boy, he became his fire hall's chief cook. Also, he cooked and baked in his own home, teaching these skills to his children.

Throughout his childhood the firemen taught him to exercise. Forever fit, he worked as a stagehand upon retirement. Having no fear of heights, he rigged sets with ease and skill.

Having learned bread baking from his mother, he baked delicious bread. His became the bread his fellow firefighters craved.

Many decades later, his son, Patsy, makes his own bread, baking the recipe Grandmother passed to his father and his father gave him. Patsy and I have a mutual cousin, Patrick, who also bakes bread using the recipe Grandmother passed to his mother and his mother gave him. Now both men serve their homemade bread when my husband and I are the guests they warmly welcome.

Grandmother's gift is the bread that fed generations. One of Dad's brothers and one of his sisters taught their sons to bake bread. They also passed on the special qualities that make these cousins Pat and Patsy "good like bread."

Our only son and daughter-in-law magnanimously named our first grandson Andino. Called by his great-great-grandmother's last name, maybe it's not surprising that Andino also makes bread. He also bakes specialty recipes my cousins Patsy and Pat send him. More significantly, he shows all the signs of becoming a man who is "good like bread."

Their Great-Great-Grandma Julia's breadmaking legacy is not the only breadmaking lineage our grandchildren share. Wisely, I married a man who learned his grandmother's bread baking from his mother. Our children enjoyed the bread my mother-in-law baked for us all the years they grew up. It is basically the same recipe used by her mother, my grandmother Julia and my great-grandmother Mamouche. Our children named Lou's mother's bread "Grandma Rochon's Famous Bread," hand lettering this name on a label of her loaf. Lou's mother was touched.

Nor did her compliments come only from children. She baked nonstop for church bake sales. Her proud husband delivered her bread straight from the oven, running the half block from home to church bringing loaves to the eager parishioners who had money in hand.

Both my husband's parents set highest standards for being spouses, parents, in-laws, and grandparents. This couple was "good like bread." My husband, Louis, followed their fine example. He is a man who is "good like bread."

Louis is not the only man from his family to bake bread. Arthur, his youngest brother's son, bakes his grandmother's bread recipe. Particularly precious is what this young man did as a teen. His grandmother had terminal cancer but she was determined to continue baking bread for all of us, often. She was slow to recognize, however, that she no longer had the strength required to knead the dough.

Louis simply filled in for the kneading stage, working side by side with his mother in her kitchen. Taking his turn at kneading was her grandson Arthur. I witnessed the spiraling weakness in my mother-in-law. This was sadder than I can say. At the same time, I was in awe of the ever-enhancing strength of character in both my husband and our nephew.

Almost to the day she died, my mother-in-law gave us the gift of "Grandma's Famous Bread." That she was able to do so is a tribute to the fine men who made it possible. That they baked bread together made memories for us all. At our annual Christmas dinner, they serve the bread they bake in their own kitchens. Grandma's recipe keeps her with us in celebration.

Louis and Arthur are "good, like bread." When Arthur was a soldier in Afghanistan we prayed God bless and protect this fine young man.

Nor are Louis and Arthur the only ones in our family to make "Grandma's Famous Bread." Camille uses the recipe and thus keeps us with her. Our oldest daughter, Jennie, baked this recipe when she served in the Peace Corps in Antigua. It was a challenge because there were periodic shortages of flour and sugar in the island country where she served. Along with yeast these are fundamental to the recipe.

Now Jennie bakes her Grandma's recipe with her young son and daughter. Her children, indeed all our six grandchildren, bake bread with their grandfather. Louis does most of the work, however, while our grandkids delight in squeezing, squashing, flinging, smashing and swinging their individual loaves in their version of kneading the dough.

All our grandchildren are too young to have known Louis' fine mother. All of them love "baking" with Louis, however. They renamed it "Poppa's Famous Bread." I do hope his mother doesn't mind.

Returning to my original question, what is this connection between bread and the men in my life?

The most important men in my life are my father, my husband, our son, and our grandsons. All have breadmaking bonds. Father and my husband had breadmaking mothers, who baked the bread of their mothers. Andino, a grandson, bakes the bread of his great-great-grandmother, whose last name is his first name.

Furthermore, we have family traditions on both sides of my family of males baking delicious bread.

As for me, I not only love to smell, eat, and serve my husband's bread but also, I love to watch him knead the dough. It is a sensual scene. I see his strong hands and solid arms, his muscles rippling with the work, squeezing, shaping, and kneading the dough.

Sometimes I see the sinew in my husband's hands. I watch in wonder as he pounds the dry flour into the sticky stuff that is the newly risen dough. I smell the beer-like scent of the yeast and I am again in my childhood kitchen baking bread with my grandmother. Perhaps part of Louis is in his dying mother's kitchen, saving her pride, kneading her bread. Maybe the sensual strength in his hands comes from an even earlier time in his life. Maybe he fortified his childhood hands by milking cows and driving teams of Belgian draft horses, working with his Mom's father on the family farm.

Lucky in love, in my long marriage my husband has always been "good, like bread." A French Canadian, he didn't hear this term of endearment when he was growing up. Nevertheless, this Sicilian phrase describes him perfectly.

In my husband's hands I see the same impressive musculature of my father's hands.

As a barber, my dad stretched and strengthened his hands all day. His work with his hands kept them flexible. I close my eyes and feel the strength of those fingers on my head as he massaged my scalp, washed my hair, and then cut my hair.

Father only lived a small portion of my life. Fortunately, I knew him as "good, like bread."

Chapter 21

Early Investment Lessons

Dad's bachelor uncles spent their youth studying investing. Dad went to work while in high school. His uncles urged him to save any money that he was not using to help support his mother, his brothers and sisters. They showed their intellectually curious nephew how to make his meager money grow. Their motto was, "A fool works for his money. A wise man makes his money work for him."

What they told my father was less impressive than what they showed him. They were the only two men he knew who worked for themselves. Other men in Dad's life worked in the steel mills, the post office, the schools, the hospitals or were employed by the city. The uncles lived during the Great Depression, when there were no jobs to be had, and began investing modest amounts as soon as they could. They supported themselves. They took care of their mother once their father died. They did it all by making their money work for them.

To say that they "played the stock market" grossly underestimates the work they did. This was not a "play the ponies" gambling game. It was day trading. They spent time daily in their city's largest library reading newspapers from around the country as well as international publications. During their everyday stock market visit, they called on their Customers' Man, the term once used to identify brokers. They watched the ticker tape to determine their losses and gains. Only when confident that this research indicated probable future trends did they trade stocks.

Modeling his uncles' investment strategies, my father learned to research current and past developments both nationally and internationally. All his life, Dad read the daily stock reports. He read and studied the daily news. He watched his barber shop television solely for news reports. Otherwise, silence prevailed in his shop when there were no customers. His quiet shop was a great place for reading. He subscribed to publications as dissimilar as the Wall Street Journal and the Algonac Courier.

Father's golfing buddy was the owner/editor of the Algonac Courier. Newspaper production fascinated me when my classmates and I toured the main street shop on a school field trip. We watched Don, a recent graduate of our high school, set the type on large trays. The boys seemed particularly pleased by the gritty mess Don created during the printing process. In the ink spattered work area the printer's big hands, smiling face, and enormous apron were black smudged.

The editor's office with its picture window to the river view was my favorite. Then, as now, ships from all over the world moved slowly along the waterway, transporting massive containers of goods. They carried freight and were thus called freighters. The editor's view of the world passing by combined with the sound of the London-based Reuters up-to-the-minute news reports transmitted by noisy teletype. These visual and auditory prompts constantly reminded the editor of the huge world beyond our tiny village.

Dad's articulate, well-educated friend wrote his editorials at a polished wood desk fit. It was his custom to wear well-tailored suits, silk ties, polished dress shoes, and crisply ironed shirts. His meticulous, well-appointed office was worthy of an Architectural Digest photo shoot. It was in sharp contrast to the blackened print area adjacent to his office. Father's friend was a local leader who had a lifelong influence on me. Dad's friend, the editor, was the first writer I knew. He showed me the power of his written words.

Dad read the Detroit News, the Detroit Free Press, and, until it discontinued publication in 1960, the Detroit

Times. A newspaper cost seven cents. Sometimes he would let me keep the change from a dime. Not often. But then, three cents is thirty percent of a dime. Why would he give me the change twice a day? He was a very thrifty man.

Chapter 22

Defining Poverty

There is an official poverty measure in the United States. It was developed in the early 1960s and was determined to be the dollar value of a minimum adequate diet times three. The multiplier of three came from a 1955 Food Consumption Survey. Data showed that food expenditures accounted for one-third of after-tax income for the average family of two adults and two children. An annual threshold was set as the standard of needs and has been fixed in inflation adjusted terms since. The U.S. Census Bureau publishes official annual poverty statistics as standards of needs. In the 1980s I administered state and federal grants. The standard of needs determined qualification for some educational programs.

Statistics sometimes cause my eyes to glaze over. Soap, however, defines poverty for me.

Some people never think about soap. To many it's just a lump in a dish next to the sink or a squirt from a bottle. To me, hand soap is much more. Every time I wash I think about the soap. I appreciate soap. It has meaning independent of cleanliness.

Grandma Julia used to give me hand soaps when I was a little girl. I thought that a bar of soap was a curious choice for a gift but I dutifully wrote and sent her warm thank you notes. It was kind of her to think of me. It just seemed like an offbeat object for a present. She must have noticed that we had plenty of bar soap in our home. She would stay with us for months each year.

It wasn't until we stayed overnight at her home that I realized why the soap she sent me was so special. Her bathroom soap was awful. It was everything that soap shouldn't be. Her soap smelled vile. It was hard and scratchy. I had to scrub vigorously with this rough, pea green, rectangular, rigid bar that left a smelly, somewhat slimy, greenish tint on my hands. It didn't lather. This was the only soap I'd ever used which made my hands red and rough and yet failed to get rid of dirt. I'd never seen such appalling soap.

Having examined many bars of soap in a wide range of cost in the years since I was a child in my grandmother's bathroom, I haven't seen soap like it since. I conclude that hers was homemade soap. Homemade soap at that time included lard and lye.

The soap my grandmother sent me was the opposite of the soap she used. It was all that soap should be. It had a delicate, pleasant scent. It produced a creamy lather that softened skin. It was even embossed with flower designs. Some bars were so lovely that I used them in my dresser drawers to freshen my things. My grandmother must have saved her meager money to buy me these lovely soaps.

Usually people see soap as one of the necessities of daily life rituals. I long marveled that something as small as soap made a big impact on me. Then I realized that soap was a symbol. It became how I measured family income.

Others have unique definitions of poverty, stark symbols which clearly show their views of the difference between those who have money and those who don't. For my father it was a matter of milk.

Fresh milk was never served in the home where my dad grew up. The family could sometimes splash drops of canned milk over their oatmeal. In stark contrast, in the home my father and mother made for us, fresh milk was regularly delivered to our door. I can see my father's smile when he would pour from the heavy glass milk jug. He was very proud to tell us that we could have as much milk on our cereal as we wanted.

His pride became my mental message. To this day I pour fresh milk carefully. This is a lesson I wanted our children to learn. They failed to take it to heart. By telling them Dad's story I thought they'd understand the importance of avoiding wasted milk and discarded food. I explained that Dad and his family often ate their mother's bread for supper along with glasses of water. But they never knew my father. They never saw the memory of hunger cross his face. They never envisioned his pride in being the provider. Hearing is never the same as seeing.

An affluent friend described the difference between rich and poor. This fastidious, smartly dressed, carefully made up woman met me at lunch after her weekly scheduled salon treatment. Her hair and nails were perfect. She confided that she had been born into poverty. By a combination of hard work and luck she was now wealthy.

Her father was poor, but finally he got a full time job with benefits. Once the steady paycheck became a reality, she saw her mother smile more and her parents fight less. This led to the day she well remembered. That day she knew she was no longer poor.

Her mother took her aside in her bedroom. Her mother glowed when she told her daughter that they could discard their "rags." They could afford sanitary napkins. She said that she earned a varied amount of money in her lifetime, but she never felt as rich as the day she learned that she could use sanitary napkins.

No one had to tell me that poor people lived differently than I did. I saw the soap. No one need describe the desire poor parents have to give their children a better life. I saw the pride in my father's face. Nor was it necessary for my friend to explain why she felt rich. I share her appreciation for basic hygienic products. Whenever I wash, I realize that I'm rich in comparison to many. Soap is my daily prompt to be grateful. Milk each morning was my father's reminder. My friend had a monthly message.

Poverty can be officially defined. The U.S. is specific in its figures. But in addition, there are the definitions of poverty and of prosperity that each of us holds in our hearts.

Chapter 23

Poverty Affected Perception

When I was two, my parents moved from Mom's Michigan hometown to the big city in Ohio where Dad grew up. Two years later they returned to Michigan. An Ohio family, the Magdalena family, who were neighbors to my dad in his childhood, happened to move to the Michigan area where my parents settled. That's how they became neighbors again, this time in Mother's home state. Dad and his once-again neighbors were thrilled at this turn of events. They quickly endeared themselves to Mother. All members of both neighbors became family to one another. They were the first friends in Father's life. Now reconnected, that friendship continued throughout Dad's lifespan. Generation after generation, the closeness continues today.

Gradually we learned about Dad's childhood from this family. They described the deprivation my dad could never discuss. Like Father's family, they were poor. Unlike them, however, the breadwinner lived. Therefore their poverty was not as desperate.

What wonderful people! Their special occasions became ours as well, and vice versa. Graduations, weddings, childbirths, we celebrated all events in both families together. To their great credit, even though they were first close to Father, they continued to befriend my mother and us after he died. Many friends with whom my parents socialized discontinued their invitations when Mother became a widow.

Our two families shared much: ethnicity, religion, "the old neighborhood," impoverished beginnings. They didn't share mutual spending habits. I understood that poverty affects perception. Deprivation affects the once-poor in different ways.

Some seem to pinch pennies, to spend sparingly, to become obsessively careful with money. Father, for instance, treated himself in a miserly manner. Others react in an exact opposite manner, spending every penny and more. Father's first friends had this reaction to their early disadvantages. They bought the best. They passed this practice on through generations.

Everyone in their family buys whatever they want whether or not they can afford it. They incur debt with abandon. They buy only the priciest. They spend years paying exorbitant interest on credit debt. They take overtime or second jobs to support their runaway spending. Every bride had a huge Italian wedding, plunging the family and the bride and groom in debt for many years. No matter. This large family felt that a show of extravagance was required. When the elders died they had long ago spent all their money. The next generation felt compelled by honor to put on an extravagant funeral with internment in the most expensive mausoleum. This is a family of big spenders literally from birth to death and beyond.

Both a bare bones budget and a profligate attitude seem extreme to me. That being said, I concede that there is much about spending that makes no sense. I am my own best example.

Having been born privileged in comparison to my father's early poverty, I nevertheless inherited his reluctance to spend money. It's hard to spend the money I have, nearly impossible to spend money that I'd have to borrow. Why is that? I have always had plenty to eat. I never worried about being homeless. I could always pay for good medical care. I never worked seven days a week. I've never been impoverished. Yet I often act as if I were poor. This is a mystery.

Once impoverished, Dad was forever affected, regardless of subsequent prosperity. Did he leave me a legacy of the dark fear of indigence? Can abject poverty mark the poor forever with generations to follow stuck in cycles of relentless saving or senseless spending?

Chapter 24

A Beloved Barber

Our father was a beloved barber. Beloved seems a strange
adjective with which to describe a barber but I cannot think
of a better word.

At his funeral, his customers expressed their grief.
There were tears in grown men's eyes, sobs moving little
boys' chests.

Characteristic of small town barber shops in the
1950s, Dad's shop was a men's community center, much
like the Greek restaurants and clubs which remained men's
domain for many years. I wandered into one in the 1980s in
Detroit's Greek Town. Total silence resulted. All the men
looked up from their meals, drinks, or games. No one asked
me to leave. It wasn't necessary. Their grave stares told me
that I was in the wrong place.

Barber shops in the 1950s were bastions for boys
and men. Women or girls didn't have their hair cut in
barber shops. Men didn't get haircuts in beauty shops.
Perhaps there was a "men only" atmosphere in barber
shops because they served some men who were still in the
process of growing up. Did they see themselves in their

"Boys Only" treehouses or roughly hammered together club shacks? A sign stating "No Girls Allowed" would have been apt at an old-time barber shop.

There were informal discussion groups in the hushed quasi-reading room atmosphere of Father's barber shop. He had the Detroit News first edition and a Detroit Free Press last edition. He sent me to the Drug Store to buy them, morning and evening. He subscribed to the Wall St. Journal and the New York Times. He was a big city man in a small village shop. He read the newspapers. His customers read them. They would discuss the latest news or stock market reports. Many would stay long after their haircuts, deep in debate.

Some of Dad's customers were executives in the manufacturing industries that were in full production during those heady economic times. They lived in our tiny hamlet but commuted to management positions. They brought trade publications occasionally and contributed to the variety of subjects for discussion.

Once everyone gleaned every bit of news and chewed over all the information, Dad would gather the publications and send me to the local library to donate them. Our library was open four days per week.

In addition to current events, they also discussed history. Some served in the Civilian Conservation Corps, a public work relief program that operated from 1933 to 1942 in the United States. This corps, also called the CCC, hired and housed eligible men and boys, unemployed and unmarried.

A family friend, Bill Pollauf, with whom Mom grew up, served in the CCC. He is one of the last friends alive among my parents' contemporaries. I am glad I talked with him at length about his work in this corps before he began to lose some of his memories.

"Bill," I said, "you must have had it hard when you were in the Civilian Conservation Corps. I read that some housing was rustic, no heat except for pot belly stoves, no indoor plumbing, eating on planks set up over sawhorses. What an adjustment!"

Bill's characteristic good-natured smile lit his face. He chuckled. Bill said, "The only adjustment was that my life got better. I met a lot of swell guys. We earned money, and money was scarce then, let me tell you. Yes, I left home but our house was heated by the stove, we grew most of our food, and we had a backyard privy. We ate at Grandma Pollauf's old oak table. I was one of eleven children but two didn't live to adulthood.

"In most of the CCC camps, there'd be some two hundred men. That's a whole lot more than Mom and Dad and the nine of us kids eating meals. Our CCC camp, like many, started up as a tent city. We loved eating outside, weather permitting. When the weather was bad we sat on our bunks to eat. Once we'd built our permanent camps we'd have barracks, kitchens, mess halls, and officers' quarters.

"We worked hard sun up to sun down. I gotta say it was easier on us country boys. The city guys had to learn how to make campfires, how to wash with creek water, how to kill ticks, and how to dig privies.

"All of us were real grateful. The government paid $30.00 a month. We had to send $25.00 to our families. We were glad to. Life was tough at home. We got that $5.00 spending money but I saved most of that. There wasn't much chance to spend money anyway. They issued us uniforms. They fed us three times a day. Nobody I knew ever ate three times a day. I met a lot of swell guys. I heard a lot about big cities. We played cards by candlelight after supper. But mostly, we worked.

"Us guys planted trees. I knew how so I sorta became a leader. We planted in the Manistee National Forest. They told us that there's more than 101,000 acres in this mammoth forest. Some guys got lonesome, but not me. I loved Michigan's Upper Peninsula. I was excited to see some places beyond the family farm. When our kids were small I'd drive the wife and kids upstate every year. We set up our families' reunion there."

One of Bill's daughter, Kathy, was the lead librarian at the Algonac Library. I attended Kathy's lecture on the Civilian Conservation Corps. Kathy's always been an environmentalist. Franklin Delano Roosevelt is her hero. She told us that in the nine years of the CCC three billion trees were planted.

Kathy said, "The Civilian Conservation Corps is responsible for more than half of the reforestation, both public and private, in U.S. history. In National Parks the CCC created paths, built flood barriers, fought fires, maintained roads and trails, and constructed monuments, towers, and benches.

"Not only did my dad serve in the CCC and tell us kids all about planting trees in Michigan, but also I've traveled through the Smokey and Yosemite National Parks and I've seen the magnificent CCC works there."

Kathy felt that in the current political climate of politician and citizen frustration, the CCC employing 3,000,000 men represents exemplary cooperation. The U.S.

Department of Labor recruited men in good physical condition from ages 18 through 25. Later the age limits changed to 17-23 and expanded to WWI veterans (housed in separate camps). Service was six months but many reenlisted for a total of two years. The U.S. War Department clothed and trained them for two weeks. The U.S. Department of Agriculture designed and managed specific work projects.

Kathy said, "More than 90% of all enrollees participated in some basic education and vocational training. Throughout the CCC, more than 40,000 illiterate men learned to read and write." My jaw dropped. Others in the packed audience were equally impressed.

Kathy's praise for the CCC reminded me of yet another reason her dad said he loved the corps. Bill said, "And then there was the food. Great big dishes filled with food. Steaming hot food. Big slabs of meat. Deep pots of soup. Mounds of mashed potatoes. And the bread! Lots of butter for it too. No butter for us at home because we hadda buy it from the neighbors. We didn't have a cow. I missed my Ma's bread but we had different kinds at the camp. Rye. Wheat. Bread called Pumpie Nickle or some such.

"And, Boy Howdy, we were hungry. The guys would rush the table. I figured out I had to do that too. But it turned out that there was always plenty. At first I just looked at the food. Gave my eyes a treat. Let my gut wait for the fill up. Gained forty-three pounds in six months! Some guys gained a little more; a few gained a little less; but we all put on the pounds. I ate my fill at every meal Uncle Sam served."

"Wow," I said. "I can't picture you with forty more pounds on you, Bill. You've always been so fit and trim."

"Well, ya," Bill said. "Ever since the camp what you see now is what I got then. After the CCC I enlisted.

"After the war I got a good job. Never missed a day of work. I'm glad I signed up for the CCC. I kept in touch with some of the guys I worked with and all of us felt we made a bit of difference by planting trees."

Bill was one of Dad's customers as well as my parents' friend. Bill survived being a World War II prisoner of war. One of his sons told me that Bill never talked about that experience until he was very old and only in response to one of the great-grandchildren. "Did your captors honor the Geneva Conference?" Bill said, "No."

Dad and most of his contemporaries were World War II veterans. Dad's customers ranged in age. Some gave firsthand descriptions of the deprivations of the Depression. There were also World War I veterans. There were disabled servicemen. Most of the men lived through one or another of the greatest crises since the Civil War. I can only imagine the conversations among them. Perhaps these reticent men, in the privacy of Dad's barber shop, in the company of others who understood, spoke of the unspeakable.

The men-only barber shop unwritten rule did not apply when Dad cut hair for Camille and me. He shampooed our hair in his deep sink in the barber shop after hours. Until his death, Father was the only one to wash and cut my hair. He massaged my head with strong fingers. I miss those moments with him. Today when I get beauty shop services I most enjoy shampoos.

When Dad cut my sister's hair and mine, as well as the times when my mother gathered the barber towels to launder them, were the sole occasions when women were welcome. The shop was a man cave. Dad hung a tarp on the wall of the back hall and he and customers practiced golf shots. My classmates perfected their swings there. Adding yet more testosterone to the barber shop building, fraternal orders rented the back-meeting room. Men's groups gathered there.

Anyone who thinks men are indifferent to hairstyle is mistaken. Walking through town last week, I happened upon Bill, my high school classmate. He told me that he agonized when the brush cut was in style. Dad cut Bill's hair all his teen years and young adulthood until Dad's death. Father told Bill that his naturally curly hair didn't fit a brush cut. Seeing his face fall, Dad tried some heavy-duty gel. It worked. Bill then looked like all the other boys in 1957.

In this precious and chance conversation, Bill said my father was very important to him. Bill's dad worked on the lake freighters and was gone sailing for months at a time. His was a houseful of twelve children. Bill didn't get a lot of attention at home. His mom used to cut Bill's hair but failed to have her shears sharpened. Sometimes hairs near the delicate temple or the ear lobe area got caught in the dull shears. Hair might be ripped out to the follicles. Bill dreaded the hair cutting and jerking process and he hated the lack of style. When he was old enough to get a job, he paid for his haircuts.

Bill said that he and my dad talked at length. Their impoverished childhoods were the link. Instead of a quick cut, Bill got the full service for his $2.00. Father gave Bill a shave. He washed his hair, massaging his scalp with his fingers and then with his handheld massage machine, moving it gently over Bill's scalp, neck, and shoulders. His haircut followed, styled with gel to ensure that Bill fit in at school. Dad sharpened his straight edge with his strop before he gave Bill close cuts.

Bill said, "Your father dusted my neck with white powder with a soft brush. I can still recall the sweet scent. Finally, with a flourish, he'd sweep away the cape that caught the cut hair. When I finished high school and left home, your dad helped me order a strop through his supply catalog. Then he made it my graduation present."

Bill related his long-ago experiences with a wide smile. He and his lovely wife invited me into their lavish, riverfront home. Bill said he wanted to show me something. It was his leather strop. I told him that my dad's original hangs in our bathroom. Bill and I savor our strops.

Bill and I have mutual high school friend, Mike, who connected with Bill's experiences in Dad's barber shop. "I never saw much of my dad either. So, your father became more than a barber. He was a very nice man. I got the feeling that he cared about me. I'll never forget the day I decided I wanted to wear my hair longer. I asked your dad for the new Princeton cut. Your dad said 'Are you sure this is going to be okay with your mother? Maybe I should give her a call first.' I was seventeen by then, well beyond worrying about what my mom thought about my hair.

"But I wasn't such a grown up in your father's mind. I did tell my mom I was changing my hairstyle. She just nodded, not particularly interested. When I assured your dad that my mother knew about my haircut I know he believed me. I knew he trusted me. He was interested in my life. He listened. I trusted him; felt confident in his barber chair that I could tell him whatever was on my mind."

When my cousin, Joe, was ten, his father died instantly in an industrial accident. Joe told me yesterday that my father immediately focused on his role as Joe's Godfather.

"He convinced me that he needed a helper in the shop. I was to walk the two blocks to his shop each day after school before I walked home. He made a big fuss about how clean his shop was now because I was so good at sweeping up the hair. When I finished, he'd take a break and the two of us went into the back room. He'd pour me a glass of cold milk and get himself a hot coffee. He'd ask about my teachers, my classmates, and my grades. He'd talk about the local and national news, but mostly he'd listen. After a few months, we became more and more comfortable in our conversations. I mentioned a girl in my history class who was pretty. It got to the point when I'd really look forward to my important job of sweeping and our time together.

"Then came the winter morning I'll never forget. My fourteen-year-old brother, and my sisters, aged eight and four awakened to find our neighbor setting out our breakfast. Within a few minutes, Mom came home. She looked terrible. Had she been up all night? Why were her eyes so red?

"Mom said, 'I have some very bad news. Your uncle died in his sleep last night.' And there is was…bam…my father died suddenly and now, two years later, my Godfather died too."

Chapter 25

So Many Summers

Concerts in the park on warm summer evenings at dusk are the stuff of lives well lived. I enjoy as many performances as weather will allow. Such concerts loom large in the pattern of my memory. Relaxing in a collapsible chair in yet another park for yet another local concert last night, I thought of Father and Mother as the young parents they once were.

He spent his nine-hour workday in his barber shop, mostly on his feet. She spent endless hours cooking, cleaning, and doing laundry without the time-saving appliances we take for granted today. She organized and lead charity projects. Their joy lay in taking us to parks. One particularly glorious autumn the year I was nine and my little sister was five, our parents drove us almost daily to play in our nearby Algonac State Park.

They packed their wooden picnic basket into the deep trunk of their chartreuse Desoto. We were recognized everywhere they drove. My thrifty father thought he was saving money buying a car others roundly rejected because of the color. Were the dollars he saved worth the loss of anonymity that our outrageously painted automobile brought?

Our parents took us to outdoor concerts in our village park. They loved music. They treasured the river forming the backdrop for every performance. No matter the weather, the river was always perfect for my father. I hear his voice declaring daily, "A beautiful day in Algonac." He was fascinated by the river surface reflecting the variety of colors from the sky.

Our annual Easter visits to Dad's hometown contrasted Michigan's fresh water beauty with the acrid soot belching from the iron mills in his Ohio birthplace. Father called his local waterway the muddy Mahoney. Those were the days when our country was king of manufacturing. The irony of the connection between Father's big, sooty city and Mother's pretty, tiny hamlet is not lost on the economics of the times.

Smelted in Ohio, iron ore was shipped to factories in Michigan. Returning from war, men were marrying, having families, and buying automobiles in ever increasing numbers. Ohio raw materials passed by our village, shipped on freighters carrying loads, using the Great Lakes as highways.

A tributary forms the border between the USA and Canada. It is the backdrop of main streets of four cities in our county. This waterway splits into three rivers that flow into the lake. These are named the North Channel, the Middle Channel, and the South Channel. No wonder small craft dominate the local economy.

Our parents joined in a love that bridged the big city/little village divide. They took us to simple summer concerts that mellowed all of us with music. Sophisticated symphonic interpretations were not the stuff of our summers. New York City had its concert stages in Central Park for magnificent music. Rather, we enjoyed the instant transformation of our postal carrier into an enthusiastic trumpet player. His sister-in-law played the clarinet. We marveled at our banker who loved to bang the drums. We admired our high school band director as he brought together the varying degree of talents our citizenry possessed to form the community band.

By high school I had attended concerts in our park most of my life. I practiced playing flute and piccolo in high school band until I minimized screeching sounds. Then I joined the other amateur performers in our community concerts. From the stage elevated above the green of our village park, I caught Dad's look of pride.

From the vantage point of time I report perusing the faces of fellow concert goers in recent Carnegie Hall performances. No patron's pride and pleasure matched the emotions on Father's face long ago.

Dad enjoyed my fledgling talent, but I know now there was another reason for his pride. He was pleased to give my sister and me the childhood he could never have envisioned. He earned the money spent on our dance and music lessons and on a used upright. Cam and I had the time and energy to develop any potential talent. At seventeen I was much older than Father was when he had to work to help support his family. I didn't have to get a job to help buy the groceries or pay the mortgages or utility bills.

With my weekly ten cent allowance, my wardrobe of two skirts, one dress, two blouses, two pairs of slacks, one pair of shorts, one bathing suit, and one pair of shoes, few saw me as rich. But to a man who never had a chance to be a boy my childhood was idyllic. He was fatherless and that was his signature state. He was my father; therefore, I was privileged.

Dad's sister, Maria, was also privileged. She often stayed with us when her times of "nervousness" arose. We'd bring her back from our visits to Youngstown when her needs arose. On one drive, Cam and I found it funny when Aunt Maria greedily gobbled every snack we offered in the car. Finally, our parents noticed.

"Leave your aunt alone. Let her rest, you two!"

Family would drive her to us some summers. Maybe quiet concerts in our park gave her some peace. She suffered symptoms psychiatrists might diagnose as Bipolar today. Perhaps our beautiful, blue river gave her some serenity.

Chapter 26

Death in a Small Town

There is no experience like death in a small town. I should know. I've lived my life in the same small town. Some would say that my small town life does not make me an expert. That would be true. Therefore, I include New York City in my reflections.

Those acquainted with the borough of Manhattan recognize it as one vast composite of many small neighborhoods. When I describe death in a small town and death in such communities as Chelsea and Greenwich Village neighborhoods, there's a commonality.

In a tiny shop, in a crowded Chelsea neighborhood, I met Frank, who loved his shop and loved people even more. No matter how long between visits he'd remember me and the little family I visit in New York City.

"How's your daughter?" he'd ask. "Their baby's doing well?"

Two years later he said with a belly laugh, "Must be glad you're here, running around the city, bringing home the bacon, so to speak. Momma and Daddy might not sleep much, now there's the second baby."

Six months later I stopped by. "How's the family? Is the little mommy tired?" Frank said.

"Well, we know how it is. Don't we, Frank? You were a young father. When our kids were babies I begged them to sleep."

"Take her some fresh liver. It's on the house. She needs nutrition to keep nursing."

An old, black-clad, tiny woman behind me in line broke out in a huge smile. I heard a snatch of comment, "Mas leche!"

Doing my daughter's errands rewarded me with meeting Frank. Proud of his skills and happy to share, Frank owned the only butcher shop I've known with comfortable waiting room chairs. I not only enjoyed his conversations, but also hung around to listen to his animated guidance.

"Here's your hamburger, Senora Sausalita, fresh ground! I've got some good-sized, low-cost briskets. You still plan on the whole family coming by on Saturday?"

"I wouldn't know how to cook a brisket, Francesco. Thanks anyway."

"Come on. Nothing could be easier. The secret's in slow roasting. 250 degrees for at least five hours. You started using that meat thermometer I gave you a while back? Now, I love this tender meat thinly sliced and in its own juice," Frank said. "But I've got a wine sauce recipe I give my special customers. I'll put your roasted brisket through my slicer if you'd like. Just bring it back and I'll slice it real thin."

One morning I walked my grandchildren to the Madison Square Park playground, dropping off dry cleaning along the way. Promising the Chelsea Park playground after Madison Square, I walked them west, picking up a prescription in the process. Our remaining errand was to Frank's shop. I went for meat. The children went for lollipops from Frank's big jar along with Frank's big smile.

Instead we got a shock. I spotted the big wreath on the door. That afternoon I visited the funeral home listed on the notice posted on the window.

There, I reflected on Frank's impact on my life; mingled with fellow customers I'd met in his long established shop; agreed that his recommended cuts of meat came with smiles broad as his waist. Young parents stated he taught them how to cook for their families. Shoppers of various ages said he showed them ways to stretch money in this expensive city, suggesting economical cuts and cooking tips to tenderize. Others worked in restaurants and talked about recipes showcasing Frank's prime cuts. We would miss our friend Frank.

Soon there was another loss. Sister Maria's solemn high funeral mass, said in a Spanish neighborhood church, brought back the morning I met the wise, wonderful woman. Ancient, short, enveloped in the old fashioned habit of her order, she approached me after a mass five years prior. She noticed me in the last pew, tears raining from my eyes. She said, "I help you?"

I sobbed.

"Was my daughter going to recover from the childbirth trauma?" I said. We prayed a Hail Mary together, hers in Spanish, mine in English.

As time went by, Sister Maria and I thanked God for my daughter's returning health and for her flourishing baby daughter. Two years later we again prayed, thankful for the newborn boy. We begged God for him to thrive and soon he did. I came to know the elderly nuns in their brownstone residence, bordering Greenwich Village and Chelsea, where they ran a childcare center. I learned that Fidel Castro deported Sister and her congregation of twelve nuns when he took over Cuba. The mother superior said, "The day after Fidel came to power we were locked out of our convent, our church was shuttered and we were deported."

The death of a friendly butcher and that of an aged, immigrant nun went largely unnoticed in this vast city. In contrast, there was the sudden death of a young, internationally known Philip Seymour Hoffman. Broadway dimmed the lights in mourning. I'd met his child in an elementary school. Grief spread through the Greenwich Village school community with his death. Parents praised these children's tear-stained teachers for sensitive responses to students' questions about unexpected death.

Youth see adults as the ones who applaud at their school plays; the daddies and moms who show up at parent/teacher conferences and Family Days. Children see parents as people, not as celebrities. Fans feel they relate to stars through tabloids and performances but real relationships are between those who know and care about each other. The world grieves when a beloved public figure dies. The family and community anguish.

In describing death in my small town I confine myself to three. Coincidentally, three is the number of funerals I attended this week.

The deceased differed widely. Dave and Carol were born, raised, and lived their entire lives in our small town.

Buck arrived as an adult and moved away in retirement. Dave was fifty-six. Carol was seventy-three. Buck was ninety and had been married seventy years. Carol was a widow. Dave was divorced. One never touched liquor and preached against drinking. Another enjoyed drinking. The third took an occasional social cocktail.

The varying locations and manner in which we gathered to mourn their deaths echoed the experiences that marked their lives. While in hospice care, Carol said, "No funeral parlor. No church. I want cremation. Then throw a party at the banquet center. Get the Achatz Caterers. They're the best. Have an open bar. I want my family and friends to celebrate. I've had a good life."

Buck had a traditional service. We packed the church and knelt in prayer. His family, unable to travel, sent their video retrospective of Buck's life. In return, church elders videotaped their heartfelt testimonials to send to his family. Sadie Smith said, "Pastor, you saved me. You turned my life to Jesus." Ron Cameel said, "Pastor told me I hadda join the choir. He said that God gave me talent but I hadda use it. Now I'm the Choir Director! I never wooda thought it."

Dave had two days of funeral parlor visitation followed by a community meal in a bar. His band played

Dave's signature songs in the background. Every local tavern's signboard posted "Rest in Peace, Dave." He played guitar in his band in each bar and in every parade in our town lifelong.

His family had a solemn holy mass said for Dave a month later. Delivering Dave's homily, the priest referred to the ties that knit our lives. The phrase "ties that knit" spoke to me. While I have often heard "ties that bind," I found that "knit" was the better. Thin skeins of yarn came to mind.

Whether we live in a New York City community or in a small Michigan town, I see invisible hands over countless years continuously knitting the netting, each skein steadily unrolling until there is no more. But ours has always been a fishing, sailing, and boatbuilding area. Nets are made to gather.

Attending each memorial, I pictured us, families and friends over decades, generations of both living and dead, knitting our netting, continuing our connections over our lifetimes, our memories the soft coverlets we lay beneath at night, our thoughts and prayers blanketing the graves of our dearly departed, our kinship the network that lies loose on our town...over us all.

There are reasons that I attended three funerals this week. Yes, I connected with each of the deceased, but also my presence brought the memory of my parents. Mom was an elementary schoolmate of Dave's father.

Dave's aged mother said, "Thank you for these old photos. I love this picture of my David at age two on a playground with your sister. Look. There are your parents, my Freddie and me watching over our children. Oh, my land, here's the four of us dancing. How we loved to dance! Sometimes Freddie and his band played for our dances in our old church hall.

"Gosh, this last photo shows the four of us, good friends, costumed for community theatre. Freddie really surprised me the time he had stage fright. Freddie was always outgoing and confident. But your shy father encouraged him and the show went on. It had always been the other way around."

I hadn't heard this story. I replied that Father told me that her gregarious, musically talented husband invited him to join the local theatre group. I told her that as a child, Dad had no time for performing arts. His family had no money for musical instruments, lessons, sports, or amusement. There was work. Father only learned to have fun in adulthood.

Buck, Dave, and Carol shared a connection to Father's barber shop. Buck and his sons were Dad's customers. He cut Dave's hair. Carol brought her son to Dad's barber chair. Father posted photos of toddler Dave's first haircut and those of Buck's son and Carol's boy on his barber shop bulletin board.

Carol's connection to Mother went back even farther. Her Swedish immigrant parents were friends with my Italian immigrant grandparents as they raised Carol and Mom in the depression years before our village became a city.

Born and raised in our small town, Dave and Carol lived their entire lives here. Buck came to our village right out of Bible College, serving as pastor more years than anyone before or since. Cam and I grew up with his children. His wife taught with my husband. She taught our children. Dave, Carol, Buck, Mother, and I shared long roots in this town. Dad had something in common with the three honored at this week's memorials. It was the love they earned from our community.

Death in a small town, death in a New York City small neighborhood, what they share is community.

Dad was a relative newcomer, and he died young. He was a local for less than nineteen years. He was late to arrive and he left early.

Chapter 27

Late to Arrive, Quick to Lead
1958–present

At my age, nearly a quarter century older than the age my father reached, I marvel that our church chose his leadership. I asked our parish priest why clergy would ask a barber to lead the fundraising to build our new church. Why select a chairman from the middle class? Then, as now, ours was a population of modest means. But there were prosperous citizens living in luxurious homes along the river. They owned businesses or were executives in the automotive or marine industries and were paid for their leadership, fund management, and marketing expertise.

Furthermore, why did so many respond very generously to his appeals for the money required to build and maintain our church? Why did so many people squeeze into our old parish hall for the spaghetti dinners my dad and mom organized? How did my parents inspire these good people to add to their long work days the jobs of cooking, serving, and cleaning up after the many fundraising events?

Father Cooney, a nearly bald, older priest recently assigned to us, pondered. Then he said, "Naturally I can't comment on your long departed father, never having known him. In general, however, we look for certain characteristics in those we ask to lead. The fact that he lived modestly and was a local barber would be in his favor. Your dad would be 'of the people.' His money worries would be theirs too. Barbers fifty years ago loomed large in men's worlds. He had to be a personable good listener. People had to trust that he'd keep their secrets because they'd tend to confide in their barbers. He had to please his customers, even those who asked for the impossible. My barber simply smiles when I ask for styles appropriate for thick hair."

Later I approached Dan, a current Lions Club officer. I said, "How had my father become a community leader?"

Dan said, "Like you I am surprised that he was president-elect of our city's leading service group. He was a relative newcomer in a village which was then, and remains, a somewhat closed community. Ours has always been a picturesque place, but it is isolated."

Dan is right. With very little industry, few job opportunities, and scant retail establishments, our area draws few newcomers. Some who moved here often felt like outsiders for generations.

This is not to say that we are unfriendly, but rather that we are comfortable with the known. We are wary of the unknown. Without intending to exclude new arrivals we inconsiderately refer to others by their links to their cousins, grandparents, or former neighbors. We thoughtlessly pepper directions with references to buildings which we identify as former banks, barber shops, stores, or restaurants.

"Our wariness of strangers slips into suspicion at times," said Dan. "We chose to live among those well known to us, in an area completely familiar. We cannot help but wonder what would inspire anyone to move into a spot where they know no one and are known by none."

Maybe the key which opened the locks to our village was Father's sense of community. He developed this viewpoint as an impoverished boy. Family and neighbors cared about each other. They divvied up what they had. No one got rich but everybody helped each other get by.

Chapter 28

Community
1917–1938

Father and his family experienced community in their
impoverished neighborhood. Grandmother raised her
children two blocks from her mother's home. She didn't
look to her family for the money they did not have. Her
parents were old and ill but they had two bachelor sons at
home who were good uncles to their sister's children. They
taught them some life skills critical to living through the
Great Depression.

The daily challenge was staving off hunger. His
grandparents and uncles showed Dad and his half siblings
how to garden in their small yard in their big city. After
their grandfather's death, the family continued to help.
Patiently they taught the children to till, plant, weed, and
harvest. With three generations working the soil together,
summer meals were bounties of fresh vegetables. His
mother and grandmother cooked together when Dad was
very young. Into autumn their fresh produce was the food
on their tables. They shared their crops with the neighbors.
They canned. Some stored the remaining vegetables in root

cellars. It was prudent to put up food for the long winter ahead.

As years passed, their mother and grandmother taught Father and his half siblings to cook. Soon they cooked for their frail grandmother and aging uncles. They had hot meals ready for their exhausted mother upon her return from cleaning houses. The cycle of life had shifted. The youth did the bulk of the cooking and canning, again using their fresh produce for meals.

Today it has become chic and creative to cook. Entire cookbooks concentrate on the Mediterranean diet. The very same recipes which today fill these graphically-illustrated, professionally-photographed, coffee-table-displayed cookbooks appeared on the dinner tables of my impoverished paternal and maternal ancestors. Both grandmothers learned from their mothers to make homemade pasta. This starch accompanied steamed or roasted root vegetables or produce picked ripe from the vines. Mother and her sister Agata said, "We ate spaghetti with swish chard, lentils, black beans, green beans, tomatoes, peas, garbanzo beans, great northern beans, mushrooms, sweet peppers, or onions."

Nor were the children's cooking lessons limited to those taught by their relatives. Dad's family lived next to a fire station. Grandmother said, "The firemen learned to love your Dad's youngest brother. Little Sam was fatherless at age two. Sammie kept hanging around the fire hall. At first he would just kind of show up whenever he smelled food cooking."

Family lore is that burly firemen began setting a place at their table for this skinny little boy. As Sallie grew older he'd help wash the fire trucks. He showed an intense interest in their cooking duties. Soon he had his own apron in their fire hall. He joined the ranks of his big city's firefighters when he grew up. No one had much but what they had, they shared.

The firemen and the nearby relatives weren't the only caring people who made this impoverished area a real neighborhood. Neighbors watched out for each other's children.

Father and his youngest brother, Sam, also watched out for their moody sister, Maria. She began to exhibit dramatic mood swings in early adulthood. Mom didn't hesitate when Dad asked her to take in his extremely emotional sister for months at a time. I well remember this aunt's vivacious personality in contrast to the childlike state in which my aunt would appear at our door. In their old age, Sam took in this sister until his death. Today a psychiatrist could help with prescriptions and referrals to therapists. But there was no such treatment years ago. Also, none in my family considered mental health treatment even when witnessing my aunt's bizarre behavior. Italians would never consider revealing family problems to professionals.

Chapter 29

Children of the Lord

Although Father died in 1962, he is still with me. I close my eyes and see his face. When my Ohio cousins speak, I hear the Youngstown of his voice too.

Memory of his voice inflection is but one-way Dad returns from the dead. It can be particular words. When someone says, "It's a beautiful day," I hear Father continue the sentence "…in Algonac." He moved from Youngstown, steel mills belching fireballs, to Algonac, a village as pristine as a park. He'd gaze at our St. Clair River and say with a smile, "It's a beautiful day in Algonac."

Father appears with the scent of bread baking or "greens" cooking. I'm back in our old kitchen, Grandmother pulling steaming loaves from the oven. Mother sets our hot supper on the white porcelain kitchen table bordered in red. The woman who gave him life and the one who led him to enjoy life are about to feed "their" man. The little me is there too, savoring the supper, basking in the presence of the first man to see me as special.

Last night, I attended a concert in our local park. The lively music drew us out of our homes, away from our televisions, and into the company of our community. Sweet sounds filled the air. Children ran through the waterworks or climbed the bright play structures. Old folks settled on their canvas chairs.

A woman called her little boy, "Time to go home, Bobbie".

"Momma, I don't wanna leave," he said, continuing to run around the playground.

His mother appeared exhausted. She screamed at him. Her words erupted volcano-like, the heat of her vocal lava rolling over all three of us, burning away the peace from the park.

I heard her hiss, "Listen to me or I'll smack your face."

My heart went out to Bobbie...and his worn out mother.

Perhaps she didn't know the four special words Father taught me. I heard Dad's whisper, "Children of the Lord."

Father would call upstairs to us, "Children of the Lord."

Maybe we'd quiet down. Soon we'd resume our mischief. Again, we'd hear Father say "Children of the Lord." We'd slip slowly into sleep.

Decades later these four words came to mind when I put our twenty-six-month-old to bed in one crib, our eleven-month-old into another, and their infant brother into his bassinet. Three babies filled the nursery. Three sweethearts filled our home. With each birth, I worried I wouldn't have the time, energy, or resources to raise our family. Three times Dad whispered, "Children of the Lord." Sighing, I put my trust where it belonged.

Settling our little ones, I often heard Father's voice. His words sprang from the nights of my childhood, Dad's voice rising from the bottom of our curved staircase. Camille and I would giggle, fight, laugh, or whatever we preferred to do rather than go to sleep.

Dad helped us to be parents. Father never knew me as a mother, never met Louis, and yet Dad's special words rang clear as we took care of our children.

We could hardly expect our infants and toddlers to go to sleep when we asked them to do so. Despite our cluelessness regarding the art of being parents, we knew enough about child development to accept that little ones have sleep schedules of their own.

We were less understanding, however, when they were no longer babies. I sometimes saw pajama-clad forms dash from our girls' room with its bunk beds to our son's room, complete with airplane wallpaper. I was upset that our kids hated sleep. As strongly as we yearned to close our eyes, they were determined to keep their eyes open. They were pleasant enough little people. They just did not want to sleep. And sleep was the one and only thing we wanted from them.

I was a grown woman begging little children to stop talking and stay in bed. Shamelessly, I tried bribes. "If you go to sleep right now I'll take you to the playground tomorrow." Had I been less sleep deprived I would have realized that for children the only important time is now. Why would they prefer playing tomorrow to playing right now?

Perhaps had I been more peaceful and less frazzled, I would have heard Father's message much earlier. In complete desperation, finally taking a deep breath and focusing within, I remembered that my worthy opponents in the sleep wars were in fact "Children of the Lord."

So I softly stated, "Children of the Lord." At the sound of my voice, their laughter stopped. Their talk turned to whispers. That first night they went to sleep more quickly and quietly than ever before. On subsequent nights when I restated these four words, the children listened.

They calmed down. "Children of the Lord" also had a profound effect on me.

This is not to say that these four words were magic, that they put rowdy children to sleep immediately. Nevertheless, the phrase replaced rancor with reality. I finally realized what Dad knew all along. These tiny wonders were on loan to us for a little while. They were simply passing through our lives. They were "Children of the Lord." And so were we.

Chapter 30

Hearing Voices

Hearing voices last week startled me. I heard my late father talking. What was wrong with me? Had I slipped into psychosis?

I know psychosis. I was an emergency room Behavior Health consultant in a hospital bordering inner city Detroit. Doctors examined the patients and ordered standard drug and alcohol level checks. When patients were medically clear, they sent them to my colleagues or me if any appeared mentally ill. The charge was to assess a patient's responses, appearance, behavior, and to research their individual and family mental health history.

If the patient was able to respond verbally, I would ask a long series of questions. One inquiry in this psychiatric evaluation was "Do you hear voices?"

Sometimes the person would say, "Of course not."

One person said, "What do you take me for? Do you think I am crazy?"

At times, however, the patient would answer, "Yes."

Then I would have to ask, "Are you hearing voices now, voices of people who are not here?" Sometimes the answer was yes. I remember a particularly articulate patient who said, "Yes, I hear voices. I know these people are not here but I can still hear them and I can see them too." She was experiencing not only auditory, but also visual hallucinations.

When a patient said he was hearing voices or seeing people who were not there, I noted a symptom of psychosis. Upon completion of the mental health evaluation I reported to the psychiatrist on call.

The psychiatrist reviewed my findings and decided whether to admit the patient to the hospital's locked ward. Sometimes a patient said voices were telling him to kill himself. A patient occasionally said that voices were telling her to kill someone. These are command auditory hallucinations. Psychiatrists immediately admitted those experiencing command type auditory hallucinations to in-patient care.

With or without the "command type" factor, an auditory hallucination is a significant symptom. Was I mentally ill? Hearing the voice of my long dead dad caused me to question my own mental status. What made me hear his voice? Then I made the connection.

Cousins who had not visited in five decades came to stay for days in our home. Conversing with them I suddenly began hearing my late father's voice.

Mine was not an auditory hallucination. My cousins' voices triggered memories. Father, the visiting cousins and their spouses grew up in the same Ohio city. Their speech patterns, tones, idioms, and cadences signaled their origins. Their voices evoked haunting connections.

This was not the first time I heard Ohio in a voice. Answering our son's home phone in Georgia, I took the message from his boys' basketball coach. The familiarity of his voice startled me. In the moments it took this stranger to tell me the time and date of the next practice, I recognized the area he was from in Ohio. I jotted down time and date. I closed our brief conversation in this way: "Thank you, Ohio," I said. "This is Michigan speaking."

Silence followed. Finally, this fellow said "Well, yes, I was born and raised in Ohio." Incredulous, he asked how I knew he was a native of Ohio. "I heard it in your voice," I said.

In the gym hallway prior to basketball practice the next day I greeted the coach I shall call Bill Blundo as soon as he completed his instructions and sent the team to the locker room. I said, "Hello, Ohio."

"You got it," he said, adding, "Hello, Michigan," with a wide smile. After the game the coach sought me out.

He said, "I'm Bill. How'd you know I'm from Ohio?" I went a step further. "You're from northwest Ohio."

"Correct again!" he said.

Then I said, "You came from Youngstown, Ohio." He paled. My grandson's coach was from the same section of the same city as my father. He grew up some fifty years ago.

Talking at length he relished the opportunity to revisit the old neighborhood. I did too. I said, "There are few people left in my life who remember such minutia as the grand façade of Father's school, Rayen High, who know where parks were located, and who can still see the long-gone candy store bearing the name of the family who owned it."

Coach Blundo agreed and then said that he's lived a long time in Georgia.

The sense of hearing is powerful. Conversations with my cousins and with the coach not only helped me hear Dad, but also to picture him.

Hearing my father's voice through the sound of my cousins' conversations connected me completely and

229

compellingly to my past. In retrospect, this shouldn't surprise. The last time we cousins were together Father was with us too.

Their voices brought his voice and hearing his voice made me happy. Their voices also brought pain. The cousins asked to visit Dad's grave. Gathered in the cemetery I experienced waves of raw grief. I felt as though it was the cold, dismal day we buried him there.

Hearing voices can be haunting. It can hurt. It can heal. Hearing can comfort the mourning.

Perhaps that's why I offered to interview and record a beloved uncle. He was critically ill. I thought his wife and children would treasure his voice. Uncle Tony agreed. Taping his recollections had to be brief. He was aged and failing by then. Cousin Nardi asked to join our uncle's sessions. She loved him too. He graciously welcomed her. I was pleased.

The three of us talked quietly, leafing through his photo albums. We laughed. We wept. Formal photographs of his young mother in the "old country" were especially precious. In his endearing accent he spoke of his long-ago youth. He described his beloved parents, his little brother, his courtship of his wife of sixty years, their children, their grandchildren. We looked through his lifetime of photos, a collection containing pictures of each of us. We savored memories that sometimes included our own.

Shortly after these special visits our beloved uncle died peacefully. He asked his wife for his favorite pasta for dinner. Uncle Antonino ate with gusto, listening to the operas he loved. Later, my aunt noticed him slumped in his favorite chair.

Hearing his voice brings Uncle Tony back. His recollections are both the pleasure and privilege that I had anticipated. What I had not expected was how much I cherish the time we spent talking together.

Uncle Tony and Cousin Nardi had always been special. We loved each other. Two listened when the third spoke. We heard each other recount events we'd shared along with experiences unique to each of us. In each other's company, we left the present. The present was not pleasant for my uncle and his niece. Both were seriously sick. And yet, in the space of time we shared, there was no talk of illness or of impending death.

It was as if they were on vacation from the stress of sickness. With the accent on the past, they held the pressures of the present at bay. Certainly we spoke of sadness, but we also spoke of joy and of the many matters in between.

231

In the process, I came to know each of them in ways I never knew them before. For instance, our uncle looked up from a photo showing him with Nardi's late father and mine. His face fell. His eyes filled with tears.

He said, "Look at the three of us smoking. We didn't know how the smoke was affecting you little ones. We fouled the very air you breathed. I feel so guilty now because you were always sneezing and sniffling and I was part of the reason."

He was right, of course, but science had not yet warned us about second hand smoke. Furthermore, the photo that upset him was taken during the 1940s, when smoking was in style. Watching the classic movies of the 1940s and 1950s reinforces the fact that most men smoked.

Both my beloved uncle and my dear cousin died within months of our recorded time together. I am grateful to be able to hear their voices.

Nor was this tape-recorded time the only instance in which the sound of family voices swept aside thoughts of critical illness. Years later while visiting Rocky, another of my critically ill cousins, I witnessed another dramatic and markedly personal rejuvenation. My family and I traveled out east to his home. Despite brief encounters at weddings or funerals, I rarely saw Rocky. He remained in my mind the virile youth when I was an impressionable young girl.

The first sight of Rocky made my heart break. Ravaged by years of chronic illness he was almost unrecognizable. But recognition returned the moment he spoke. His deep voice was strong, despite his body's weakness. He hadn't forgotten his intonation in Brooklyn when he left the old neighborhood.

Hearing his voice brought back all our shared experiences. Not only was the "real Rocky" still there, trapped in a body that was giving out on him but also, he and I quickly became the teenagers we once were.

Rocky and I eagerly scrutinized the huge scrapbook I brought, filled with my oldest photos of shared times. We delighted in seeing him at age seven in his First Communion portrait. We laughed to see ourselves decked out in the latest of fashions of the 1950s and early 1960s. Our family members chatted as they enjoyed his wife's delicious brunch. We were gone from them, awash in our memories.

Hearing each other's voices gave Rocky some relief from his suffering and gave me back a bit of my beloved cousin. That time together was our last. Both of us now old, we spoke on the phone across the country before his death.

233

His weak voice was recognizable from his accent and the emotion it always conveyed. Even in his decline his voice had the power to move me in the same thrilling ways of our youth.

A window into this phenomenon pictures the time when I was nearly sixteen and he was nearly fourteen. Our differences were vast. Our connections were complicated. He lived in Brooklyn. I was growing up in Michigan. He was big city. I was village. He was younger but worldly. I was older but clueless.

Rocky was Mother's first cousin. Sometimes he and his family would fly to visit our family. Twice my parents drove my sister and me the long miles across pre-interstate roads and into the congestion of New York City.

With Rocky's family and mine, we enjoyed a long visit. Our parents gave us some money, suggesting that Rocky and I see the city. We dressed in our finest. Rocky confidently navigated the neighborhoods. We were on and off the subways. We saw the Empire State Building, Grand Central Station, and Central Park. We ate lunch at a Chinese Restaurant. Then he took me to a world apart. He introduced me to the weird wonder of Coney Island.

On our second visit to their Brooklyn apartment, the attraction I felt toward Rocky must have been obvious to

Mother. She said, "Do not fall in love. Rocky's mother is my aunt. At your age I fell in love with my older cousin. My parents forbid us to even consider a match. I forbid you. You must bear in mind that cousins should not marry." The science of genetics was then in its early days, but experts described dangers. Having spent part of her childhood on a farm, my mother knew well the hazards of inbreeding.

Ever since he took me around his city, I loved Rocky. It was impossible not to fall in love. My love lasted fifty plus years despite the complete lack of any display of affection between us, not even a kiss.

When a beloved uncle heard Mom's voice, it led to another sweet family story. She described her visit to her special Uncle Salvatore. When Mom arrived at the hospital, he was semi-comatose.

When Mother spoke his name, Uncle Sal opened his eyes. He spoke. He told her how glad he was that she had come to visit him from so far away. They talked about the good times. Those around his deathbed wept to hear Sal speak. The quiet conversation between Mom and her uncle was the first he had in months. It was also the last time he spoke.

Many decades later Mother was the one dying. The sense of hearing again became the special stimulus. Hearing enabled comforting.

One of her best friends, the nun who was my second grade teacher, had become a hospital chaplain. She visited Mother in her hospice bed. Death was eminent. For weeks our family as well as the hospice staff asked Mom if there was something we could do for her. When Mother was alert she would shake her head "no" and smile. When she lapsed back into repose she didn't respond at all.

When Sister Beatrice leaned over our semi-comatose mother, she softly said, "How can I help you?"

To our collective amazement Mother opened her eyes. She said, "Pray with me. I want to pray the Memorare...in Latin."

Tears streamed as we witnessed, hearing our frail mother pray in a strong, sure voice. We watched two old friends pray in a language much older than anyone.

Hearing Mother and Sister Beatrice pray in a language I last heard as Sister's grade school student brought me back in time. Knowing that the child that still lived within me was soon to be motherless, I was awed. Who, other than this elderly nun, could have given Mom this special gift? None of us could pray with her in Latin.

Days later, peaceful in the company of all her family, Mother died.

Six months afterward, Cam, her husband, Louis and I attended a memorial service organized by the hospice group who cared for our mother. Their spiritual counselor led the event. She was a sister of St. Joseph, as was Sister Beatrice.

When we mentioned Sister Beatrice she became sad. She said, "Our congregation asked Sister Beatrice to retire because she was seen driving erratically on her way home from visiting your mother. She moved from the convent to their infirmary the day after."

This surprised us. We told her that Sister had never seemed reckless. She informed us that there had been increasing signs of memory loss. Sister Beatrice needed care. I requested the motherhouse address and I sent frequent cards to our family's dear Sister Beatrice. Within the year she was no longer able to comprehend my correspondence.

Sister Beatrice's voice was the last to voice rouse Mom. Also, there was only a small window in which she could come to Mother's deathbed. This makes the matter of hearing the two old friends pray together in Latin not merely magical but, indeed, mystical.

There was another touching matter. The middle-aged doctor who treated Mother for many years was there for her in her last days. He was an immigrant who connected with my mother in an exceptional way, her immigrant parents having shared the same lilt in their native languages.

When she heard her beloved family physician's voice, when he described the comfort care in hospice services, she quietly and quickly made this choice. He then coordinated her case with a hospice doctor so that they worked together to give her the best the medical community offered.

Her family doctor came to her funeral a week later, his presence a gift to my sister and me.

Four months later, this healthy doctor took his daughter out to lunch. While they ate he began to feel ill. Within minutes he died of a heart attack at the restaurant.

Attending his funeral, I reflected on the fact that this doctor had a short life. He lived long enough, however, to be there for my mother. In his care, in his very voice, Mother found comfort. They connected.

Regarding the power of hearing voices, language itself is a significant factor, regardless of the individual speaking. The Roman Catholic mass in Latin is an example. A friend, educated in parochial schools, no longer formally practices her religion. Together we recently attended a funeral mass. The family of the aged deceased requested the use of incense and hymns sung in Latin.

Later my friend confided that, even after all the years since she was a schoolgirl, the Latin words of the hymns came back in a rush. No doubt many of her senses were on alert. There were the colors and shapes of the long familiar vestments of the priest and altar servers. There was the heavy, acrid scent of the rarely used incense. There was the beautiful church. What she mentioned, however, was hearing voices, hearing voices sing in a language she had not heard since youth.

On a less personal and much broader scale, famous people's voices become familiar to all of us. Like everyone else they have unique characteristics in such aspects as tones, lilts, and accents. Unlike the rest of us, however, they speak and the world listens.

If we hear them often, they deposit their voices in our memory banks. I hear the voice of a famous figure such as Beverly Sills, Hitler, Dan Rather, Jimmy Carter, John F. Kennedy, Mr. Rogers, Lily Tomlin, James Earl Jones, or Elvis and I slip back in time.

Seeing some of these famous people on television, I may have trouble recognizing their appearance over time. But I instantly recognize their voices. Hearing them brings me back to my former age and circumstances, evokes the people they were and the person I was.

The force of hearing voices is much more intense when it comes to recollecting my father when I hear my Ohio cousins talk. This comes as no surprise. After all, I heard my father's voice much more often and in many more circumstances that I ever heard the voices of famous people. Also, there is no comparison between my emotional connection to my father and my distant and impersonal link to those who are famous.

At the sound of my voice, the last of my gaggle of aunts returned from wherever she wanders in memory. The first time Aunt Aggie responded we were sitting on her porch. Sun warmed and lulled by waves lapping at the edge of the river, we shared hours of silent contentment. I wrote. I looked up from my manuscript, noticed that her unfocused eyes were open, and asked if she would like to hear a passage. No response, neither verbally nor through eye contact. Nevertheless, I began reading the piece I was writing about my parents' wedding. Sometimes reading aloud helps me identify a discordant phrase.

Scarcely into my second sentence, I heard an unfamiliar sound. Startled, I turned toward my aunt. Aunt Aggie locked her brown eyes on mine. I was enchanted. Clearly, she and I were in the moment together. Again, I heard the sound. It was her utterance, rising from her rusty voice box, unlocked through her sheer force of concentration.

With repetition, I understood the garbled sound. "Talk about the cookies," she said.

"Of course," I said. "You're right!" Italians serve specific wedding cookies. I'd failed to mention them.

With that, Aunt Aggie smiled broadly, closed her eyes and returned to her resting state.

Inspired, I described our cookies. It was easy. Every Italian wedding in my long life appeared before me, beginning with the one that happened to be the wedding of the aunt who sat beside me, the first wedding of my memory. I was the four-year-old my aunt chose as flower girl.

High drama ensued. We four preschool cousins dressed in velvet and lace of identical style but different colors. In all our family scrapbooks is the duplicate faded photo of little girls smiling. Closer examination reveals forced smiles on three tear-stained faces and the triumphant look of the fourth, the one holding the flower basket.

The cookies served at this 1948 wedding are the same cookies at Sicilian weddings today.

Hours later, I had a rough draft describing her wedding and identifying traditional wedding cookies by name, ingredients, appearance, and taste. Once more I read to my seemingly sleeping aunt. Again, she returned from whatever date and place where she was comfortable.

Grinning together we connected completely. We savored my glory as the focus of attention. She is my Godmother and I had her favor. The rest of the little girls just had to cope. I delighted in my triumph. Maybe she was also relishing the sighting of her handsome groom. A nineteen-year-old bride, she was widowed at thirty-two.

Other thoughts surfaced from the depths of my aunt's mind. She haltingly stated, "Remember. Depression. Rationing." Then she closed her eyes once again.

Framing 1940's weddings in the context of the times, I began to gauge the magnitude of Aunt Aggie's contribution to my writing. In her I had a firsthand account of the wedding that preceded my birth. Not only had she been a member of my parents' wedding party, but she also served as my eye witness to this event seventy-plus years later. In addition, our "conversation", as constricted as it was, returned me to the tiny flower girl at her wedding.

Prompted by hearing each other's voices the past became the present and, briefly, I was not fatherless.

Chapter 31

Brought a Dad, Took a Dad
2014

For years, I was sad, thinking of my father posted at our village wartime Navy Base. Was he lonesome for his large family? Did he yearn for his home, friends, his big city lights? Last week I realized that Father was not alone. Dad left his close knit family for the first time but was soon surrounded by a community of military men.

When I arrived at the Veterans' Walk, many memories surfaced. The meeting point was our town's memorial. I reflected on Dad's name and those of many uncles, classmates, neighbors, and friends.

Breezes blew the crayon colored autumn leaves. Sun warmed my upturned face. This morning's walk had distinct differences from my daily walk through our small city, soothed by the gentle lapping of the blue water waves to my right, off the boardwalk of our river.

The new backpack I wore was a difference. It's emblazoned with a black silhouette of a soldier in uniform holding a little child's hand. The lettered promise is "Walk for veterans. You'll never walk alone."

Indeed, I did not walk alone. The large crowd consisted of all ages of men, women, and children. We walked in support of veterans. Some were enlisted personnel. Some who walked were veterans, certain of them wore VFW garb.

Our local VFW sponsors this annual walk. This was my first year but it won't be my last. I thought of Father in the 1940s. The military did for him what recruiters still promise today. By serving his country he saw more of the world than the ethnic neighborhood where he was born and raised and from which he could never afford to travel.

The Navy sent Dad from urban Ohio to basic training in Chicago and from Chicago to our Michigan village, the birthplace of the Chris Craft Boat Company. During World War II Chris Smith converted most of his production to build landing craft for Normandy beach.

As we walked, quiet companionship reminded me that Father was not alone. He found a brotherhood in the military. While there were differences in religion, race, personality, age, ethnicity, home states, education, and economic backgrounds, men had the military in common. Maybe Dad, at age thirty-two, served as an older brother to the youngest among them. Father was used to that role in his family.

VFW members and their Valor auxiliary coordinated the Veterans' Walk. Camaraderie characterized this event. It was good to walk together, each at our own pace. Organizers accommodated those who could not walk or chose not to do so. They provided a parade-perfect vehicle decorated in red, white, and blue suitable for bussing many.

Before walking, we recited the Pledge of Allegiance. Then, in commanding voices, soldiers sang the National Anthems of both the USA and Canada. Both shores of our bordering river honored our nations. A bagpiper added his talents.

Nor did song and bagpipe music provide the only melodies. The parade vehicle's loud speakers broadcast a patriotic medley including "Yankee Doodle Dandy," "America the Beautiful," and "The Caissons Keep Rolling Along."

Some songs put a march to our steps. I matched my steps to the speed and rhythm of my many walking companions. That's when I remembered walking these same streets with Father. The combination of music and marching prompted some sounds that I alone heard. Softly at first and soon more distinctly, I heard Father's voice. It seemed natural for Dad and me to walk together again. I saw his beautiful smile, brighter with an otherworldly glow. Father picked up the pace, saying, "Your left two, three, four; your left, two, three four; I had a good home and I left, two, three, four."

This little marching ditty was quite telling given my father's circumstances. He did leave his good home and it was in fact the military which ordered him to leave. The US Navy not only drafted my father during World War II but transported him to the same peaceful place where he lived out his life and where I live mine.

His duty station was a most unlikely oasis of peace in the middle of war.

World War II brought me a father. That was very good luck. It was a different story for my pre-school friend. The war took his father's life. Both his mother and mine married handsome Italian American men who were in the US military. Three months married, his mom became a war widow. She gave birth to their fatherless baby eight months later.

Chapter 32

A Fatherless Father and a Fatherless Friend
1948—present

Can anything be worse than to be born fatherless to an
impoverished, young mother who twice loses the men she
loves? Yes. It is worse when the mother of a fatherless
child cannot cope. I shall set this scene in Youngstown.

Mine was a fatherless father. Also, I had a fatherless
friend. Both began life with loss. Each took a different
path.

Mother and my friend's mom were young,
strikingly beautiful Italian women. They looked like the
ravishing star sirens of the movies produced during their
lifetimes, Gina Lollobrigida and Sophia Loren. Each met
and married young Italians serving in World War II.

Father and my friend's dad had been friends
forever. They grew up in the same city and graduated
together from Rayen High School. They had their World
War II military service, their nationality and their Italian
wives in common. I shall call this couple Sal and Vicenza.

Dad's friend, Sal, and his newlywed Vicenza came
from Youngstown, Ohio, to Algonac, Michigan to celebrate

my parents' wedding, thrilled that the marriage took place when Salvatore was on leave.

Three months into their marriage, Salvatore was killed in the line of duty. At Sal's funeral, Dad vowed to honor his friend's memory. He assured Vicenza that he and his wife would stay connected to her. "I remember how hard life was for my widowed mother," he softly stated in a rare reference to his tough childhood.

Vicenza gave birth eight months after Sal's death. Everyone described their baby as a beautiful boy who had his handsome father's features. She named him after his dead dad. Dad felt so sad for his friend's fatherless infant. Now that Vicenza was a war widowed mother, Dad was even more determined to be good to his friend's little family.

That Easter, like every Easter, my parents drove to visit Dad's family. By this time my parents were awaiting my birth. They took the time to see Vicenza and her baby who had moved to Berlin Center, a bucolic community on the outskirts of Youngstown.

When I was two we moved back to my father's hometown of Youngstown, Ohio. Other than her in-laws, my mom knew no one but Vicenza. She often called upon her widowed friend. She brought me along on each visit as well. Because our mothers passed so much time together little Sal and I shared playtime often. He was a quiet child. I was not. He had little energy. I appeared to bounce. In fact, Bounce became my nickname. Sallie was like a little old pre-school man. He was solemn; I grinned, laughed, and smiled often. We seemed unlikely pals. But we would play for hours.

Gradually, our mothers had less time for their visits. Vicenza was supporting her son by cleaning and decorating homes. She kept her own home clean and neat. My mom had begun the process of sorting and packing. In a year we were going to move back to Michigan in time for me to start school.

"I am feeling less comfortable at our friend's house," Mother told Dad. "She always says she's glad to see me, but she seems less and less gracious each visit. Today when I finished my coffee she whisked my cup from the table. She took it to the sink and she scrubbed it over and over again."

Dad's face fell when he heard Mom's description, a faraway look in his eyes.

They talked again days later when Mom and I returned from lunch at Vicenza's home. Mother complained that it had been awkward. "In the past we'd feed the children. They'd play with Sal's toys while we talked. We'd linger over our own lunch, clean up the table, and catch up with news in our lives. One of us would wash. The other would dry. But today she grabbed up our dishes and washed each one with great care. She refused to let me help. She spent an awful long time cleaning the dishes, drying, shining, and buffing each glass. And then, with me still at her table, she whipped away the tablecloth. Immediately after, she swept the floor beneath my feet.

"She's the one who invited me. But she wouldn't sit and talk. Instead she acted like I was keeping her from cleaning her already immaculate home! I never want to visit her again."

"Honey, please don't give up on our friend. I'm sure she doesn't mean to insult you."

"That's easy enough for you to say. You weren't the one trying to make conversation. Vicenza didn't listen. I pointed out how nicely our cute children were playing. She gave a quick nod. I asked polite questions about her cleaning and decorating jobs. She gave a word or two back."

Although taciturn, Father began speaking. Mother's words seemed to have reached the fatherless boy deep inside. In an unusual reflection on his childhood, Dad talked about his twice widowed mother. He described how she changed when his stepfather was killed. He said that it was as if black, the color of mourning, spilled over like ink and stained all she could see. He watched as she spent most of her time scrubbing. He realized she could never reach clean. "It took a long time," murmured my father, "but by now she does more than just scrub."

Moved by the memories my dad shared, Mom continued to visit Vicenza often. She knew that her friend wanted her company. She dismissed her own discomfort. She knew in her heart she was needed by someone who was in great pain.

When we moved back to Michigan, we saw Vicenza at Easter when we visited Dad's family. A once a year visit made for a different relationship between Mom and her girlfriend. They missed so much. There were no more long afternoons spent in quiet companionship, no chances to share daily happenings, and no time to watch as their small children grew. They could not note the gradual changes that occur daily, monthly, or after a season or two. Therefore, the sweeping changes were staggering.

Our brief yearly stopover was telling. For one thing, the voluptuous Vicenza was still beautiful but now she was very thin. Her formerly clean home had now become antiseptic. She stuck a sign on her door telling visitors to take off their shoes. She took our coats in the vestibule. She shook each outer garment outside before hanging it in her closet. Each closeted item hung in perfect order as if in a high-class clothing shop.

In addition to the increased cleanliness there were things that should have changed but did not. Sal's baby toys remained constant. He had nothing to play with that a boy his age would enjoy. When my parents first noticed this pattern, they brought Sal new toys and games each Easter. Also, Vicenza let her decorating skills lapse. She used to rearrange her furniture and accents often; now she kept each in place. For example, Dad moved an armchair to a slight angle to converse without twisting his head. I saw her put the chair back immediately when my father stood up to leave. Her furniture was getting older. This surprised me because she used to buy the latest style. But nothing looked shabby or soiled. She had each piece covered in transparent, thick vinyl.

After a few years Vicenza remarried. Dad's family buzzed with the news. They spoke of her groom as a "catch." With an insight uncommon at my age, I found that term insulting. In my mind brides and grooms married because they fell in love with each other. It made no sense to catch or to be caught. That was a matter for fish. Adults found my opinion amusing as they talked about Dan, the rich, handsome bachelor who married Vicenza, the beautiful widow.

A few years after their wedding Dan and Vicenza had a baby girl and named her Dannielle. When my parents visited Vicenza and Dan, Sal and I would play with the board game gifts that we brought. One day my cousin, Mary, happened to be visiting Sallie's half-sister. Mary and Dannielle both loved to ride Dannielle's horse. I greeted Mary when I arrived. I said goodbye to her later. I noticed that she was wearing different clothes when she left.

Later that day, at our grandmother's house, I asked Mary why she had changed clothes. She explained, "That's the part I hate about going riding at Dannielle's home. When we come in from the barn we've gotta take off all our clothes at the door."

"What? You've got to strip naked?"

"Yep, and sometimes it is cold outside."

Seeing the shock on my face, my cousin continued. "Her mom is weird. She leaves two bathrobes just inside the door. I bag up my clothes and go right to the bathroom. After I shampoo and shower I put on the set of clothes that I brought from home. Then Dannielle and I gotta use the washtub to rinse out her riding clothing along with the bathrobe and towel I borrowed. Next we've gotta wring them out. Only after all that does her mom allow us to put 'em in the washer. Then Dannielle must shower and shampoo. We've gotta add her robe and towel to the washer. Finally, we put everything in the dryer. It sure is a lot of time and trouble just so we can go riding! But it's worth it. Her horse is great!

"Once I said we ought to skip the washtub routine but Dannielle won't take that chance. She said her mom found a horse hair on the floor one day and screamed at her. Her mom grounded her for a week. Dannielle's mother is the cleanest person I ever met.

"Dannielle always wanted a horse. Now she rides all the time. She's almost always in their barn. Her horse is her playmate. She takes good care of him. She loves to be with him. Dannielle and I know that her big, gentle horse understands when we talk to him as we brush his hide. His big eyes show that he's thinking. Her horse, he loves Dannielle as much as she loves him. Her horse is really her best friend. I love her horse too."

"Well," I replied, "I'm glad that she has her horse but there is something that I can't understand. Why did her parents buy her a horse when her mom gets so upset about horsehair?"

A dark look took possession of my normally cheerful cousin. At first she gave me no answer. Then she sighed deeply and said, "Dannielle got a horse after her puppy died."

Unsettled by Mary's swift change in mood, I made an awkward attempt at empathy.

"It had to be hard on Dannielle to lose her little pet."

Now it was as if my cousin's face fell to the floor. She opened her mouth but she did not speak. Intrigued, I decided to wait her out. We sat in silence until she finally whispered the account that cut to my core.

Mary told me that Dannielle saw Sal kick her dog one day. She yelled at her brother. She screamed that she was going to tell their parents. Sal smacked her in the face. Dannielle got scared and kept her mouth shut. But the next time that she saw Sal kick her puppy she ran right to her folks.

They grounded Sallie but he simply smirked. He must have badly injured his sister's puppy. Within a week Dannielle's sweet little dog was dead.

Mary said, "I know you think Sal is your pal but I don't like him at all. Dannielle hates her brother and I understand why."

Now it was my turn to be silent. I was shocked. Black memories bubbled up. I once saw Sallie with a matchstick frying a fly. One time he showed me the legs he had pulled off a frog. I didn't want to play with Sal anymore but I had to go to his home with Mother.

Several years later into Vicenza's second marriage there was "trouble in the family" as I often overheard my mother tell my dad. This was no surprise to me. I was no expert on marriage but I knew it would be hard to live in Vicenza's home.

The Easter when we were halfway through high school I noticed that all signs of Sal's good looks remained. Yet I soon saw that Sallie had changed. While once he seemed solemn, now he was sullen. There was something else different as well. Salvatore told me he had a new name.

Having met as newborns, played together as toddlers, and visited yearly, we were both used to each other's Italian names. I told him that I was our town's only Angela and that he was the only boy I called Sallie. I exclaimed, "How'd you get a new name?"

He scowled and explained that he was still Sal but his stepfather had changed his last name. He had often heard his mother screaming, "You treat our daughter better than you treat my son." Sallie said that in an effort toward peacemaking his mom and stepdad came up with a plan. They would have her son's last name changed. His stepdad said that Sal would feel more like a member of the family.

His face blood red in anger, Sal said, "That's just stupid. I've always known I was the baggage that came with my mom. Soon after their wedding he started to treat my mother like dirt. I don't like my stepdad. He doesn't like me."

Knowing Sal was really upset I later told my mother, "Sal doesn't have his dad's last name anymore."

That night Mom whispered to Dad when they thought I was outside, "By bearing the name of the man heading the family, Vicenza must've thought her husband would warm to her son." Dad made no comment. He shook his head slowly.

At dinner I brought up the subject of Sal. "His American new last name sounds odd with his same old Italian first name."

At first father said nothing. He just sat at our kitchen table, a haunted look in his eyes. Then my quiet Daddy began to talk.

"A few months ago my mother phoned to tell me that they'd changed Sal's name. How could they do such a thing to this young man? First he was born fatherless. Now they took away his dad's name!"

Father continued, saying that at a time in his life when a boy is just beginning to become a man, they changed his identification.

"Sal must wonder just who he is and who he's gonna be. A young man's gotta figure out his future."

Dad pointed out that all Sallie had from his dad was his name, his nationality, and the memories shared by those who loved his fine father.

Father said, "Sal's name no longer signals that he's his father's son. How can he connect to a name that's not his? A boy with no father builds an image of one."

Dad supposed that a fatherless boy might fashion his life like a saint, a strong protector, or a hero of some sort and that his connection with this image would help him shape his life path. Dad said that he feared for Sal, for the man he'd become.

"Venera," Dad said to my mom, "I know Vicenza's our friend. But she made a big mistake marrying a man who treats her badly. Now she and Dan better be careful. They could break her son's spirit."

Dad acknowledged that his mother's second husband favored their children. He thought that perhaps it was just human nature.

"But my stepdad was good to my mother and their children. He treated me okay too."

He felt that it would have been wrong of them to change his name when he was Sal's age, soon to be grown. Father reminded us that his mother and stepfather called him by his stepdad's last name from the day that they married. Dad therefore knew himself by that name since he was a little boy.

Sadly Father said, "A name is a complex matter. We well remember that my father's family acted badly when they learned I had lost my father's name. They struck out against us unfairly for a decision I had to make."

He shook his head slowly as if to push away the dark shadows in the background of his life since birth. He asked, "Why can't family just love one another? Why make it so hard for us all?"

When Father stopped speaking there was silence. We were stunned that he told us so much. Never, nor again, did he tell us the thoughts he'd held all these years.

Vicenza's husband divorced her in time. Who can know all that goes on in a marriage? Why did he run off with a young girl? I know that Vicenza was difficult. Also, it was clear that her husband never loved her son.

Eventually, I found nothing left to like in Sal. He and I went in different directions in high school. I studied. When we visited his family at Easter he was usually out. He skipped school. Eventually he dropped out of school. Always quiet, Sal now became surly.

We lost touch and did not reconnect.

He fathered two babies with two girlfriends; married one, divorced her; neglected both of his children; physically and emotionally abused his ex-wife. He went into business. He went bankrupt. He refused to try to work after that. Sal never became a good man.

He began to eat obsessively, burying his good looks under fat. When he became diabetic he would not take care of himself. He could not control his appetite and he became morbidly obese. Doctors amputated both of his legs due to diabetic complications. Sal died young.

Mom and her friend Vicenza had holes in their hearts ever after.

Our fathers' long-ago friendship tied Sal and I together as playmates. I was drawn to Salvatore his whole life in a way that I can only now see. I was repulsed by the wreckage Sal spewed, the cruel things he did. And yet I feel badly when I think of the sad life he lived. His father was dead. His stepfather was clueless. His mother could not cope. Her untreated obsessiveness laid waste to her family life. Her compulsive cleaning made everyone's lives unhappy. Her second marriage was miserable.

Sal, my former friend, had something in common with my beloved dad. Both had been born fatherless. But my dad's life was a triumph of hope. Very early in life Sal succumbed to despondency. The despair that swallowed him up was yet another tragedy in his sad life. What would I be like if I had lived a life filled with loss?

Who can blame Sallie's mother? What a sad life! When her son died she began a swift descent into dementia.

I had a fatherless father. He had his mother and her family to help him. I had a fatherless friend. His mother had no family and she was unable to help her son. My dad lived out his short life contributing to his country, his family, his church, and his community. My friend also died young but he spent his time taking care of nothing and no one, including himself. My friend never left his hometown. Sal contributed nothing but trouble. Dad was forced to leave his birthplace. My father became a leading citizen in his new community.

Both men began life with loss. My father was kind and loving. My friend was cruel. Each took a different path.

Chapter 33

Premonition

One September Sunday at the end of my sixteenth summer, my forty-nine-year-old father did something he'd never done before and never did again. In doing so, he gave me a priceless present. He took me for a little drive. That picture-perfect time became a moving image on my memory's screen. I love to watch the sweet scenes.

Driving along the river, sun sparkled on the waves, Dad was happy that I was recovering.

Pervasive malaise was my diagnosis. The categorizing an illness as an autoimmune disease did not exist in 1962. That summer, doctors noted a rapid slowing of my vital signs, a marked decrease in my energy, and a deterioration of my blood levels. They ordered bed rest and weekly medical visits with hemoglobin injections.

Dad said, "I'm sure you'll soon be well."

"I feel much stronger," I said. "The doctors should let me get back to school soon."

Then Father and I settled into a silence that suited me quite well. Still wondering about our destination, I sat back and enjoyed my unaccustomed front seat status.

Without my sister's chatter and our mother's lyric voice, I savored my father's company in the cushioned comfort of our big Desoto.

Father passed familiar parks in our village and the next before he chose a park made special by school year-end picnics. We celebrated summer's start, a continuing tradition with our kids and now their children.

By unspoken agreement, we passed up the train that kids climb on and walked the park's woods south of the playground. I suspected something serious, a reason for our drive alone. Dad led me to a park bench. We sat in silence for a little while.

This time was our treasure. He and I were present for each other. We had no distractions as he talked. Within two months he was dead.

He gave me all the wisdom that he had, all the tools that I'd soon need to become an adult.

Father didn't give me a profound lecture. He did not tell his story of poverty, pain, and the lingering loss with which his life began. Dad didn't speak of his joys.

Instead, he talked of birds.

He scanned the trees surrounding us, ablaze with autumn colors. He saw a nest snuggled in the branches filled with red and golden leaves. He pointed out the bird nest.

"Honey," Father said, "we can learn a lot from birds."

Wondering where this conversation was going, I simply listened.

"Birds build their nest. They feed and shelter their precious chicks. Then, when they know the time has come, they push their young out to fly. It's nature's way. Fledglings must learn to make it on their own. It's the same with all of us. We grow up and move on. Good parents help us do that. Then good parents must move on too."

September shadows dimmed our light earlier each autumn day. Perhaps Father somehow sensed that the winter of his death was soon to come. In 1962 we did not know that sometimes changes in our heartbeats warn us we need care. Today there are medications that help stave off massive heart attacks like the one that caused my dad to die in his sleep that December.

I recognize now what I barely noted then. A month before, he told us that he could no longer visit his beloved sister-in-law. She'd been a beautiful blonde teen who loved dancing at his wedding. Multiple sclerosis reduced her to an invalid requiring total care.

"It breaks my heart to see her. I love her so much. I pray God takes me quickly. I couldn't suffer stoically like she does."

Indeed his heart was literally breaking, although none of us knew.

Also, there was the stress which science says can kill.

His dentist broke his office lease. His florist tenant died. The stock market had a setback. Although recovering, I had been very ill. Like every local merchant, he counted on abundance from our annual village fishing festival. This year, pickerel tournament organizers scheduled a go cart race route down our street. Their decision closed his barber shop to traffic and cut his business down. Storm clouds threatened the sunshine of his marriage. He recently joined a men's golf group. He was spending less time golfing with Mom. She was not pleased.

Maybe he had a feeling; perhaps a premonition prodded him to make some special time for me. I'm forever grateful for our short drive that day. A possible forewarning did not seem to make him sad. We sat in quiet contentment, sweet time together in a peaceful park.

Father was a quiet man. Yet I hear him even now; his simple story resonates. Our long-ago connection still binds.

Chapter 34

Friends Helped

1944, 1962—present

At two significant gatherings, friends enabled my family
and loved ones to get together. First was my parents' World
War II wedding when villagers shared their ration cards.
Second was when friends provided my father's funeral
meal. In both instances, their generosity was a sacrifice.

Flash forward seventeen years since my parents'
wartime wedding. Picture the same village where my
parents settled. This time see it in a blinding blizzard. As
soon as reports predicted dangerous winter weather, Aunt
Aggie phoned with the bad news. She said, "The grocery
sold out all their staples. Lee said he's phoning the two
villages closest to ours." Imagine the challenge of feeding
the many guests who came to pay respects at Father's
funeral.

Mom and Aunt Aggie's brother Calogero drove
Mother, Cam and me in the lead car. Uncle Calogero
followed the hearse from the funeral parlor to the solemn
mass, to the graveside prayers, and to the church hall for

the supper where mourners paid their respects, sharing precious stories of how Dad earned their admiration.

Emerging from the cars packing the parking lot, we saw women opening their trunks to trays full of bean salads, tossed salads, jelled salads, pans of macaroni and cheese, platters of pickles, carrots and celery, big cakes, cookies, and picture-perfect pies.

The father of one of the largest families in our village had just returned from a successful hunt. He shot a deer, dressed it, and froze it for the family's winter provisions. He was not a man of means and was glad for the meat that meant sufficiency for his family. Nevertheless, he and his wife quickly made a heartwarming change in plans. They gathered their oldest children and together cooked and served their venison at Dad's dinner, one of the largest funerals ever held in our community.

Suffering from the shock of Dad's sudden and unpredicted death, Mother, Cam, and I were initially unaware of the sacrifice this hunter's family made in order to make a funeral meal possible.

In the days and months of the long, cold winter that followed, however, we had plenty of quiet, lonely time to think about the magnificent meal quickly organized to feed so many so well. First to come to mind was the family who gave, cooked, and served their winters' venison.

A tiny village is filled with people with long memories. In the half century since my father's funeral, my heart still swells with gratitude for this kind couple who gave what they had and did so without hesitation. Over the many years that their family experienced weddings, births, funerals and other major events, my family always responded to their needs.

The military representative appeared at their door in 1963. In full uniform he gravely announced that their oldest son stepped on a land mine on his first day in Viet Nam. Theirs became the family with the hollowed eyes; ours became the family who fed the funeral guests. We gave what we could to this family who, in our greatest need, gave us all that they had. It is in their memory that I help serve church suppers after funerals.

Gatherings of loved ones renew and refresh both in celebration and in comfort. I'm grateful for family friends.

Chapter 35

Prediction

1962

Had Aunt 'Fina's screaming prediction come true? Was my illness killing my father? In August 1962, she had warned me to "pull myself together before I killed my father." Had my failure to do so led to his death?

I was much better. Initially lab tests produced alarming results, but they improved. I no longer had to visit Dr. Mayhew every other day to monitor my weight, blood pressure, and white blood cell level. My rapid weight loss slowed. This sudden and severe weight loss had ravaged my already slim body, leaving me weak and wan. My allergist Dr. Briggs recalibrated the dosages of my weekly allergy immunization injections. He conferred with Dr. Mayhew. They decided on a treatment of bed rest and vitamins and minerals in high doses. Together my doctors assessed whether to admit me.

Dr. Mayhew said, "I'm avoiding hospitalization because Angela is so susceptible to infections." The doctors agreed. Their treatment plan seemed to be working because although July, August, and September marked my lowest points, October and November showed improvement. By the first week of December I was strong enough to return to high school for my senior year. I no longer had a regimen of weekly B-12 injections.

No further medical details remain in my memory. I recently asked an allergist what might have caused this malady in my teens. He said, "Treatment of allergies was in the Dark Ages in 1962." This was a grim time in my life and a very difficult time for all who loved and cared for me.

No doubt Aunt 'Fina loved me but her frantic and emotional responses upset all of us. In the heat of the August sun she shook me by my then skinny shoulders and screamed that I was going to "be the death of my father."

The fury and frustration Aunt 'Fina vented that summer revisited me four months later. The howling cold of the winter of 1962 was not as chilling as the thought that my ranting aunt may have been right when she said that I was going to kill my father.

Did I cause my father's death? I did not know.

Nor was I particularly concerned about either my dad's death or the cause of his death when she awakened me from a strongly medicated sleep. Aunt 'Fina said, "Your father died."

273

Her brown eyes were as dark and big as they were the day, months before, when she predicted that my illness was killing my dad. Her eyes pierced mine but made little impact. Minutes later, half awake, I looked out my upstairs bedroom window. By streetlight I saw a hearse pulling out of our driveway, disappearing into the dark.

Sleep stumbling down the banister-bordered stairs, turning the curve from the second floor landing I saw relatives surrounding Mother and Cam. I realized that my father had died. Nevertheless, I soon returned to bed and went right back to sleep. Guilt waited for me to waken.

Chapter 36

Fatherless Child

1962

On the morning of December 7, 1962, my reprieve from reality ended. Sleep no longer shielded me. Death had arrived in a snowstorm. The full force of my father's death the night before blasted through denial. My reaction to Dad's death was to hate him.

Guilt and anger were appropriate. I had been literally commanded to honor him. Likewise, I was charged with honoring his now seemingly shell-shocked wife. The commandment was unambiguous. "Honor thy father and thy mother."

With Dad dead, what about me? How could he leave me? Now I felt I had to guide Camille, my thirteen-year-old sister, and take care of our obviously crazed mother. He left without saying goodbye. Was it true? Would he never, ever come back? Gone was the man who had lavished me with love every moment of my life, the man for whom I was named.

What had I done to deserve a father who suddenly deserted me, Camille, and Mother? With his sudden death he made me what he had always been. Now I was a fatherless child.

A seemingly healthy man, Dad celebrated his fiftieth birthday three months prior. Snow blanketed all of us as evening approached. One of mom's neighbor friends, Mrs. Fairchild, stopped by. Dad welcomed her, visited briefly but then excused himself.

Mother later said, "You were kinda rude, honey." I thought the same.

Father said, "You're right. I sure didn't visit much. It's just that I don't feel too good. I made myself vomit and now I feel better. I'm going to bed early."

Camille and I went to sleep. Then our mother went to bed that dark December night. Hours later Mom said she felt a little rustle in their huge, wood framed bed. She awakened to find her husband dead at her side.

Chapter 37

Who was this man?

How could the man I loved so much become the man I
hated? Who was this man? Vehemence flowed through me
as though it was a substance. My blood boiled, simulating
hot water heating, as if in a steaming blood surge through
my veins/pipes. Liquid heat made me flush whenever I
thought of the man, the object of my intense wrath.
Outwardly appearing so serene, who could have noticed my
pulse pounding, my stomach churning, and my broken
heart aching? Seemingly stoic, I held my anger on the
inside, agitating my innards.

Was he a hateful man, this object of my fury?
Indeed he was not. He was a good man, a loving, and kind,
soft-spoken guy. He was both a gentle person and a
gentleman. How could he do this to me? Who was this
man?

One way for you to know him is to learn what he
loved and did not love. He adored Mom, Cam, and me. He
loved his country, his community, and his church. He
cherished his mother. He was kind, loving and generous to
his half siblings. He loved basic food, rejected processed
products, and confined his diet to healthy meals. As a

mature man he learned to golf and loved the game. Mom and friends urged him to audition for a community play. He discovered that acting was fun. He enjoyed swimming, a skill he learned in the Navy. He valued physical fitness. He loved classical music. He read local/national/international news.

He hated noise. He couldn't bear rudeness, particularly when parents permitted their children to be impolite. He hated hot dogs, refusing to eat anything that's contents were unfamiliar. Gossips turned him off, along with people who nagged. An employee talked obsessively. This constant chatter bothered him very much.

His was a devout Catholic with an old world Italian upbringing. He valued vows. He took duty seriously. He was intolerant of those who allowed their separation or divorce to distance themselves from their children. Father hated things that broke. He had no skills for fixing anything but he hated to pay anyone to do the repairs. Heavy drinkers offended him. He loved a good night's sleep and hated anything that kept him awake. He didn't like to spend money. Having lost teeth in a renovation accident, he hated wearing dentures as a young man. He hated his early onset baldness. He grieved the loss of his teeth and his hair. Those who flaunted their money repulsed him.

He was suspicious of males who showed an interest in me and was uncharacteristically curt with them. At the top of worst offenses were fathers who didn't take good care of their children.

Clearly, I did not like any father who didn't take good care of his children either! Why did he leave me? Why did Father die?

How I hated him! Enraged, I railed against him in a silent scream. Now Dad was dead. How could he do this to me?

He loved me like none had ever loved me. The palpable hate that rose in me was equal to, or greater than, the love I always felt for him. In addition to the hate I had overwhelming guilt.

Had I killed him?

Chapter 38

Called Away, 1962

Looking back over a sea of solemn people on December 9, 1962, my eyes blur. Many dressed in black, a tradition at Sicilian funerals. Others were in priests' black vestments. All men wore hats.

Familiar faces passed through our village furniture store's funeral parlor. The back room parlor was packed with people, filled with flowers, and distinguished by attractive, modern and sturdy furniture. Huge floral sprays expressed sympathy. Years earlier the florist next door said, "Funeral flowers are a major income for flower shops."

Young as I was when I hung around the flower shop, I remember thinking it made no sense for people of limited means to buy expensive flower arrangements. Perhaps cost is the reason why there are few large floral arrangements today. Maybe expense explains why there are fewer funerals. But everyone had a funeral in the 1960s and it's possible that mourners thought the size of their funeral sprays reflected how much they valued the deceased.

One arrangement contained Bird of Paradise flowers, the first I'd ever seen. Some say the scent of flowers covers any offensive smells in crowded funeral parlors. Perhaps this is also why incense was widely used at funerals. The scent of incense or the sight of a Bird of Paradise bloom bring with them my father's funeral, its dirge like Latin hymns and the mourner's hollow eyes.

There were those dressed in black but with a touch of white. The bib-like wimples of the nuns' habits identified them as Sisters of St. Joseph. They taught Camille, our cousins, and me in elementary school.

Funerals are designed to comfort the living in the process of honoring the dead. The nuns said we were obligated to comfort those who mourn, such comfort being a corporal act of mercy, an action of great value in the hierarchy of charity.

Grade school students of varying shapes, sizes, and ages wore navy blue slacks or skirts with white shirts or blouses. Cam and one of our cousins were eighth graders. Not only all their classmates, but also most students in kindergarten through seventh visited the funeral parlor with their families. My public high school classmates and their parents came too.

Every student prayed at Father's funeral Mass. All pupils attended daily morning mass prior to the beginning of classes. The nuns adjusted the school schedule to accommodate the midmorning timing of Dad's Mass.

Camille's classmates' families and many parents of students in the entire student body came as well. We were touched.

Our parish pastor and associate priests celebrated mass with tears in their eyes. They led the largest church in our village. At Father's funeral, however, they appeared as vulnerable and clueless as their flock. Monks, priests, and seminarians came from every parish in our diocese to honor my father, arriving, in large part, because Dad's leadership and the priests' guidance raised the funds to construct our new church.

The bell of our new church could be heard for miles. The sound was especially clear to my family. We lived a block from church. It was built in 1959 because we'd long outgrown our picturesque wooden, mission church with its tall, white steeple.

Black clad mourners mark my memories of Father's funeral Mass.

Women's black dresses and men's black arm bands were familiar. Every Italian I knew had a black dress in the closet, a dark suit in the wardrobe, a black band in the drawer. We didn't need to shop prior to the traditional three-day visitation, funeral mass, procession, interment, and the meal which followed. Black was the color of comfort.

Mother's was the only Italian family in our village until my father arrived, lonesome for the traditions of his Italian family. Perhaps my parents and Mother's family earned respect in our village because many mourners wore black, including those who had not been immersed in centuries of ethnic mourning traditions.

Stunned by the shock of his sudden death, I was overwhelmed by the presence of so many mourners. During those three days of public mourning and in all the years that followed, Father's funeral served its purpose. I treasure those who valued the life Dad lived and who cared about Mother, Cam, and me.

Time in that week appeared dreamlike then; nightmarish later; surreal today. Did every person I'd ever known come to the funeral? Every guest at my recent sixteenth birthday party, those whose hair Dad cut, all our local and faraway relatives, customers of the florist shop next door, all our friends moved by us in a long, slow moving, black-clad, red-eyed, shock-faced procession.

Grieving family, friends, colleagues, and neighbors braved the worst of winter storms to arrive from New York City, Youngstown, Canada and Detroit to mourn the man each cherished uniquely. They arrived by plane, train, automobile, ferryboat and on foot. My father's funeral was the largest ever held in our 1.4 square mile Michigan village.

Respect was the signature sentiment of those who came in collective grief. And it was good. Not only was it good, but also it was a tribute. Consider that my father was relatively new to our village, to our close-knit community, and to our state.

Comfort comes back to me with every funeral I attend, with every visit I make, in every sympathy note I write, in the weeks, months, and years that followed Father's death.

Through the long and gut wrenching grief honored by funeral traditions I came to see that Father had not left me. The friend with whom I have the longest link in my life came to my father's funeral. Claire Rozelle was twelve when she met me as a newborn. When she spoke, her signature soft voice and her consistently calm manner cut through the funeral fog through which I was sleepwalking.

Claire connected with me. I confided in her. I shared my aunt's prediction that I was "killing my father" and that I had best "pull myself up by the bootstraps and get over my illness." Her response was immediate, emphatic, and unequivocal.

"Your sickness didn't kill your father. You were not responsible for his death."

Her quiet conviction severed the chain that linked me to the weight of guilt. Free of that burden, I realized not only that I hadn't killed Father, but also that he had not left me. He had been called away. Neither Dad nor I caused his death.

Chapter 39

"You Made Him Happy."

1962

On the December day when Father's sister Helen arrived in a snowstorm for his funeral, she gave Mother a gift. Aunt Helen, her big hazel-colored eyes liquid with tears, softly told Mother, "You made him happy."

Maybe other family members said comforting words. Certainly Mother's glass-eyed expression, wooden walk, and obvious exhaustion would inspire kindness. I do remember that someone said something that gave no comfort; words that instead caused pain.

In the quiet of the crowded funeral parlor there were conversations in hushed tones. Grandmother Julia began to shout. She said, "You poisoned him. Get an autopsy. My Angelo was strong. He couldn't work all day, eat dinner, go to bed, and die."

Father's grieving doctor came to pay his respects. He spoke to Grandmother, "A massive heart attack caused quick death. High blood pressure is a silent killer."

Grandmother seemed to listen. She respected doctors because of their education. She accepted his explanation that, although Dad appeared fit and despite his relative youth, his high blood pressure had been a serious threat.

Within an hour however, her rationality disappeared. She began to dance at the funeral parlor. Every mourner stared as this short, elderly Italian lifted her black dress, revealing her black nylon stockings rolled at the top, and danced the Tarantella. Translated to "Spider", the Tarantella is a traditional Sicilian folk dance associated with grief and madness.

Many assisted Grandmother. She was in shock, deep in grief and exhausted from the long drive. Years later, Aunt Helen said, "Momma was never the same after her Angelo died."

Aunt Helen again turned to my mother, whispering that she was grateful to her. She reminded Mom that her brother loved her very much. She said, "You gave my brother joy."

Everywhere there is evidence that good words, good thoughts, and kindnesses are gifts at the time and treasures ever after. Aunt Helen's gift was one such kindness. All Mother's long life she found comfort in her sister-in-law's message.

The years immediately following my father's sudden death were very difficult for my mother. On her darkest days I would remind her that Aunt Helen told her, "You made him happy." In deepest grief it is hard, sometimes almost impossible, to look beyond the immediate, painful moment. Without exaggeration, I say that Aunt Helen's kindness helped save my mother from the abyss.

Chapter 40

War Between Women
1943–1965

World War II raged when my parents met in 1943 and married in 1944. That war ended in 1945. But the war between the women had just begun.

As with any war, history is written by the survivors. In the absence of other potential war correspondents, I share the following near verbatim report Mother repeatedly described to me throughout my childhood.

This 1944 interchange was between Venera and her mother Giovanna, called Jennie. A year later Venera and Angelo became my parents, making Jennie my maternal Grandmother. My parents' marriage, which took place weeks after the conversation below centers on Venera's soon to be mother-in-law, Julia. Eventually, Julia became my paternal Grandmother.

The location is Grandma Jennie's kitchen table in the house her husband and son built in Algonac. Thick, strong, black coffee came from an angular, silver colored appliance. The scent of homemade sauce lingered in the air. A fig tree reminiscent of Sicily grew incongruously in the backyard. I walk by this trim, little ranch style often, nearly seventy years later.

"Mom," Venera said. "I love Angelo and he loves me but his mother hates me."

"No," said Grandma, "she doesn't hate you personally. She wouldn't like anyone her son wanted to marry."

"And just why not? I'm always nice to her. I know he loves his Momma and I treat her with respect."

Grandma Jennie stopped stirring cream into her coffee. She looked at Venera and said, "You don't seem to understand, honey. Angelo's mother doesn't want him to marry you or anyone else, ever. First, Julia's in shock. He was twelve when her husband was killed and her Angelo became the man of the family."

"Well, that's true," Venera said. "Angelo told me he got a job to help out and he took care of his half siblings. He watched over Julia's aged mother along with her brothers. It was like Julia was married again, but without sex and her duties to a husband. 'Her' Angelo never had a serious girlfriend. She probably figured he'd be like her bachelor brothers, content living at home, supporting their widowed mother. Instead, the Navy took him from

Youngstown to station him in Algonac, a village the map doesn't show."

"And then," said Grandma Jennie, "he falls in love with a much younger woman his mother never met. He tells her they'll marry as soon as possible to avoid the wait the church requires with the Easter vigil."

I can well imagine that Mom's mother paused and said a silent prayer. She loved Mother's betrothed. Grandma Jennie found in her daughter's fiancé a gentle spirit, notably absent in her own strong, confident, but crude, demanding, and brutish husband. She hoped Angelo would be patient as his young wife grew into maturity. She knew her daughter was smart, but she also recognized that her girl had a lot to learn.

Grandma said, "Angelo is wise, kind, and mature." Venera nodded. "I'm proud of you, honey. You immediately agreed to continue financial support for Angelo's mother."

"Of course," Venera said. "You raised us to honor our parents. I'm glad that my sweetheart and I are of the same mind."

"Her son's closer to my age than to yours," Grandmother Jennie said. "Look at it from Julia's viewpoint, sweetie. She can't believe he's going to 'leave her,' to marry a young, pretty girl he just met."

"Well, that's just too bad," said Venera. "We're getting married and that's that. She'll just have to get used to it."

In the end, many years later, I understood that Mom was wrong. Her mother-in-law never did accept her. Nevertheless, the two were always polite as they waged war over their man. Their fierce fight was no less destructive because it was a quiet conflict. For the first sixteen years of my life, I heard their brief, strained conversations.

Grandmother Julia sweetly said, "Venera dear, you don't keep a clean house." She often pointed out grime. I heard her say, "Down home, women wash the walls every spring."

Mother smiled tightly and said, "Well, you're not down home now." That retort, delivered in the softest of sounds, served to stop the comparison. I only hope that it was not a cruel, subtle reminder to Grandma that this was Mom's home, not hers.

When Mother complained to her mother, she got no sympathy. In retrospect I understand that my grandmothers had much in common. Both born in Italy, they were raised in poverty, married for love at age fifteen and sixteen respectively, and were often with child. Grandma Jennie had nine pregnancies and raised the five live births. Grandmother Julia had eight pregnancies, lost a four-year-old son to pneumonia, had a miscarriage and raised six children. They didn't drive. Both were subservient to their husbands. Neither they nor their spouses studied beyond grade school. All my grandparents worked hard to raise children during the Great Depression, were faithful in their marriages, and helped their extended families.

But my two grandmothers were different in many ways. Grandmother Julia no longer had her mother to talk to regarding her Angelo's marriage. She could no longer seek the comfort of her mother's kitchen. Grandma Julia's first trips out of Youngstown were to her son Angelo's betrothal and then to his marriage. All her future travel consisted of driving back and forth to Algonac. In contrast, twenty-seven years into their marriage, Grandpa took Grandma Jennie to Italy to meet his parents. They often visited her aunts, uncles, and cousins in New York City. They established and operated businesses all their lives, the first being a corner grocery in Detroit to supplement Grandfather's income as a boilermaker. Grandma Julia always had robust health. Grandma Giovanna had Type 1 diabetes and childhood osteomyelitis and died at age forty-nine.

When Mother complained to her mother she got no sympathy. Instead Grandma Jennie reminded her daughter that the rules of the relationship between Mother and Grandmother Julia had been firmly established for centuries. Grandmother Jennie said, "Venera, I know you don't have warm feelings toward your mother-in-law. She is rather dour. That's understandable. She's had a difficult life."

At this point Mother interrupted. She said, "Yours has been a hard life too and still you are pleasant and kind."

Grandmother Jennie reacted. She locked her brown eyes laser-like onto her daughter's hazel green ones. Her expression was stern, her voice was quiet. She spoke in measured tones.

"There is no comparison. Julia's been widowed twice and their first son died. She was her children's sole support. I've always had your dad. Together we've worked our way out of the poverty that still marks Julia's life, and that will be her lot always. Your father and I have a difficult marriage but we are no longer poor...far from it...at times we were seen as rich. We've supported my mother and family while Julia's and her mother's family have been dependent on the charity of others. Ever since our house and all our possessions went up in flames, we've worked hard and been blessed. Living in this lovely village on the river reminds your dad of his early childhood in Sicily. Julia's home grows more dilapidated in a neighborhood ever more dangerous. She's lonely, envious, and unhappy."

Mom lowered her eyes in acknowledgement and shame.

Grandmother Jennie said, "So, she makes it clear that she doesn't like you. Nevertheless, you are required to be civil and courteous at all times."

Grandma Julia and Mother were bound by strict Sicilian traditions requiring respect. The letter of the law applied to both women. While both accepted the conditions without question, neither combatant fought by the spirit of the law.

Grandma often sweetly stated that Mother didn't keep a clean house. Mother would ignore the remarks, silently leaving the room. As our bedrooms adjoined I could hear Mom crying, telling my father, "Honey, I do the best that I can. Our house is not dirty!" Dad would agree and comfort his wife.

Perhaps Grandma thought that her years of taking in laundry and being a "cleaning lady" qualified her to comment on Mother's housekeeping. This was a particularly sensitive subject given that Mother became a housewife in the 1940s and 1950s, a time when a woman's worth was tied to her housekeeping skills.

Grandma Julia's gleeful grime reports continued unabated. She took pleasure insulting her daughter-in-law. Again, Mom turned to her mother for advice. She and Grandmother Jennie came up with a plan. The next time Grandma Julia said that our house was dirty, Mother was ready with a witty reply.

"Well, Mother dear," she sweetly said, "our home is your home. We want you to be comfortable here. You are always welcome to clean whenever you wish and in whatever way you choose. You're an expert at cleaning."

Grandma Julia was delighted. She swept, scrubbed, and polished. Proudly, she showed her son the many ways in which she made his house sparkle. She got his attention. Sensing a truce in the turmoil, Dad complimented his mother, thanking her for her work. Out of her eyesight, he winked at his wife.

Mother thanked Grandma Julia and walked out the door. She'd return to an immaculate home. She repeated compliments to her proud mother-in-law who responded with broad grins. Unknown to my parents, however,

Grandmother Julia was simultaneously complaining to her daughter Lizzie about her lazy, cruel, dirty daughter-in-law who treated her like her slave. Thus began the years of accumulated animosity Lizzie felt toward my mother. Ultimately Aunt Lizzie erupted as if her loathing was a lava belching volcano, burning me long after Grandmother Julia's death. Clueless, I assumed that the war between the women ended with the death of one and the dying state of the other. I underestimated the depth of hatred. But that's a different story.

Now that Mother was free from cleaning, she did what she did best. She led. She volunteered to serve on charity works. The Village Council appointed her to the board of directors of the area's hospital. She spearheaded a committee, submitting a grant proposal by which the federal government funded a medical/social services center for the needy that operates to this day.

Mother experienced desperate times in childhood and knew that Dad did too. Maybe that's why she spent her time and energy in charitable work. Another, perhaps more basic reason, is that Mom liked being in control. Always personable, she directed others in such a pleasant manner that they did what she strongly suggested. Mother was a managerial woman ahead of her time.

Grandmother Julia's matter of money, however, was never really resolved. There was no social security or aid to dependent children in the early 1900s when she was raising her children. This money might have blunted the blow of Grandma's pervasive poverty. Having no savings, she spent her later years living in the homes of each of her six children. The six months she chose to spend yearly in our home was decidedly disproportionate to the time spent with each of her other children. I knew Mother was glad when she returned to Ohio.

Grandma arrived each summer, smothering the sunshine of my Mother's days. They greeted each other with the purse-lipped politeness that thinly covered the coldness between them. They immediately resumed their war. I intuited that Father hated being both the link in their lives and the source of their constant conflict.

Both Mother and Grandmother were dependent on Father's income, compelling these two strong willed women to live together yearly, locked in constant competition. Perhaps poverty made grandmother bitter. Was she jealous because Mother spent money on my sister and me? Maybe the memory of her young children's unmet needs haunted her.

Grandmother cleverly capitalized on her son's fixation on finances. Grandmother recruited Dad into battle, playing on his fears of again being poor, wily pointing to ways that his wife wasted money, loudly criticizing Mother's expenditures. She saw our music lessons as unnecessary. Grandma decided we had too many toys and said that our clothes were too fine. She declared that piano practice and study took too much time away from our learning to clean and to cook.

Dad soon began to oversee all the expenditures Mother incurred. I sensed Grandma's glee when she listened to them quarrel.

Dad had always reluctantly doled out money. He spent little on himself and now, influenced by his mother's insidious inferences, he watched Mother's spending even more closely. Therefore Mother was incensed by father's occasional splurge for his mother. I remember Mom's scowl the day he bought a choice cheese his mother enjoyed. Grocery shopping was always a tense time because Dad often examined Mom's shopping cart.

An older man's darling, Mother filled her home with beautiful music, fine food, parties, and fun people. She introduced her solemn spouse to ballroom dancing, church leadership, and community theatre (activities he learned to love). Mom did all this in spite of the dour mother-in-law to whom she was bound by the rules of respect, paramount in our old world Italian family. She was insecure, caught up in her mother-in-law's criticism and her husband's financial scrutiny. But Mom was clever.

Mother cunningly coupled her antagonism for her mother-in-law with politeness. Mom made me her little ally, disrespecting Grandma and saying, "Act nice to your grandmother but you need not be nice. Don't listen to her. Don't help her at all."

I well recall an incident. Grandmother called down our long, winding, polished, wood spindled staircase for me, "Help me lace my shoes." Mom shuffled me out the door, saying, "Let's just let her tie her own damn shoes."

It was a tough situation for Mother and Grandmother. They were undeclared enemies forced to live together in a pretension of peace. No one in our home was fooled by this falsity. I became collateral damage in a war between the women. So much has finally become clear to me. I know now that Grandma never meant to hurt me.

When I was small we shared tender moments as she scratched my back or combed my curly hair, we two sitting silently on our little back porch. Sometimes she allowed little Cam and me to bake bread with her.

Baking was the best of our time together. Grandma baked beautiful bread and perfect pizza dough. Camille and I focused on the fun of kneading the dough. We would sling it, smash it, and roll it. Out of Grandma's watchful eyes, Cam would sometimes treat bun dough like a bocce ball plaything. We were proud to work with her in the kitchen; mystified by the magic of the dough as it rose; enchanted by the aroma that spread through our home.

Every part of the process brought its own pleasure. I can still see Grandmother dip her elbow into the water, testing the temperature (warm enough to activate but not so hot as to kill the yeast). Then we'd pour in the yeast grains and watch them come to life, wiggling in the water, releasing their special scent. Next Grandma poured from the big bag of flour. We delighted in the puffs of flour-filled air drifting up from the bowl.

Together in our old kitchen, our times are my treasure. My fingers still feel the dough as we kneaded. My nose smells the unique scent of yeast. To this day I hear the crunch as the knife cuts through the crisp crust. I see the butter melt down the tiny holes in a steaming fresh slice. Eager and impatient to taste the freshly baked bread, I was careful not to burn my tongue. These baking memories are pure joy, little gems of good times, respite from the vile scenes I witnessed between Grandma and Mom.

Unfortunately, by the time I was about eight, my affection for Grandma Julia was a casualty of their war. The ways Grandmother and Mother maltreated each other saddened and scared me. I wanted to please my mother and so became her ally.

Mother and Grandma Julia were as fierce as gladiators in their constant competition for the responsiveness of "their" beleaguered man. Over time they became entrenched in the arena, fighting literally until death and, even beyond. They waged war for the seventeen years of my parents' marriage, until the night Father died. Perhaps the simmering stress contributed to Dad's early and immediate death of a massive heart attack.

At Dad's wake, Grandmother's animosity surfaced. In the packed funeral parlor she screamed that Mother had poisoning her son. In the depths of her shock and grief, Grandma dropped all previous pretense of politeness. Cam and I never saw our Grandma Julia again.

When Dad died, Grandmother Julia never visited Mother's home, where she'd lived half of each year of her son's marriage. She neither phoned nor wrote. I wished she would call. I fantasized her wanting to talk to me, the namesake of her beloved Angelo. I wanted to bake bread with her again, to enjoy our brief interludes alone, times of truce in the ongoing war of the women. I should have phoned my grandmother when Mother wasn't home. My instant reward would have been the sound of Father's voice in her tone. I have asked myself why I lived in Mother's home until I married. Why did I let Mother's wishes rule me?

Was it because I had suddenly lost one parent and feared losing the affection of the other? Did I feel as though I was taking care of my sickly mother? I was taking care of her financially in that I saved my salary and paid back Mom the money she spent to help finance my college education. To her credit, Mother never asked for money. I was aware, however, that I had the qualifications to earn more money than she could. I was also healthy in contrast to her sporadic illnesses.

Mom sorted her assets to put aside some money for her mother-in-law. When Mother traveled twice to her mother-in-law's home several years later, it was only the money that was welcome. Mom and Grandmother dropped all pretense of connection. Grandmother died three years after her Angelo's death.

Mother refused to take Cam and I to our grandmother's funeral. I regret not driving myself and offering Camille a ride. Grandmother Julia was Father's mother, after all. She, Cam, and I were not enemies. Sometimes I feel as though I was a noncombatant, born on a battlefield. Mother said, "How could you even think of going to that wicked woman's funeral? I can't even imagine going to grieve her. You make me angry!" Then Mother went to bed with a "sick headache." I wish I had shown some courage and done the right thing.

The weird war between two women waged on even after the death of our father, the object of their contested affection. The war did not end when Grandma died, although she was one of the two engaged in the fight. I was still stepping on landmines fifty-some years later.

As for Grandma Jennie, she died before her Venera gained the maturity and wisdom her mother longed to see. It was only when Mother became my husband Louis' mother-in-law that she gave me this wise insight. "Angela," she said, "you know that I love you but Louis doesn't know me as you do. I must show him my love and support. Therefore, I praise him often, look for qualities to admire, ignore the shortcomings I see, build him up. I remind you in his presence that you married a wonderful man." Early in my long marriage I noticed that the more Mother focused on Louis' attributes, the more he showed his best features. Grandma Jennie would have been proud of her daughter.

When raising children I realized how hard it is to bring up responsible, compassionate people of worth. Furthermore, I recognized that my mother-in-law had done just that. Therefore, I was grateful to her for having raised the best man in the world so that I could marry the best man in the world. We needn't become girlfriends. We didn't have to have anything in common besides him.

But who am I to judge Mother and Grandma Julia? Unlike these women at war, my mother-in-law and I liked each other. Also, I have never been widowed or impoverished, have always earned enough to support myself, and, perhaps most significantly, my mother-in-law and I never had to live together.

Chapter 41

Talking Houses
1955–1962

"What do you mean, Grammie? Houses can't talk!"

Sighing, I realized how hard it might be for eight-year-old Melissa to understand that many houses in our hometown talk. I explained that they speak eloquently about the past, define the present clearly, and whisper future possibilities.

Houses began talking when I was in elementary school. Our family moved from the apartment over Father's barber shop to the home on the corner built for a lake ship captain.

When the barber shop closed nightly, Dad passed our flower shop and walked half a block to our back door. We'd be in the kitchen on the door's other side, ready to serve dinner. The sound of Father's steps announced his arrival.

Dad's work ended with the last customer. Camille and I set the table by the closing time listed on his shop door. But I waited until hearing Father's approach before awkwardly pouring milk from the glass gallon jug.

Melissa said, "Wait. What glass gallon? What are you talking about?"

"Milk came in heavy glass bottles. Our milkman carried the number of bottles Mom ordered in strong, wired baskets with handles—something like the cardboard six packs that hold your soda pop—but more heavy duty." I said, "Mr. Lake would set the bottles into the silver-colored box near our door. Mom put the milkman's money right next to the door."

"Wow," said Melissa. "You didn't even have to go to the store."

"Well, yes, honey. And that's not all. If we wanted cream or additional milk we'd leave that message. Sometimes Mr. Lake just left our order but mostly he'd knock and Mom would serve him coffee. He'd tell us the neighborhood news. After all, he'd be going door to door."

What I didn't tell sweet Melissa was that Mr. Lake's friendliness led to the neighborhood scandal. He and a customer fell in love. She'd invited him in for years. He left his wife and five children.

"During the four to six months that Dad's mother lived with us, both Mom and Grandma Julia would make dinner. They put hot foods on the table when we heard Dad's steps," I said.

Melissa seemed interested so I continued my description of an evening when Grandma switched on the light in her borrowed oven to look at her loaves. Mother taste-tested steaming meatballs from her simmering sauce. Mom spent the day cooking. She mixed the ground meat, bread crumbs, eggs, garlic, green peppers, parsley and oregano. Mother showed us how to stir by hand. Cam loved to mix meatballs. I didn't. I tried mashing the cold meat combination.

"Yeech! It disgusted me," I said. "With washed hands my mom and sister squeezed the stuff between their fingers. They hand formed meatballs.

"That was the end of child friendly cooking. We were too young to use mother's old, green stove, which stood on little feet against a wall. Mother flash fried each meatball before dropping it into tomato sauce, stirring often, keeping the fragrant sauce from sticking to the pan.

"Grandma Julia spent the day baking. She had me run the just-warm water into her borrowed bowl, testing the temperature with her elbow. She asked Camille to stir in the yeast. We waited. When the yeast bubbled we got to add flour, sugar, salt, and water or milk."

Melissa was familiar with this breadmaking routine, the same she followed when making bread with her grandfather. Melissa, Louis and I love the bread baked from our grandparents' recipes.

I told Melissa that my Grandmother Julia rinsed a towel in hot water, wrung it nearly dry with her big, muscular hands, and laid it over the bowl. Again, time had to pass. We waited with Grandma, two little girls, each savoring a lungful of yeasty scent. We relished the sight. The dough swelled so very slowly that we could never see it push up the damp towel. But every time we checked, the rise increased.

Always amazed, we watched it double, triple, and bulge from the bowl. Then Grandmother floured her hands, dusting flour on the dough. Punching, squeezing, kneading, she slammed her strength into the dough. Straight as tin soldiers, hands washed, we awaited her call to action. Finally, Grandma sprinkled flour on our outstretched hands. We three took turns punching fat, warm, soft dough, releasing air pockets. We loved kneading. There was more fun ahead.

Grandma pulled the orb, separating the dough— small balls for bread loaves, tiny balls for buns. Grandmother kneaded globes, shaping dough to fit the pans that we had greased and floured. We worked on the buns-to-be. We smashed them on the floured porcelain kitchen table, pounding our little fists. With Grandma in the bathroom we threw them, catching bun balls tossed from corners of Mother's kitchen. We rolled dough strings and swung them overhead. There'd be no air in our buns!

Just about then Melissa saw a friend. She ran to play in the yard. Just as well. Unpleasant memories surfaced—ones I wouldn't share with her.

Grandma and Mother kept busy but found time to cut to the quick. I watched them from the sidelines. They nimbly avoided each other in our cramped kitchen. It was choreography. My pretty, young mother pirouetted on our kitchen floor stage. My prematurely aging grandmother slow danced a parallel performance.

Intent on perfecting her specialty, each deftly expressed hostility. Wisely and skillfully Mother and Grandmother avoided eye contact. This was a safety issue. Accidental connections caused emotional injuries. Eyes drilled deep, bores directed at each other's hearts.

In our kitchen I heard their caustic conversations.

"Like I tell my son, 'Meat is dear and your wife should mix less meat and more breadcrumbs into her meatballs and sauce.' Venera, yu'uns eat too much meat."

"That's an interesting opinion, Mother dear." Mom's voice was saccharine sweet.

310

"You waste money on swim lessons, Venera, dear. My son shouldn't allow it. He was a poor boy. My children didn't need to learn to swim and yours don't either. They spend too much time playing. You should teach them to clean, garden, iron, and to tidy the yard."

Silence followed.

Mother took us to the movies. She never invited Grandma. Mom treated us at the dairy. She brought no ice cream home to Grandma.

The relationship between the two most prominent women in my youth was icier than the Cold War waged internationally. Some sources say the Cold War ended in 1980. Others say it was over when the wall came down in 1989-1990. Still others cite 1991 when the USSR disbanded. As for my world, the war between the women began when they met and ended when Grandma died.

In their competition, each woman anticipated the reward for her efforts. Each expected her man's smile. His appreciation alone made the work worthwhile. He loved the scent of bread baking, the aroma of spaghetti sauce as he climbed onto the porch. Inside he'd see bread browning and meatballs simmering in the sauce. His salivary glands were already engaged.

Special scents would greet and please him. The bread of his boyhood waited, bringing warm memories of his grandmother's recipe. Happy to see his mother baking and his wife cooking, he thought they were working together. Walking in, he saw his wife drop pasta in the boiling water. A steaming meat sauce would smother the perfect noodles she'd test "al dente." There would be meatballs! Meatballs and meat sauce signaled financial success.

Growing up, neither Dad nor Mom ate spaghetti with meat on weeknights. Meat was an extravagance. Dad worked in his grandparents' garden. Mom labored on her parents' farm. They helped grow the produce which flavored their meals. There might be spaghetti with Swiss chard, peas, peppers, broccoli, cauliflower, tomatoes, or simply garlic or onions.

Tonight's weekday meal reflected Dad's success as a provider. Unlike his boyhood bread that his mother was glad to sell to the firemen next door, he would eat it fresh baked. He was no longer the little poor boy delivering steaming bread to the firehouse. He was the man who made enough not only to support his wife, their daughters, and his widowed mother, but also to treat them to meat anytime. For Camille and me a meal with meat wasn't exciting. We had never lived with want.

But, for me, every meal Mom and Grandma prepared jointly tasted of animosity. Tension between them in Mom's kitchen exerted a tightness which squeezed my soul.

Was Father oblivious to the war between the women he loved? I felt as if I was collateral damage. Didn't Dad see that they wore the armor of steely smiles, cleverly camouflaging their open conflict with perfect politeness?

Old timers say, "If this old house could talk!" But who would really want their home to talk? It might serve up family secrets, describing hard feelings bubbling like the spaghetti sauce in our kitchen.

Our house would speak of antagonism, of exasperation, of cooking, of baking, and of the impoverished youth of Mother, Father, and Grandmother.

Their family homes must have talked to them too. Mother's house must have screamed the night it burned to the ground. Everything her family owned incinerated. At seven years old she stood pajama clad in a Detroit street holding the hands of her five and three-year-old sisters. Family friends welcomed them to rural Algonac. Perhaps their old farmhouse spoke encouragingly as the family started anew, learning to farm.

Dad's dilapidated childhood home in his unsafe neighborhood probably spoke of insecurity. His mother's scrub woman's wages and the family's thrift were all that stood between them and homelessness.

Grandma's breath must have quickened with any nighttime knock on the thick wood door of the home in which she raised her children.

Our home must have verbalized serenity to Father and Mother. I felt the peace. I'd play piano softly, Dad smiling up from his newspapers. Camille, an early artist, sprawled on our hard wood floor, drawing on butcher paper rolls Mom bought her in bulk. For hours she'd paint, color, or cut. Mom, delighted, framed her pieces, hanging them on our walls.

There were precious, quiet moments when our house spoke of the love our parents shared. I'd see his arm around her; notice them cuddle close on the antique loveseat he bought her; observe as they watched Ed Sullivan or followed President Ike on our tiny, black and white television. Our home promised security to our family, until the night it didn't.

That night Camille and I went to sleep. Hours later our parents did the same. Only three of us awakened.

Ours had been the house that announced Dad's arrival, signaling us to put dinner on the table. Now it repeatedly stated the saddest of news.

Despite Dad's funeral I'd hear his footfalls on the porch. Hearing Father's steps I calmly waited for him to open the door and walk inside. Even when the sounds of his steps softened I waited for him. He would not enter. The same scene repeated. Each evening brought hope followed by hollowness. One night I didn't hear his footsteps. My grief changed. I was bereft. I ached for the momentary solace of the sound of his steps, a kind of comfort, false though it was. I'd lost those moments of promise. With the sound of silence our home told me to stop waiting. It finally and completely closed the door on comfort. Our house announced that Dad was dead.

Chapter 42

When Christmas Changed
1962

When I was sixteen I celebrated Christmas in the same old way. Never again.

On December 6 of the following year Father died. Christmas that year was when the Christmas party ended. Sorrow stole the celebration. Stark reality trumped fantasy splendor.

As in the case with anyone whose parent dies when they are young, many things change. Christmas changed for me. The party was over.

The faculty chose Cam for one of the two most important roles in the pageant put on yearly in her parochial school. She was the Blessed Mother. Her lifelong classmate was St. Joseph. The live infant in the manger was the real star of the show but he was unaware of his celebrity status.

Dad died a week before his little girl's big performance in eighth grade. Our parents were proud for Cam. It was her elementary school's capstone experience for the nuns, the parish priest, the students, and their families.

Although Father couldn't see his little daughter shine, Mother and I were in the audience with all our aunts, uncles, cousins, classmates, neighbors, and friends. Mom wasn't dressed in the cherry red dress she had chosen for the occasion. She wore the black of mourning. Mother wore black for a year in the tradition of Sicilian people.

Nor did the customary hush and awe occur when the Holy Family appeared with the background chorus of the student body. Instead collective grief marked the faces of all the audience, and many of the students whose stage make-up could not mask the tears shining on their little faces.

And why not? Our dad cut hair for most of the boys in this little school. Their fathers brought them to their barber for their first haircuts. Their families' albums held the photos of this minor moment of transition from baby to boy in Dad's barber chair. Father posted their first haircut pictures on his bulletin board. Our parents spearheaded many fundraisers to support this school. Dad would not be with us to celebrate the Christmas fast approaching.

The Good Shepherds (in their bathrobe costumes) stood tall and proud as they held their simple staffs (no doubt the canes they borrowed from grandparents). The sheep gathered around them in fluffy outfits fashioned by their mothers into wool-like looks. The Wise Men were resplendent in their regalia. But Dad's death was a damper on the long-awaited event.

Nor was the school celebration the only experience my father wouldn't share. The summer before he died I studied flute at Interlochen Music Camp, having won the local Music Study Club annual youth competition for a scholarship. It was with great pride that my parents drove me the long miles to this celebrated educational site. All my family, as well as my piano teacher and my high school band leader, were impressed by the quality of this music camp. They knew I would learn from the expert instructors and that I would be in the audiences of some great musicians. For instance, that summer, I heard young Van Cliburn play piano at that camp.

The Interlochen Music Camp capstone was the recording of our outdoor concerts. This recording was to be my Christmas gift to my father, who had taken such joy in listening to me practice on our upright piano and on my silver flute.

Recording, editing, and packaging took lots of time. My family and I eagerly awaited the box which would contain my concert performance. It arrived during Father's funeral.

There was the absolute irritation of the Christmas carols Mr. Smith played on a loud speaker. He owned the radio store a block from our home. We heard the same songs play endlessly. Every year all in our neighborhood dreaded the constant carols. He disregarded the repeated requests, "Please turn down the volume on the songs you play night and day from Thanksgiving week to New Year's Day."

A half block between his radio store and our home was a tiny shop, located in the front section of the small home of an elderly woman. It was the Emla Shoppe. Who knows? Maybe the name came from her own. Perhaps her first name was Emma. As for the "la" she wasn't a "la ti da" sort of woman, if such a type exists. Nor was she refined or sophisticated or given to grandeur. She was crabby and small minded, as evidenced by the scolding she once gave me when I was seven. I'd picked one of her day lilies to give to my momma.

The Emla Shoppe proprietor was quite hard of hearing. She yelled at our mutual neighbor, "Turn down that incessant music or turn it right off. I took out both my hearing aids and I still can't shut out your music. Stop it. Stop it. Stop it."

But the music played on.

319

In addition to the loudness, there was the limited selection. He rotated his collection of High Fidelity records but they were nevertheless few in number. Even the most enthusiastic music lovers among us learned to loathe these Christmas carols.

The month Father died, the constant carols changed from highly irritating to a real source of pain. Even as Mother, Cam and I heard the words "Have a holly, jolly Christmas" repeated endlessly we knew that this just was not going to happen that year.

Even prior to Father's sudden death during the holidays, Christmas had never been my favorite. The over-the-top festivities did not seem to connect with what our nuns taught us about the humble birth of the baby Jesus. Perhaps my attitude was also reinforced by our family's Sicilian custom of quiet celebrations at Christmas and of Little Christmas on January 6. The Italian accent was always on the special foods and the joy of the family getting together.

There was the hectic preparing for and the letdown which followed December 25. Despite our delight in being with each other, someone among the family or friendship groups would drink or eat too much or say hurtful things. Often there were hard feelings.

Christmas always brought quarrels. My parents were normally quite compatible but inevitably they had issues regarding our Christmas tree. Long a leader in the local Lions Club which cut and sold fresh Christmas trees, Father would insist on buying our tree at the Lions Club stand. That sounds innocuous enough. But no.

Dad hated Christmas trees. He well knew that he had no expertise in buying the right tree and he understood he wasn't handy. He had other talents but had none among those required to put up a tree each year. That being the case, he avoided the dreaded task.

Mother would suggest we buy the tree at the first sign of the sale at the stand. Dad would drag his feet. Mom would suggest more strongly. Soon she was nagging. That brought out the stubborn streak in her man. Then they would argue.

Finally, just before Christmas, we would all get into our car to pick from those little more than limp saplings and the overgrown trees which remained on the lot. Naturally, there was a limited selection among these leftovers. It was also inevitable that the remaining trees were not exactly fresh cut anymore. There were puddles of needles beneath them by now. Mother always berated my father's belated purchase. It was never a pleasant family outing.

What a job it was to estimate how high and wide our fresh tree should be! My parents could never quite get this right. It was an awful job to wrestle our annual tree up onto the car roof, off the car, up our icy stairs, and into the front door. The French door vestibule was a lovely entry to our home but an impediment to any large object, especially an inflexible tree dropping needles in all directions. Then they would have to move the tree through yet more French doors to our living room. When they stood a giant tree up it was sometimes too tall for our ceiling. Dad would root through the garage for his rusty old saw and grump as he chopped off the top to make our tree fit.

Dropped needles clung to our carpet as if they were miniature men clinging to the edges of little lifeboats. The job of securing our pathetic tree in the tree stand drove my dad to distraction. My mother was not sympathetic to her husband, who had never been skillful with Christmas trees. Nor did it occur to her, in the pre-Women's Liberation days, to just do the job herself, or even to pay her handy brother to do this bothersome task.

Our awful trees usually had crooked trunks. This made it very difficult to secure the twisted trunks securely in the stand. The listing limbs appeared incapable of supporting even the lightest, most delicate decorations. Often the shakily secured tree would overturn. This could happen anytime but most often occurred when we had completely decorated the tree. Actually, it was better when it happened immediately afterward. That eliminated the sound and shock of the crash in the middle of the nights before Christmas.

Each Christmas tree bulb was made of very thin glass. Whenever a bulb broke it smashed into tiny, sharp slivers which required an immediate and thorough clean up. Disposing of the mess was difficult and dangerous. Blood was usually involved. The small shards cut quick and deep.

Decorating our tree included silver strands of icicles which were neatly wound on cardboard packaging. Neatness did not impress my sister and me. We grabbed handfuls and threw them on the tree branches with reckless abandon. Our parents soon stopped our fun. Then we had to follow their example. What had been entertaining became a tedious task. Strand by strand we would drape each branch with individual silver icicle strands. It was a joyless job.

The dreary decorating process got even worse when we draped the tree branches with the used, individual silver icicle strands from Christmases past. Our thrifty,

Depression era parents reused everything. Each previous year we had carefully removed the decorations and rewound the individual silver icicles strand by strand when we took down our tree on Little Christmas. For every tree trimming we took each strand from the cardboard on which we had stored it. We would have to run our fingers down each strand to straighten it. A crinkled icicle did not reflect the same luster as a smooth one.

As I bemoan this labor intensive, highly boring process, I must concede that it could have been worse. My extravagant Aunt Fina decorated her tree each year with expensive spun glass "snow" that she discarded when the holidays ended. It was fabricated from fiberglass. She bought new each year but my frugal family might have tried to recycle that "snow." We would have been cut and scratched in the process!

Christmas tree lights brought their unique challenge. If one burned out the whole line worked no more. We had the task of checking for the clunker. It took time and patience and there was so little of both. Sometimes, just to avoid this tiresome task, Dad would turn the tree around so that darkened light strings faced the back wall. But that trick worked only once. After that we again had the onerous job of checking each bulb after crawling under the tree to unplug the string and extracting it from its spot where it was now useless for light.

Many years later, when I was a young wife and mother, we always had a fresh and beautiful tree. We bought it as soon as the tree sale stands opened. One year, and one year only, we had a little family outing to cut down our fresh tree. It was such a disaster that we never repeated the experience.

Our oldest daughter was fifteen months old. Her baby sister was three weeks old. Louis' mother offered to watch the baby, giving us a little getaway. I declined. "We'll just bundle up both, Mom. Thank you anyway, but the baby has colic."

"Now don't you worry. I can handle a crying baby."

"No, really, she's a little doll but she cries all the time."

"Go on. Have a good time."

When we returned two hours later, a tree strapped to our hood, our oldest sporting rosy cheeks, we found Gramma Rochon in tears.

"I tried everything. She cried and screamed."

A few years later a relative added a tree farm to his assorted businesses. He gave us a fresh cut tree early in the holiday season. After about five years, however, I noticed my pattern of illness at the holiday and observed that two of our children had the same teary-eyed, runny-nosed, labored breathing symptoms. At long last I recognized an allergy to trees, explaining the symptoms that began in my childhood. No wonder I never liked Christmas trees!

Finally savvy enough to put up an artificial tree each year we avoided the allergic reactions to pine scent. Also, we established a tree trimming tradition. We bought boxes of plain glass ornaments. Each year we'd review with our kids the names of new babies in our extended families and the new schoolmates, neighbors, or friends that year. Then we'd write the name of new special people in each of our lives. We'd use sparkly paint on shiny bulbs. It was fun to pull past year ornaments out of the storage boxes and read the names of favorite people as we hung their bulbs on our tree once again. Most were still in our lives. Sadly, some died. Some moved away and we'd lost contact. Our family decided that if someone became unworthy of our friendship over the past year we wouldn't hang the bulb with that name. Instead, we would smash that bulb. I'm happy to report that no bulb was ever smashed by anyone in our family.

Then there was the matter of Santa Claus. In fact, I had long harbored some resentment about the Santa subterfuge. Not only had I been quiet, serious, and scholarly, but I was a naïve youth. I believed what my parents told me. I can remember childhood conversations in which I reported hearing the reindeer hooves on the roof top just above my bedroom ceiling.

Mom and Dad must have been bemused or astounded that I was so gullible. Nor did I believe my friends and classmates who had early figured out the Santa story. It was not until I heard the truth from my parents that I gave up the fantasy. I can still see myself that day in our living room when I decided that, should I ever have children, I would not feed them this lie.

Years later Louis convinced me to keep Santa Claus in Christmas. I compromised, given his promise to soften the accent on Santa. Mainly because of my attitude, the emphasis was never on Christmas gifts in our family. Many enjoyed shopping. I did not. I avoided the harried crowds. Louis would venture out into the heavy traffic and spend endless hours searching for whatever item each of our children especially wanted. Often he would get tired and frustrated.

All our children seemed to want the same toys because they were the targets of each season's marketing. Therefore it was not unusual for parents to wait in long lines only to learn that these items were sold out. Louis never returned home emptyhanded but he was discouraged as he wondered if our kids would like "Santa's" choices.

While Louis did not share my complete distain for Christmas gifts, he did finally accept my proposition that we should not give each other Christmas gifts (or birthday gifts either). He understood my logic in that gifts "required by a specific date" were not always the most desirable and the deadline for gift giving made shopping stressful as well.

From that point on we embraced the habit of buying whatever we thought each other wanted whenever it came to our attention. The diamond ring he bought me when I happened to admire it in The Detroit Institute of Art gift shop showcase is an example. I have enjoyed wearing that exquisite ring daily, a sweet reminder of the lovely afternoon we spent together at an awesome art show some thirty years past. Last week he bought me beautiful blouses that I happened to see in a glitzy shop. As I emerged from trying on slacks in the dressing room I was surprised and delighted to see Lou at the checkout buying the pretty blouses. That same day I bought him a fine leather belt when he declined to spend so much on himself.

Spontaneous generosity is a quality that both Lou's father and mine shared. His mother and mine had to hold back any comments they might make unless they truly wanted an item. Otherwise their spouses would surprise them with the purchase. That is how, in fact, my mother got an ocelot fur. She happened to admire the coat as she and Dad saw it while riding the escalator from one floor to the next at Hudson's Department Store in downtown Detroit.

It makes great sense to me to get gifts for anyone you love whenever they want them and if you can afford them. On the matter of having enough money to buy gifts, Lou and I have always agreed. We never understood friends, colleagues, and acquaintances going into debt to buy the latest and greatest. Often they were still paying off the credit card purchases (with interest) that they purchased for last year's holidays when this year's Christmas came along. They felt that this defined them as good parents. We did not.

Christmas shopping always overwhelmed me. That is why I was delighted when Lou's sister and brother-in-law proposed that we pick names among the sixty plus extended family members. One adult picked the name of another adult at Thanksgiving dinner. One child picked the name of another child. They also proposed a price range. Many years ago it was a $5 to $10 limit. Gradually it went up to $10 and then to $20. This thoughtfully insured that not only did we have lots of time to shop leisurely from Thanksgiving to Christmas, but also that even the most cash strapped could participate equally.

Money was not the only excellent consideration in this policy which the family embraced. There was also the joy of concentrating time and effort and thought on one family member. Shopping was fun because I could use the time to find something unique to that relative's personality or need. Each of us gave and received something very special.

And every year I liked my gift very much. One Christmas my father-in-law bought me a selection of teas. All year I'd think of him whenever I enjoyed quiet time with a hot cup of a different type of tea. Having picked my name yet another year, my father-in-law bought me a red flannel, one piece, footed pajama. I loved it. I looked like an elf in Santa's workshop. I'm scrawny and short, a grown up packaged as if I was a perpetual child. Some call me "skinny Minnie" and I often feel chilly. The flannel pajama kept me warm as toast.

It's a testament to Lou's sister Joan and her late husband Carl that this family tradition remains, forty-some years after their suggestion. His sister Sue had another idea recently. "Why don't the adults simply donate the money we'd have spent on another adult? We could give the total to the Old Newsboys Charity in Dad's memory." We loved Sue's suggestion. Their father, Louis, our son, and a son-in-law used to be newsboys. This local charity gives Christmas money to needy families.

It was my dear father-in-law who donned a Santa hat each year, sat by the tree in his home bursting with all of us, and handed out each gift. He would call out the names to and from on the package. He began with the youngest child and ended with the oldest adult. The recipient would step forward to receive the gift and sit in the middle of the family who had encircled the room. When the package was open and the gift revealed, all of us would applaud and cheer.

It's a tribute to Lou's father that this gift opening extravaganza continues long after both he and my mother-in-law passed on. The youngest grandchild cried non-stop when her "Poppa Rochon" died. She was afraid that Christmas was over. Her mother hugged her and said, "Don't worry, Denise, Uncle Louis has always been Poppa Rochon's elf. Uncle Louis is ready to wear the Santa hat now. We'll all miss Poppa Rochon but we'll still give and get gifts."

As a child, my mother emphasized that the best is homemade. While I have come to realize that handmade is wonderful, it is also labor intensive. I am left feeling a bit guilty when I buy a gift. I never feel that anything store-bought is good enough, never have enough time near Christmas to make all the presents, never plan enough to make gifts all year long. Also, I have no talent with crafts, sewing, baking, or other skills.

Louis and I picked and chose among the holiday traditions. We took our kids to family friendly events. Our emphasis was on community and on experiences. We hosted annual Christmas carol sings in our home, inviting legions of family, neighbors, colleagues, and our friends as well as those of our children.

Flashlights aglow we sang at the doors of the aged, the sick, and the handicapped. Our home packed with the people who were precious to us, we ate Christmas cookies and drank hot chocolate and steaming cider. These light refreshments were delicious. With no alcohol or heavy meals served, we had no issues with drunkenness or gluttony.

To this day each child receives a card Santa hand-writes. He congratulates them for this year's specific accomplishments. He encourages their current efforts. He tells them to be good. He includes candy bars and puts his request in writing. "Please leave me some cookies and a nice glass of milk."

Here's some 2016 examples of the nineteen total letters. The first went to our oldest grandchild. The second to the youngest family member, a grandson of Lou's youngest brother, Joe.

Dear Jessica,

This has been one amazing year! You completed high school successfully and now have moved on to EMU. Your high school graduation party was a complete success. It was also very thoughtful of you and your friends to have a Spaghetti Dinner for the benefit of the food pantry. You have a good heart! I saw you were honored at swimming. Your coach had only good things to say about you. It must have been bittersweet to move on from the swim team. Maybe you'll swim at EMU. You were beautiful at the prom. I guess you have grown up to be a young lady. Is college going well? The variety of classes and teachers can make it overwhelming—not to mention that you're basically "on your own." I know you can handle it.

And now for the sad part of this letter. Adults have a tough time believing in me and the magic of Christmas. Since you're now an adult (by age) and acting like an adult (on your own at school, driving, working…) you probably find the Christmas letter and season "childish." I don't want to embarrass you among your friends. So, this will be your last Santa letter.

But be assured that I will still be watching you! Be "nice" and not "naughty"! Also, know that my heart will be glad at your many future successes; my heart will quicken when you face future choices and challenges; my heart will be sad when life treats you poorly or you experience difficulties.

You are a special person who deserves only the best.

Have a Great Christmas. You are blessed to be able to share the season with a family that loves you. Love, Santa

Dear Ezra,

My elves tell me you have finished potty training this year. An accomplishment that makes it easier on your mom and dad. It also lets you go to day care when it is necessary for your mom and dad to work. I see you have a lot of energy and climb and jump all the time. Maybe your sister, Lily, will read to you, so you can relax. I see you like dinosaurs—so do I! Keep being affectionate and kind. You are blessed with a big, loving family. Love, Santa

Chapter 43

Christmas Revisited
1988

Jennie, our oldest, belonged to a service group when she
was a student at the University of Michigan. This student
group fed the hungry in a church basement. Jennie phoned
home near Christmas break in 1988 with a suggestion. She
thought that her grandmother, her sister Julie, and I might
want to arrive early the day we were scheduled to bring her
home from college.

Jen said that we might want to help the group which
shopped for, cooked for, and served about sixty people,
most of whom were homeless. She said, "It is always fun.
There are plenty of us and we all work together."

Her grandmother declined the opportunity, stating
that she was feeling tired. Julie and I decided to try this
new experience.

Julie and I drove to Jennie's university dormitory.
The three of us then went to St. Mary's Church basement to
check out the dinner needs. There were boxes of noodles in
the pantry. Restaurants and bakeries had delivered their
day-old bread. Markets had contributed ripe blueberries,
past peak apples, and almost fresh green beans. We decided

on a spaghetti dinner menu and made a grocery list for the items we did not have.

The other students hadn't arrived when it was time to shop. We guessed that they were tied up with final exams and would be there when we returned with the groceries. Curiously, they were not.

Getting right to work, we soon had bubbling pots of spaghetti sauce. I looked up from the green beans that I was snapping. I checked the clock.

"Shouldn't the other workers be here by now?"

The look on Jennie's face told me the answer. She made frantic phone calls. No answer. We later learned that the student crew thought that this week's dinner had been cancelled due to Christmas break.

Then a lone student wandered in, wondering if we needed some extra help. "I have never done this before, but I heard about the program," she said. Soon the four of us were rushing wildly through the food preparation.

Time ticked on. There was no time to prepare the quantity cooking recipe we'd planned for dessert. Instead, Jennie washed the blueberries, dumped them in long pans and topped them with flour, sugar, and butter.

"What is your recipe?" I asked Jennie.

"I am kind of making it up."

"Good grief!"

Julie and I were stirring the spaghetti sauce when I heard some people come through the door.

"Thank goodness," I said. "You're late. Please set up the tables. Get the chairs out of the closets. Then wash your hands quickly and put on these gloves. After that you could set the tables."

They looked at me wide eyed but did exactly as I had asked.

"What's that smell? Oh, no, the meat sauce is burning!"

Jennie, Julie, and I carefully spooned off the top sauce from the scorched pan to a fresh one. Jennie's boyfriend, Mike, stopped in to say hello. He was on his way to his next exam but had about a half hour to spare. He helped us lift the heavy pans and pour the sauce.

Meanwhile I ran back to the ever-growing arrivals, giving directions. "Please wash the apples. Don't forget to wash your hands first. Then you can work with the other helpers to finish setting the tables."

As I began to assign workers to the steam tables to serve the food, Jennie looked up from the spaghetti sauce. "Who are you talking to, Mom?"

"What do you mean? They're the workers, of course."

"Oh, no, those are our guests!" she said. Then she whispered, "In fact, that's Crazy Eddie over there setting tables. Mom, he really is crazy."

"Oh!"

"Listen, Jennie, he's doing a good job. I don't care if he is dancing around as he does it."

And thus it was that my two daughters, one other student, and I, together with the needy, fed the needy. In fact, we all ate together. There was a kind of family dinner atmosphere. We said grace together. The four of us sat at different tables and talked with our guests.

There were some fascinating conversations. All of us were famished and exhausted. Dinner tasted delectable. There truly was no clue that the sauce had burned. Our meal was simply scrumptious. The blueberry cobbler was delicious.

After we ate, we all cleaned up together. No one asked our dinner guests for help. There was just a spontaneous recognition that help was needed. Within two hours our meager crew of four and our sixty-plus guests had washed the dishes, cleaned the kitchen, put the chairs back in the closet, folded and stored the tables, swept, and mopped the floors.

One scruffy old man seemed to smile all night. He asked me if the girls were my daughters.

"Those two are my daughters," I replied.

"You must be so proud," he said. And indeed, I was.

None of our fears were realized. There was plenty of food...more than enough. We boxed the leftovers and offered them to all. Some guests took food with them. By some miracle, the dinner destined for disaster had become a fabulous feast.

It was the most wonderful Christmas dinner I have ever had.

A crate of large, red, delicious apples remained. I urged people to take some. I'll never forget the conversation I had with the big, burly, soft spoken man with whom I had shared dishwashing duties.

"Joe," I said, "take some of these apples home."

"Well, mam, I don't have a home. I could take two for the boys down at the corner, though. Thank you very much."

His simple statement of fact hit me with force, like a body slam to the wall in a racquetball misstep. The lifestyle differences between me and this lovely man who lived on the streets were immediately clear. For a few short hours, all of us worked together, ate together, and talked together. Then, we shared the jobs of clean up too. Now I was about to drive my daughters to our home. He had neither a car nor a home.

One tray of blueberry cobbler remained. I put it in our car and drove my sleepy daughters the two hours home to Algonac. We served the cobbler at our Christmas caroling party the following evening. Guests raved about it and asked for the recipe. We laughed and assured them that none of us had any idea how much of any ingredient had been tossed into this delicious dessert.

Christmas changed when my father died. I was seventeen. Years had passed. Now I was a happily married woman with a wonderful family. Many experiences had transformed my life. Perhaps the most poignant was my Christmas conversation with a thoughtful homeless man. I learned to appreciate all that I had. Again, Christmas changed.

Chapter 44

I Just Saw Your Dad
2015

It was July 15, 2015…at least for me. As for Carl, there's a
question about time. His words startled me.

"I just saw your dad," Carl said. "We had a good
visit Tuesday."

I was astounded. Dad's been dead for fifty-two
years.

Carl said, "We talked about our Lions Club building
the pool. Us guys are so excited. We're gonna have a pool
to be proud of. Kids'll learn to swim there. They gotta learn
to swim. We've got the river, the canals, the marshes, and
the bay. We can't have our kids drown.

"Your dad wishes he could work with us. He wants
to know everything that's happening at the building site."

While Carl and I sat in our church basement, we
occupied different universes. I decided to just listen, not
knowing what to say.

It was noon. I remember details. The question
"What?" bounced on my tongue as if poised to dive high

into bewilderment. One glance at Carl's smile was enough to abort my dive and swallow my surprise.

Confusion became wonder. Wonder became joy. Carl's been eighteen years traveling the way his memory leads. His words invited. My eyes accepted. We walked awhile together in his world.

Carl and I ate together after the funeral of his best friend, Bill. Bill and Jeanne were my late parents' friends. Carl serenely recounted the distant past, that time being for him the present. I joyfully experienced his past in my present.

Mary brought a coffee pot, "Want a fill up?"

"No, thanks, Mary," I said.

"Sure," said Carl, "Top me off."

Mary said, "Saw you today, Angela, walking to the pool. Have a good swim?"

"Sure did. Early swims start my day right. Sometimes, sun sparkling off the water, I feel as young as when you and I—our classmates, friends, neighbors— swam there most every day."

That morning, I cut through time with each stroke, swimming thoughts flowing from present to past to future. I felt fully in the moment. Childhood pool memories warmed me. I thought about a granddaughter's upcoming swim test.

Emerging from the pool, I shook off swim sensations, memories, and plans as if they were water droplets.

I wondered if my lingering scent of chlorine prompted Carl's thoughts of our community swim pool.

"Ya know," said Carl, his eyes alive with excitement, "I had my doubts. I couldn't see how the bunch of us could build a swimming pool. But, it turns out that some of the guys know what they're doing. Harold and John are in construction work. They supervised the bulldozing last week. Now the rest of us just do whatever they say. I'm beginning to see a real swimming pool instead of what looks today like a big hole in the ground."

Carl pulled me out of the present, propelling me to the past, disoriented and amazed. I landed in Carl's world at age twelve in the heat of the summer of 1957. There was no escape from the scorching sun; no air-conditioned homes; no air-conditioned businesses.

Dorine, my seventh-grade classmate, said, "Awful summer! Our apartment above the bar and grille is a furnace. Mom and Dad take turns climbing upstairs to shower. One tends bar while the other cools off. Our bar and grille is so hot! My parents take two, sometimes three, showers a day. Dad called your father about your barber shop window awnings to find out if they help cool the shop

344

and your apartment above. Our old, cinder block buildings are alike, solid but stifling.

"I sleep with puddles of sweat in my eyeballs. I mope around like a slug. Good thing we've all got the Lions' pool. It's great! Mom and Dad don't let me swim in the river. I'm at the pool every day except when our Girl Scout troop camps at the Algonac State Park. Breezes come off the river. Big trees shade paths through the woods. The camp sites are mosquito-ey but we're a little cooler."

It felt odd to be young and to be with my equally young-again friend.

Dorine and I learned to swim in this pool, as do the generations after us. The best swimmers become the lifeguards and swim teachers. That morning I watched lifeguards encourage children all around me, students alternating between swimming, flopping, and shivering.

Carl still belongs to the Lions Club. Fellow members treat him with dignity, a respect he earned, and that reflects their charitable organization. Father was their president-elect.

Because Carl has forgotten that Dad died, he is uniquely able to bring Father to me. My memories are Carl's current events.

Carl said, "Lions and other leaders go door to door. We collect donations from fifty cents to twenty dollars for our pool. People are glad to give."

Yellowed photos show Carl, Mary's dad, and fellow Lions with their shovels reinforcing the excavated dirt of the hill that houses our treasured pool. But old photographs can't compare to the experience of being on the construction site. That's the gift that Carl gave. He took me to the scene where work is still in progress.

Reluctantly, I forced myself to concentrate on Bill's funeral lunch, knowing that my presence brings my late parents to his elderly widow and their ten children. Cam and I went to school with two of them.

Three weeks prior, in his hospital room, I showed Bill and Jeanne my parents' album. The pictures brought the past, making this old couple young, transporting them to happier times.

Soon after my hospital visit, I brought this photo album to Bill's funeral, along with sticky notes, pressing my message on the cover. "Write your name and address and stick your notes to photos you want. I'll have copies made and send them to you."

Aged mourners looking at the weathered photographs returned to their appearances within them.

346

Fragile pictures featured them dressed up, dancing with friends. There were shots of picnics with other parents, their children at play. They shared milestones: baptisms, confirmations, graduations, and weddings.

Sideways glances at Carl's wife, who hovered nearby, sent my signal that I was fine, he was fine, and she should savor her moments of freedom. Her smile beamed gratitude. With other quick breaks in the eye contact that held Carl and me, I was pleased throughout our meal. She was luxuriating in the joy of conversations, those in which all parties lived in the same world.

Time passed, as if on parade. Carl became increasingly eloquent. I listened intently.

"Your dad's got his barber shop on Saturday. That's his busiest day. He can't work with us on the pool, but he does a great job chairing the fundraising. And he donates cases of beer each week!"

Carl said that the guys also appreciate all that my mom does. "She's a real good organizer. She's got the other wives and all you kids making sandwiches and cookies." Carl grinned and thanked me, adding that a man loves a good meal when he's working hard outside.

Aware that the eye contact I maintained was my return gift to him, I fought the urge to look away. He must

347

notice every day that people avoid looking at him directly. It's natural to avert the pain of seeing the man they love and respect disappear more deeply into his own universe.

So, I locked my eyes on Carl. I listened with my eyes. I moved into our communication, allowing my body to speak silently. In this way, we both participated in our "conversation."

Yes, I acted out of sympathy and charity, but so much was returned to me. Listening is love. This fine, old man was bringing back the first man who loved me.

Carl talked on. I listened with rapt attention. Here was a man who daily loses more and more of himself giving me back more and more of my beloved father. I thought of the Methodist motto: "Do all the good you can, in all the ways you can, as long as ever you can." I realized that Carl is rapidly losing his abilities to achieve anything. And yet, through the dreamlike disorder in which he lives, he was sharing with me what no one else could give.

Dad did a lot of good. Had Father been a reprobate, Carl might have recounted horror stories. Carl lost the ability to screen his thoughts, so he would speak whatever was on his mind. Instead, Carl's words reminded me that it is the good we do that is our legacy.

Carl mesmerized me with his joyful voice as he reported the events that connect us. Carl had me hooked and the pull of the past was reeling me in. I was swept up in his current, feeling as if the two of us were floating on gentle waves. A warm wind moved the clear water of the pool. We were like two children in swim class, our faces in the water, our bodies flat on the lolling waves, and I held his hand.

When I lifted my head to take a deep breath before I put my little face back in the water, I knew I had entered Carl's state of mind. The elderly in our presence now looked young.

In my daydream, Bill's widow was in her thirties again. Jeanne somehow shed the hollow look, the dark-lined eyes, and the half century of history she had when we last visited in Bill's room. Now Jeanne appeared to me as she no doubt always seemed to Bill when he looked at the love of his life. No one except Carl and me would ever again see her in her prime.

Jeanne and my parents' other friends appeared as if they'd stepped out of their vintage photo album. Bill, too! He lost his pallor as he rested in his casket. He did, however, seem a bit solemn without his usual wide smile and twinkling eyes.

349

Background music for Bill's memorial video came from the 1940s, 50s, and 60s. The music coupled with the photographs created a reverie. I cherished my father's favorites: "Once in A While" and "Let Me Call You Sweetheart".

With wonder everywhere, I saw my parents' young-again friends. For a moment, I joined Carl in that I saw Father. And he was smiling.

Chapter 45

Walking Backwards

Living in the town where I grew up means that I walk where Father walked. Wandering frees the random reflections tucked in the crevices of my memory, making my hometown my favorite place to walk. Also, there is very little traffic. Most drive slowly because few people are in a hurry. Many honk and wave. Some pull over to chat.

Although I try to remain aware of my surroundings for safety sake, entertaining thoughts often distract. Just what is so interesting in this little location? There are many old homes. Some show their age. Most store my memories. I often pass the house where my parents brought me newly born. I gaze at big trees. They form background: scenes of Dad's Algonac years, backdrops of my lifetime. I alone see images of long-gone treehouses where my friends David, Christine, and I played.

Some see the now rundown home of my late Aunt 'Fina and Uncle Larry. I see it alight with our family gatherings. When Mother took to her bed in response to our father's sudden death, Cam and I did our best to grocery shop and prepare simple meals. Appraising the situation,

Aunt 'Fina said, "Come to my house for dinner every night." She eased her grief and provided her solace through cooking. This decision produced several results. Mother got out of bed and took us the two blocks each night to her sister's home. Aunt 'Fina relieved Cam and I of the bulk of meal planning, shopping, and cooking. Our aunt, uncle, their daughter, Mother, Cam and I ate a good dinner each night. The dinner table was a place of conversation for all of us. And lastly, Aunt 'Fina loved control. Nightly dinner meant she was in charge. When I look at the big window facing their dining room, I see us enjoying her meals; I smell her spaghetti sauce and taste our uncle's fresh produce.

Shifting my gaze from that window to their backyard, I sometimes see Uncle Larry's shadow working his huge gardens. Orphaned early, he became a foster child on a big farm. Many overworked foster children. He learned to garden. Uncle Larry relished fresh vegetables. Not only did he enjoy growing and eating fresh foods, but he also loved to give his produce to neighbors, friends, and family. I think of Uncle Larry's generosity with every garden-fresh taste.

Old structures keep my childhood clear. Over the years a variety of attorneys have practiced in the Kane professional office building where another of Mother's sisters was a legal secretary. I close my eyes and see her at her desk, open my ears and hear her clipped answer to the phone ring. Fortunately for us, Aunt Aggie learned a great deal in this position. She took over Mother's bill paying, checkbook balancing, rental collections, tax preparation, and insurance claims. Eventually rousing herself from nearly year of slumber, Mother awoke to find her affairs in order. To this day, I am grateful.

Some houses, trees, buildings, and boat launch areas are exactly the same as when Father and I passed them. Nevertheless, everything changes even as it stays the same. I filter every image through my memory. There are quaint words that I've heard elders use to hedge their remarks, "years ago," "If memory serves…"

If memory does indeed serve, it often does so imperfectly. Sometimes I concentrate intently. I want to bring back an experience from years ago. My effort can produce surreal results. At times I experience passing down a long, dark tunnel…backwards. Images surface and recede. Sentences and phrases form and drift away. The more I try to reach and grasp images or words, the more ephemeral they become.

Trying, reaching, and grasping are not as effective as when walking awakens the memory genie. I clear my mind, glance up at big trees, and look around at old houses. Strolling along the boardwalk I breathe in the scent of fish off the river and listen to the constant lapping of the waves. Then, sometimes, "memory serves."

Near Aunt 'Fina and Uncle Larry's Victorian home is a brick house with leaded glass doors and windows. Outside, it looks the same as when my husband was first my sweetheart. I wonder how it looks on the inside now. I have not entered through the magnificent front door since it led us into a Halloween Party forty-seven years ago; Louis dressed as a white knight in aluminum foil shining armor; I was a damsel in a long dress. We confirmed something very special about each other that night on the other side of that leaded glass. One of Lou's colleagues phoned Mother the next day to say, "I was at a Halloween party last night and saw that your daughter is in love."

Chapter 46

Love

Louis and I know that we were proceeded in this life by a love story.

A love story also led to our children's lives.

Love at first sight defies logic. It seems impossible that a person's initial look at another can impact that human being so profoundly that it creates a connection that lasts from that moment onward. And yet, love at first sight worked well for my father and mother, my mother and father-in-law, and for Louis and me.

1944-1962 Dad first saw Mother as the maid of honor at her sister's wedding. Venera was a slim, young, gregarious woman with curly dark hair and a bright smile. He looked at her and that was all it took. Mom, on the other hand, had to think a bit. Her parents urged her to marry the son of their friends. Her dad said, "Bill's a decent man. He'll take care of you financially."

"Bill was okay," Mom told me years later. "He was well established in business, owned his own home, was nice to me, and respectful to my parents. But Bill was kind of dull."

And so, she talked to her parents about Angelo, the Navy man invited to her sister's wedding at the last minute. She asked them to invite Angelo to their home for dinner. "We know he's lonely," she said. "Angelo yearns to be with Italians and we are the only ones in our village. He's so far away from his Italian family and community in Ohio."

The family dinner took place the week after her sister Sara's wedding. My mother, and her mother, saw a magnificent man in Angelo. Within two months, Venera and Angelo married. It was war time and GIs knew they could be called to the front at any time. They loved with all their hearts until death parted them.

1944-1986 Around the same time that my parents met in Algonac, in the Village of Marine City eight miles away, my mother-in-law noticed another Navy man in uniform. She watched as he strode self-assuredly down her street. She turned to her girlfriend and said, "Who is that guy? I am going to marry him." Within a year, she did just that. He returned to their village on leave and they moved to his duty station in Oklahoma. Later he was sent overseas.

Some say that opposites attract. Mom Rochon was accomplished, a fine mother and devoted grandmother, a top woman golfer and bowler, and an excellent seamstress, cook, and bread baker. Nevertheless, she never had her husband's self-assurance. When he entered a room others noticed. She admired his self-confidence.

Through lean years and good times Lou's parents were good to each other. Mom and Dad Rochon loved children, had six, and always grieved their baby boy, little Art. He died soon after birth.

As all their children and grandchildren sat around their dining table each Sunday I saw my in-laws treat each other thoughtfully. Dad Rochon was genial and kept the table conversation interesting. Mom Rochon quietly smiled at his stories. She would cook and he would leap up afterwards to clean the kitchen. I remarked on this to Louis one day.

"Oh, yes, honey" He smiled. "When I was growing up, every night after dinner Dad urged Mom to visit her neighbor friends. He would then wash the dishes. He told me that everyone needs a work break and he knew that Mom worked hard.

"When our wedding approached, I asked Dad if he had any marriage advice for me. His answer was quick and brief. 'Eat what she cooks and thank her for all the effort.' It made sense to me because I sure never wanted the job of cooking.

"Mom and Dad worked hard. Money was tight. They built our home with a little help from her brother. They volunteered for jobs at church. But they also had fun together. They loved dancing when he courted her. They joined other couples in the big band ballrooms prevalent in Detroit in the 1940s and 50s. Once, hearing their favorite song on Dad's 78 record I peeked into our little kitchen. Hearing 'I'll Get By...as Long as I Have You,' I saw them dancing past the stove and 'fridge.

"My parents bowled on a Ma and Pa League and they golfed in a couples' league. Our family had fun. My brothers and I bowled with Dad on the Father and Sons league; Dad bowled on the Men's league. Mom was on the Women's League. Dad financed our bowling by keeping the scores manually. The bowlers elected Dad as League Secretary because he was so good with math. He taught me the process. As League Secretary I paid for the Ma and Pa bowling we enjoyed with other young, married friends. Dad and I loved math but we lost our jobs when computerized scoring began."

When my fine father-in-law died all of us could see that part of my mother-in-law died too. Once, during the sixteen years she was a widow, I wanted to introduce her to a nice widower I knew. I thought they could golf or bowl, attend Mass together and go to breakfast afterward, or go out to dinner.

"No," she said, "I've had the best of men. I have no interest in anyone else."

1945 Louis and I were born less than two years after my dad fell in love at first sight with my mother and my mother-in-law likewise instantly decided she wanted to marry my father-in-law.

1969–the present Twenty-five years later Louis says he fell in love with me at first sight. Louis noticed me through an open classroom door. I was a substitute teacher in the elementary school where he taught.

The feeling was not mutual.

For one thing, I hardly noticed Louis. A stand-in for a very permissive teacher I shall call Mr. Melki, I was focused on keeping order in an "Open Classroom." This was a passing fad in education that encouraged students to "express themselves." When I told the fourth graders that they must stop jumping rope, typing on the old black Remington, or tossing a volleyball across the classroom they fell silent in shock.

Louis' classroom was just down the hall. He noticed the absence of the usual din in his colleague's class. Walking his fifth graders to their recess Lou peeked into

Mr. Melki's classroom door. According to Louis there was an aura around me; he says he sees that aura still.

Another reason that I did not instantly fall in love with Louis is that I was engaged.

Louis asked my aunt, another teacher in the school, to introduce us. She told him I was to be married in two months. Always a perfect gentleman, Louis did not approach me. But he did not forget.

Months later, my fiancé and I called off our wedding. My aunt told Louis. He immediately invited me to dinner and dancing. I felt very comfortable with Lou on our first date. I said to Mom on my return home that night, "I'm so glad I wasn't married when I met Louis."

Louis and I grew up in loving families. His mother was helpful and steadfast. Louis had a wise and wonderful father. "How do I know when love is real?" he asked his dad. His father said, "You just know."

Marge, my teen friend, visited me in our home so we could work on our high school newspaper. We entered through the French doors and sat at our big, wooden table in the formal dining room. The second set of French doors was also open and led to the living room where Mom and Dad sat on the upholstered loveseat. His arm lay loosely around her shoulder. He was reading the stock reports. She was mending our socks. Marge and I could hear my parents' voices above the soft music of 1940's love songs. Sometimes we heard quiet laughter.

The next time we had a looming newspaper deadline I suggested we work together at her house. Marge was quick to respond. "No," she said, "it's better at your home."

Again, my parents were in the living room while we sat at the dining room table. This time Mom worked on the wording for one of their land contracts while Dad checked out the futures on the Wall Street Journal. Again, we heard strains of Bing Crosby and The Andrews Sisters.

When Margie and I finished our work, she rose to leave. Walking toward the French-doored vestibule she stopped by living room to say goodbye to my parents. Mother said, "Good to see you, honey." Then, as if the words rose straight from her heart, Marge said to my mom, "There's peace here. I can tell that you and your husband love each other."

Of all the things said and heard when we were teenagers I remember those sentences distinctly. Marge described the atmosphere of our home.

1975 Decades later, our babysitter, Kelly, said to me, "I'm glad to be here. You and your husband are good to each other and kind to your children. What a happy home!" Her insightful words brought back Marge's reflection on the home my parents made for my sister and me.

Louis' kid sister, twelve years younger than him, sent us an anniversary card when she was a young wife with two small children. She added a personal note to say, "You two share a love that inspires me. Ever since I was a junior bridesmaid at your wedding I have watched you. Perhaps you never knew that little eyes were always on you. I see the gentle way you treat each other and your patience with your children."

1982 Once, my mother twenty years widowed by then, a girlfriend my age, and I sat at Mom's dining table.

The girl said, "My husband just doesn't understand."

Mom, ever the discreet lady, said, "Well, honey, during your 'tender moments,' just talk to him honestly."

Sadness closed the conversation. My friend smiled wanly. She said, "We don't make love. We have sex. We don't have tender moments."

The Present Dad, my husband, my mother-in-law, all fell in love at first sight and loved unconditionally from that day on.

Both Mom and I took a little longer to fall in love. I had been engaged twice and I had begun to question my judgement. I soon realized, however, that the love I felt for Louis was more intense and certain than any emotion I'd ever experienced. Mom quickly decided that her persistent boyfriend paled in comparison to her Angelo. Did my parents fall in love in part because they felt comfortable with each other? Did Louis and I do the same? Certainly, all of us quickly made the most important decision of our lives. Mom and Dad married within two months of meeting each other. Louis and I were engaged six weeks after our first date and married within eight months. I regret that we wasted that much time.

Not really.

It was good that we spent time planning our big wedding, fixing old furniture, and finding the cheap upstairs flat to rent as newlyweds. We got to know each other better as we made decisions, budgeted, worked together, and paid off our wedding.

Louis continued to teach in my hometown. I got a high school teaching job in his hometown. I paid Mom the last of my university expenses. My education had earning potential while my widowed mother's finances were tenuous. Louis paid off his used, midnight blue Pontiac Le Mans.

We entered marriage with optimism. Louis had $5.00 to his name. My assets were a few dollars more. But we had jobs that would resume in a month with the new school year.

"Have a honeymoon," said my mother. "You'll be glad you did."

"Why not?" we agreed. We had each other. We had time. We were delighted to find that we had some gift money left after we paid off our wonderful wedding. We were debt free.

So, we drove off in Lou's highly polished car. It was a beauty but it didn't start when it rained. Ours were mostly sunny days.

On the wet ones, we'd just stay a bit longer until the car worked again. We drove across the Blue Water Bridge into Canada until we found attractions in nearby Sarnia, then Toronto, then Montreal, followed by Quebec. Returning to the USA, we toured Maine, New Hampshire Rhode Island, Massachusetts, upstate New York, New York City, New Jersey before driving across the state of Ohio to our Michigan. Ours was a glorious, three-week honeymoon.

The trip was also an excellent decision. Within thirteen months we were parents. Travel ended for a while.

Was it love at first sight that brought us together?

Yes. And no.

While passion is evident from the beginning in the form of love at first sight, such chemistry is not the only factor. Research says that such arousal can be infatuation. * Love is also a commitment, an action instead of a feeling, a decision.**

Indeed, just like our parents, fellow travelers down the trail marked "Love at First Sight," we entered a marriage contract. None of the three of us couples took this decision lightly. In our mutual faith, matrimony had the significance of a sacrament. In addition, everyone in each marriage liked their spouse, wanted the best for each other, and felt a warm closeness. Marriage, based on shared values, was reinforced by generational patterns on both sides.

My family is lucky.

Looking back, I realize that intimacy was present and intensified over the years of support. Additionally, many extended family members lived nearby and gathered often. Long distance travel to other relatives was a priority, despite cost and effort. Marriages were not untroubled. Family was there for each other in troubled times.

Mom considered leaving Dad in Youngstown, Ohio. Her mother said, "Don't try to make this good man choose between you and his mother. Find a way that the two women he loves can still be in his life." My parents learned to compromise.

There was a crisis in Lou's parents' marriage.

Louis said, "Dad was transferred. Most of my childhood, my father worked close enough that he could walk to work. When his new job relocated him to Michigan's upper peninsula from our hometown, we prepared for the move.

"Mom's brother had helped them build our home. Now, Uncle Duke hosed down his cattle truck from their family dairy farm. He disinfected the hauler. We packed it with all our furniture and other belongings. Dad drove all us kids in our American Motors Rambler, Mom and her brother followed. We had a two-vehicle caravan for our twelve-hour drive.

"It was a long, cold, lonely winter for my mother. Snow mounds deep in the uppermost Michigan. With all us kids in school and Dad working ten-hour days she missed her village, her neighbors, and her family. She became unusually quiet. Patches of her hair fell out.

"We traveled downstate for the family reunion. Uncle Duke told Dad, 'Your wife's not gonna make it, Art. She's at the end of her rope.'

"Shortly after that Dad and Mom worked out an arrangement. We moved back and Dad worked away from our hometown four to five days. He returned home on weekends when possible. Dad put in for a transfer back and that transfer came through."

Louis and I faced challenges too. Married thirty-nine months, Marc was born when our Julie was eleven months old and our Jennie was twenty-six months old. We were overwhelmed. Relatives helped whenever we asked. One baby stayed with my mom, another stayed with my mother-in-law while I grocery shopped with one child for an hour or when I took one little one to the doctor. My sister offered and took care of our children for a weekend yearly for the ten years after our first baby was born. How we looked forward to those weekends alone!

Our family realized many advantages due to the children's closeness in age. Age appropriate playgrounds, amusement parks, and sports appealed to all of them at the same time. Following each other through the school system they knew each other's teachers, classmates, friends. Moving through dating, marriage, and into parenthood they reunite our family regularly. Their children cherish each aunt, uncle, and cousin.

Many mothers, fathers, aunts, uncles, grandparents, cousins, in-laws, siblings on both sides played supporting roles in the dramas, comedies, tragedies, romances, and shorts that documented our family love stories.

My mom, Mother-in-law, and I married kind gentlemen. Louis and I had parents who loved each other throughout their marriages and mourned their late spouses all the rest of their lives.

How I wish my father had not been born fatherless! Fate was doubly cruel when his stepfather was also killed. His mother must have communicated to him the love she shared with the two good men she married. Somehow my fatherless dad learned to be a loving husband and father. Certainly, many in the neighborhood cared about him, including his grandparents and bachelor uncles. But nothing helps youth learn the dance of diplomacy a good marriage demands more than seeing their parents treat each other lovingly over the years.

After the death of their widowed mother, one of the bachelors, Uncle Tony, married late in life. He and Aunt

Sue had a son and a daughter, both a bit older than me. Maybe they showed Dad that he was not too old to marry and have children.

1969 When Louis and I married, I had "Love is eternal" engraved on his ring. These were the words Abraham Lincoln used for his wife, Mary Todd Lincoln, but, most importantly, these are the words Louis' parents lived, and my parents too. This was the feeling that drew me to Louis.

While we were dating, Lou and I visited his infant goddaughter. His sister Sue's newborn cried inconsolably. Everyone in the family tried to quiet Baby Christine. Louis held her tightly in his arms in Gramma Rochon's rocking chair. He softly circled his finger on her temple. She immediately went to sleep.

Any man who could be so gentle and perceptive with a newborn would be a loving husband and tender father, I thought. It turnout out that I was correct.

We wanted children. I was especially eager to become a mother. I remembered how glad I was to be my father's daughter. When I observed Louis quiet the baby I saw in him the kindness I knew in my father. I sensed that together Louis and I could be good parents.

After we'd been married two months I remember crying because I had my 'monthly visitor' (as my refined mother used to say). "Louis, I'm afraid I'll never get pregnant." Soon after, our full-term pregnancies came one after another until I could have no more babies. We cherish our children and their children.

The present Louis is kind, strong, and smart. He is a man of integrity. And there is the indescribable attraction that drew me to him on our first date and that has changed only to intensify for forty-seven years. I am crazy about him.

Two weeks ago, Louis and I went to an outstanding concert. We appreciate classical music. As the notes swept us into a world of beauty I had a delightful thought. I realized that, while Louis fell in love with me at first sight, I fell in love with him before I even knew he existed. I was in love with the idea of him. I well-remembered attending concerts by myself and yearning to share this enjoyment with someone special. Now, in our forty-seven years together, classical music has filled our homes and hearts. The sounds we love became the background music of our marriage.

As we dated, I learned he and I both studied in our respective university libraries, fascinated by the huge worlds of books open to us. I wished that we could have been two nerds studying together.

In addition, he was attending lectures and art shows alone on his campus while I was doing the same at mine. He toured museums. I loved to visit museums also.

Love is love. Sometimes it is between two people. Other times it is one, a person loving art, libraries, music, museums or other passions. When people in love with each other find that they appreciate the same pleasures it increases their mutual attraction. I was indeed in love with the idea of Louis long before we met.

Certainly, we have much in common: the same education, age, religion, small town upbringing, profession, values, and love of family. We're different in temperament, habits, nationalities, and book, movie, and food preferences. Commonalities trump our differences.

In the end, love defies explanation.

*Mary-Lou Galician 2004: Sex, love, and romance in the mass media: Analysis and criticism of unrealistic portrayals and their influence. Mahwah, NJ. Lawrence Erlbaum Associates. Dr. Mary-Lou Galician said, "There is no such thing as love at first sight."

**R. J. Sternberg 1986: a triangular theory of love, Psychological Review-93 (2), 119-135. Sternberg specified three kinds of love. One is passion define by infatuation, increased romantic or sexual desire, physical arousal or, perhaps, love at first sight. Passion is chemistry. Two is Commitment, consisting of making a contract. The third type is Intimacy, referring to closeness, caring, sharing, supporting each other; the individuals relate to each other; they like each other. Passion, Commitment, and Intimacy are the three sides of the Love Triangle, the length of each side changing during different times in the relationship. Research stresses that if all three of these factors exist, the lucky couple share consummate love.

Chapter 47

My Father/Myself
1919-2016

Another family fatherless? Just as I was about to conclude these memoirs, our adult children almost lost their father. In the middle of the night, Louis turned to me saying, "I have a pain in my heart."

I said, "We have to go to the hospital. Take your blood pressure and check your blood sugar level, honey. I'll phone the emergency room, give them your vital signs, and alert them that we're coming."

Doctors examined Louis and got his blood test results. Despite their somber faces I chose to be hopeful, but my internal alarm system rang as soon as I heard the word "procedure." Optimism is one thing. Semantics is another. While I may not know exactly what happens in a heart catheterization, I do know the meaning of certain words. Healthcare providers may call it whatever they choose, but anything that a doctor does in an operating room and under anesthesia I say is "an operation." Any surgery petrifies me.

Soon, strange sounds came from behind the stall door. I was in the Women's Restroom just off the Surgical Lounge. These were awful noises. Choking, gasping. Not just sobs—racking, heaving, shuddering sobs. At first I imagined them being animal sounds, guttural, visceral, hauntingly horrible, the emissions of a being incapable of speech. Gradually I recognized I was hearing a human being; a human in circumstances so dark as to render words inadequate. My entire body flash-froze. I realized it was me.

Minutes before I sobbed in the bathroom, the cardiologist told me that he could not continue the heart catheterization "procedure" as it was too dangerous. Stents were not an option. Open heart surgery was Lou's only hope.

The cardiologist showed me the photo of Lou's heart, pointing out the blocked arteries. I found the photo helpful although I got a little confused with the left lobe, right lobe references due to my directional dyslexia. I registered the words "eighty percent blocked." Then, the words "impending death" sunk in. Doctors seldom say the word "death." At times, I've heard "unexpected outcome," "abrupt reversal," "rapid decline," among other euphemisms. He's the first physician I've heard describe a clogged artery as the "widow maker." I've heard people use this colloquialism when referring to strangers with arterial concerns. When the doctor used the term, however, I found it flippant, considering that this night I may have changed from wife to widow.

Perhaps the specialist chose his words carefully. Obviously, English was not his first language. Maybe he noticed my somewhat spaced-out demeanor and wanted to make me understand. He may have thought I was ignorant as I sat before him, wide-eyed, slack jawed and silent. Whatever his motivation, his word choice did the trick. I straightened my spine and focused on his face. Concentration and action replaced confusion and denial. "Death," I said. "If this is the situation, proceed immediately."

The cardiologist patiently said, "My colleagues and I consider the situation urgent as opposed to immediate. Upon consultation with a cardiac surgical team, we shall stabilize after the trauma of the attempt at catheterization. We anticipate surgery in one to two days and are prepared to operate sooner if necessary. The cardiac surgeon shall talk to you soon."

Walking out of the Surgical Lounge restroom I faced Louis' compassionate, tall, young nurse who had two

375

hours before read aloud the patient permission document. It was the standard "cover our corporation" paper that is "just a formality, everything is going to be all right, just outlining all the unlikely possibilities." Louis signed and I co-signed in advance of my husband's heart catheterization procedure.

Scared is what I felt to find Louis' nurse waiting for me outside the restroom. "Quickly," she said. She was no longer calm and composed. "The cardiac surgeon is waiting to talk to you."

Can this really be happening? This was my brain talking to my wooden legs that responded to Lou's nurse as if I was a sheep and she was the sheep dog. Although aware that she was mouthing encouragement, the only words I could hear were those of the cardiologist. I was still struggling to understand the difference between urgent versus immediate when Lou's nurse arrived and led me, dazed and stumbling, to meet with the cardiac surgeon.

Surgeon school must include "how to deliver the worst of news in the best of angles" because that is exactly what he attempted to do. "As a cardiac and thoracic surgeon, I rarely get extensive time to prepare and closely monitor the patient prior to open heart surgery."

His words "open heart" caused my own heart to stop. My brain tried to buy me some time by means of an escape from reality. My lifelong fascination with language kicked in, prompting me to wonder if the cardiac surgeon was born in the same mid-eastern country as the cardiologist. Their voice inflections were similar. They used the same very proper English in communicating.

The cardiac surgeon brooked no more of my denial of the truth. He fixed the black pupils of his very large eyes on my black pupils. He said, "My team and I shall attend to every detail, plotting the course in a manner that concurs with his current fragile state. Normally the patient is scheduled to arrive on the day of surgery and my team begins the process. In your husband's case, we are giving him prescriptions in the cardiac unit. He shall remain on a monitor. I have the great advantage of time to assess his reaction to each aspect of his preoperative care due to his urgent need. We must acknowledge that your husband is very lucky." He said, "Fortunately, he came to the hospital instead of disregarding this warning sign. Otherwise he would be dead. When that artery ruptures, death follows."

Although I nodded, I felt like screaming. I wanted to say, "Enough already with the word 'death.' Gimme a break."

377

As blunt as he was, the surgeon had a job to do. I was not his patient. He had no time to waste. He was trying to tell me that they may need to operate at any time. Louis was medicated and the surgeon needed my signature for an informed consent.

The problem was that I was still having trouble accepting that Louis and I should even be in a hospital. We were enjoying parties with our family in New York City and in Atlanta, Georgia from mid-August through the mid-September evening when we flew back to Michigan. In the vast Atlanta airport Louis seemed exhausted. I said, "We're here in plenty of time for our flight. Let's just sit at this gate until your fatigue passes. There's nobody waiting here. We'll rest. We're both tired. Then we'll walk slowly to our departure gate."

Two days later, Louis again said he was tired. That evening, near midnight, I woke up when he got out of bed. "What's going on, honey?"

Lou said he felt a pain in his heart. Louis was not particularly concerned. He said, "It's not excruciating pain." Despite being half awake, I knew it was important to go to the hospital.

Lou and I chatted calmly along the way. Halfway there, Louis said, "The pain is gone. I think we should go home. If we go to the Emergency Center and it turns out to be heartburn our insurance won't pay the bill."

I said, "That doesn't matter, sweetheart. Let's keep on going to the hospital. Heartburn would be good news."

Lou nodded. "Probably we should. I have had this pain, on and off for a month."

A month! I fumed. Why hadn't he told me? But, I thought, I'd better focus. We can discuss this matter later.

A physician waited at the door while the nurse completed the quick triage process. He reviewed Lou's condition and reported to the cardiologist who immediately admitted Louis.

As they transported Lou's gurney to the operating room, I said, "Darling, I would give you my heart."

"Honey," Louis said, "you already did…forty-seven years ago."

This story has a happy ending. Pride glowed on the face of the cardiac surgeon when he said, "Surgery went well. I did three bypasses while operating on his beating heart. He is responding well post-operatively."

As we held hands in the Intensive Care Unit, Louis smiled wanly. "That was a close call, honey. Your family history could have repeated. You might have awakened, as your mother did, her husband dead in the bed."

Early death, mostly unexpected, often traumatic, recurs in my immediate and extended family history. This pattern began with Luigi Marcheoma's death due to pneumonia at age four. His father died a few years afterwards when he was run over by a train, leaving my dad fatherless at birth months later. When Dad was twelve, his stepfather, Pasquale Andino, was killed instantly by a drunk driver. Vito Andino, Pasquale's brother, murdered the drunk driver.

Mother's side of the family tree is also scarred by death. Mom was the first of the nine babies but only five lived past a year. Her thirty-two-year-old sister's husband died in an industrial accident at age thirty-two, leaving their four children. Their thirty-six-year-old sister died, leaving her grieving young widower and their sixteen-year-old daughter. Mom's mother died at age forty-nine. When Dad died of a sudden heart attack at age fifty, Mom was thirty-eight.

Our son and daughter-in-law lost a baby through miscarriage.

Louis and I have grown old together, grateful for our blessings. His recent heart attack and his severe anaphylactic reaction to a bee sting last year are the exceptions to his good health. I am also healthy. I had three pregnancies resulting in three live births, all healthy newborns. Our three children and six grandchildren are all well and strong.

The contemplation of my father's life led me to consider my own. I reflect on Dad's father's death. It is impossible to know my grandfather's thoughts as he lay splayed across the track, broken-bone-helpless in the path of the approaching train, but he had just demonstrated his deeply spiritual nature by walking the pilgrim's way.

Grandma said, "We were so young. We loved each other since we were children in our neighborhood and I'll always love him. When our Luigi died, it was as though we became old instantly. Later, when we knew we were to have another baby, hope, joy, and our youthfulness came back to us. We were so happy. My dear husband, Angelo, made a pilgrimage to thank the Lord."

Grandma described her young husband as eagerly anticipating their next baby. They would name a boy Angelo. I am comforted in my conviction that my grandfather's last thoughts were hopeful, not harrowing, peaceful, rather than frightful.

While I do not wish to die, I do not fear death. My near-death experience and those of others who confided in me reassure me. I was driving alone when I had a single car roll-over accident on an icy overpass above an expressway. As my auto smashed first into one guard rail and then slipped across to the other rail and back and forth again, I knew I could not prevent a crash. But I never felt fear. Instead, I experienced a profound peace. I felt myself serenely moving down a tunnel with a light at the end. I was glad to be there. Suddenly, however, Louis and our three teenagers came to mind. I said, "God, please let me help raise our children." The light dimmed and I left the tunnel. I emerged with a small facial gash from my totally wrecked car, much to the amazement of the witness who phoned for an ambulance.

Cousin Nardi felt that same serenity during one of her many critical health crises. My mother-in-law viewed herself from above during a heart catheterization. She said she felt tranquil. When she died, years later, she smiled and blew a kiss to her oldest daughter minutes before. My mother emerged from her weeks of coma, beaming her smile just before her heart stopped. My friend's eighty-two-year-old father awakened moments before dying and turned to an empty corner where he greeted his long dead brother.

A year ago, Lou was cutting the lawn when a bee stung him. He reacted with a complete anaphylactic shock, staggered into our house, fell forward and struck his forehead on the tile floor. The gash required twenty-two stitches in an emergency room. Louis was alone. He was gasping for breath, his tongue, lips, eyelids and extremities grotesquely swollen. He lost control of his bowels.

Later Louis said, "I felt no pain. I didn't panic. I wasn't afraid. At first I felt guilty for the mess of my blood and body waste. But soon shame disappeared and I felt content. I just wanted to sleep. I felt a wonderful peace. I recited the Act of Contrition. Relaxed, I was aware I was dying. Then I thought about you. I felt badly you'd come home to see my bloodied face. You'd have the awful smell and mess. So, I dialed 911. The dispatcher said she would wait on the line until the ambulance arrived. I told her that she need not, after all there would be people calling with emergencies. She insisted. I had to put the call on speaker phone since I couldn't keep holding the receiver."

When the ambulance arrived, Louis was unconscious.

Lou's recent near-death experiences play over and over on the screen of my thoughts and my dreams. Every trauma awakens my long-ago losses, hibernating deep within me, releasing the terrors to fill me with fear.

When terror arrives, my father comes calling.

Father says ever so softly, "Don't worry, honey. You're a child of the Lord."

Dad's words bring the serenity that I knew near death, the calm that enfolds me. I think "Children of the Lord" and remember the love that lies waiting when we live no more.

Legions of loved ones arise from my genes. The earliest elders carried each tattered valise with all they had when they came to America. Their strength lay in courage and they give me that gift.

Comfort comes to me, a blanket smothering my smoldering sorrow.

Joy arrives expectantly, this year right after shock. Lou's heart blocked in September and yet, this December each child again gets a card Santa handwrites. As Mrs. Claus, I'm very happy that Santa is alive and gets better every day. Neither the elves nor I could express his love the way that he can. My already aching heart would have broken if I had to tell the children that Santa couldn't write his letter this year. Their parents would've been very sad too. Santa sent them letters when they were children. Forty-four years ago, he sent his first letter to his sister's toddler, the first of his parents' grandchildren, and his first niece.

By next Christmas, "God Willing", he'll write to that niece's first grandbaby. *

Wisdom is my last visitor. I am the eldest, sealing the door to sadness forever, acknowledging the truth of our lives. Fifty years of rejection laid waste to our family. Reconciliation celebrates the love we still share despite the strife. Yes, our family knows loss upon loss. More surely shall come. But, always and ever, our legacy is hope.'

Chapter 48

Bless Your Heart

Is someone here? My eyelids flutter as I feel as though someone brushed me. I've felt this before.

As a child, I slept under a mound of blankets. Our old home was drafty; my frugal parents dialed down on fuel oil. I'd fall asleep under the weight of warmth but soon felt hot. I'd stick my feet out from the covers. On his way to their bedroom Dad would softly shift a blanket to lay across my toes. Dimly aware for a moment, then slipping back to sleep, I'd cherish Father's kindness, his effort to warm me, unaware that I was overheated. Soon I'd stick my feet out to cool them again.

On a black of night in December 1962, I awakened from the soundest of sleep by my Aunt Sara's frantic voice and her tug on my shoulder. Ignoring the persistence of my closing eyelids, she said without preamble, "Wake up! *Your father is dead.*" Instantly, I woke. Crazed, she sobbed wild-eyed, "Your dad had a heart attack. He died in his sleep. When your mother woke up he was already dead."

She led me to my second-floor bedroom window. The two of us stood shivering in the dark. I was a skinny seventeen-year-old in my home-sewn flannel nightgown. She was the emotional equivalent of a two-year-old, stock-still in pajamas covered by her coat. We watched in solemn silence. The hearse pulled out of my driveway and made its slow journey the short block to Gilbert's Funeral Home.

Her words pierced my heart. But I did not cry. My brain refused to register, saying, "Go back to sleep. This is a nightmare."

So many years later I wonder, "What was the urgency in waking me up?" Surely, this news should have waited until morning. I have had a lifetime to grieve my father. Roused, I experienced further trauma when I heard a rich relative say to my mother, "Don't ever ask me for money, Venera. I told you not to marry a man so much older than you." His cruel selfishness served as another blow to my mother. He dealt this injury in her darkest hour.

But that's family history. Some would say it is ancient history. One glance at the spots on my hands show I'm no longer a teen. I'm much older than my mother was when Dad's sudden heart attack widowed her at thirty-nine.

Who insists on waking me now? It's coming back to me slowly. My eyelids resist the tug of sleep, my body yearns to return to the deepest of dreams. I know that gentle touch on my face. It's my great-grandmother, Mamouche.

It is 1948. My father has taken the three-year-old me to his grandmother's white bedroom. There is Mamouche, a little lump sunk in the huge crest of her feather comforter, her ice-white hair fanning softly across her deep pillow, her broad smile, reflecting the mouth and teeth she gave to her daughter, who gave them to her son, whose gift they are to me.

When I approach her bedside, she lifts her shaky hand to make a little cross over her heart. Then she extends her fingers to lightly touch my face. She says, *"Dio ti benedica. Ricevere."* My robust, young father smiles in reaction as he translates her Italian, repeating his Sicilian grandmother's blessing in English: "God bless you. Bless your heart."

I am flooded with joy. I realize that God did indeed bless me. I am not my mother. Family history did not repeat the death of a husband in bed. Yes, Louis and I were asleep. But we had enough time to get to the hospital after his heart attack. Plus, the doctors had tools inconceivable in my father's time of need. Also, I do not have children to raise.

Father recognizes my own time of need. He comes to me, bringing along his beloved Mamouche. My loving dad remains with me.

"I fell asleep in the sunlight," I tell my father.

"What!" Dad says, "How could you sleep when your husband is in the Intensive Care Unit after open-heart surgery?"

"That's exactly how," I say. "The Cardiac/thoracic surgeon said the operation was textbook and Louis would sleep deeply for many more hours due to anesthesia. The doctor said, 'You can take a quick look at your husband but be prepared. Louis' features will be engorged.'

"Well, Dad, I'd had quite enough with swollen," I say. "I saw Louis' handsome face grotesquely unrecognizable in anaphylactic shock from a bee sting last year. It gave me nightmares. I couldn't bear to see that dear man with his features ballooned again."

Smiling, sighing, releasing the lock fastening our identical brown eyes, father fades away. "Bless your heart," the last of his words.

I talk with our daughters, Lou's siblings and cousins, and our friends packing the Intensive Care Unit waiting room. Our younger daughter fields international phone calls from her brother. She arranges for her husband to install home shower equipment for her dad's recuperation. Momentarily, I hope, our loved ones can peek in at Louis, in the two by two pattern of scant visitor time this department permits.

Lou's youngest sister, who just arrived from Las Vegas, along with his local siblings, need to see Louis soon. They have demons to dispel. Their family horror history came in 1986. Surgeons declared their dad's cardiac bypass surgery a complete success. Rejoicing with relief, they were unprepared for his post-operative plummet. After thirty days of intensive care in a coma, their beloved father died. They became yet another heartbroken, fatherless family. I could only pray that Louis did not dwell on his dad's death on his gurney route to heart surgery.

Leaving our loved ones to their waiting room vigil, I walk across Port Huron's main avenue. The hospital sits across the street from Pine Grove Park. Thanks to the foresight of long-ago planners and architects, patients and families can see the lovely park on the teal waters of the St. Clair River arched by the Blue Water Bridge.

My view includes a sapphire sky. It reduces my anxiety. Beauty becomes my sedative.

It is summer in September. The day is a gift of peace. Sunshine, trees, blue skies, and the river. Nature soothes my soul. Walking a mile along the boardwalk and through the winding parkway I listen to the lapping waves.

"Thank you, thank you, thank you" my mantra with each step. This is the second time in less than two years that Louis eluded death in the adjacent emergency room.

Leaving the park, I feel a mix of relaxation and fatigue, following the euphoria of evading tragedy. Because of the compassionate Willard family, I don't have far to walk. I go to their Hunter Hospitality House on Lincoln Avenue across the street.

The Hunter Hospitality House had already helped our exhausted oldest daughter and me. She swapped her briefcase for luggage and slipped from her suit to her jeans before flying from New York City. The complimentary bed and board helped us rise refreshed at three that morning and walk across the street to be with Louis in preparation for his open-heart surgery. Just before leaving, we enjoyed fresh grapes and herb tea. A posting on the refrigerator thanks the grocer who donates a rotisserie chicken each week. An odd question pops into my muddled mind. When is a chicken more than a chicken? My answer is clear. When it nourishes both body and soul.

Making a sandwich in the Hunter House fully-stocked kitchen, I look out a big window, read a sign in the yard acknowledging the Port Huron Garden Club for planting and maintaining, spy the proliferation of flowers. I see the backyard alive with butterflies.

Plating my sandwich, adding a handful of warm, homemade cookies, I hold both the dish and the steaming mug of hot milk. I walk out the back door to their private garden. A cushioned chaise lounge calls me. I sit in the sun and eat with the hunger I'd ignored all day.

Subtle scents surround. Like me, beds of flowers revel in this off-season summer. Blooms tip their petals to take in the warmth. Boughs wave in welcome. I feel as if I dropped into Wonderland. Not to be outdone by the flower display, the sky spreads the clouds in a slow slide show above.

Warmed by the sun, nourished by both food and nature, I fall sleep.

And what a sleep it is. Slipping into serenity I feet Lou's arms hold me, secure in knowing we'd again share our bed.

The sun sets, the air around me cools, I open my eyes to a profusion of colors that delight and soothe. Twilight slowly replaces azure blue with soft pinks and violets, giving way to hints of indigo.

As the all-time winner in the fatherhood category, I've had a sterling dad, a tender father for my children, a loving father-in-law, and a son who cherishes his children. Our two sons-in-law are also devoted to their little ones. All our grandchildren have kind fathers.

During our brief engagement and in the first year of our marriage I avoided calling my father-in-law by name. It was awkward, what with me walking over to talk with him directly instead of calling him across the room; waiting to establish eye contact before I could ask him to pass the peas at Sunday dinners at their table each week; clearing my throat to catch his attention. It must have been uncomfortable for him also because one day he took me aside, asking me to call him Dad.

Tears appeared in my eyes because I admired my father-in-law and I didn't want to hurt him. In honesty, however, I declined his request. "I had a father. He is dead. In calling you 'Dad' I would dishonor his memory."

"Please reconsider," said my father-in-law…ever the gentleman. "I'd never presume to be your father. But, I'll always be there for you just as I am for my own and for their spouses. You and Louis will be together forever. I knew that the night he introduced you to me. You two love all of us. You're part of my family. I want to be more than 'Mr. Rochon' to you."

Out of respect, I began to call him Dad. Over the years, I saw the direct connect between his example and Lou's character. Watching his father treat his mother with courtliness and consideration taught Louis the definition of manliness. Because his father was patient with his houseful of children, Louis was easygoing as our home filled with our little ones, their cousins, and friends.

Because his father was a gentleman Louis never heard him swear, not even in their small town, smoky pool hall or the combination bar and bowling alley where both would shoot pool or bowl on Father/Son leagues. Lou does not curse, nor does our Marc.

Lou's parents enjoyed each other's company. They bowled on the Ma and Pa League; golfed on the mixed league; served on church charities; and enjoyed their respective annual family reunions. They were good to each other. They resolved their disagreements promptly. They loved each other and cherished their children.

Back in the 1940s Dad liberated Mom Rochon from the kitchen clean up. Sharing our household chores was the pattern Louis learned.

Both Louis and Dad were masters of math. Lou followed Dad's pattern of sharing these skills. Dad set up a newsboy ledger so Louis could record his weekly collections. He said, "You'll know at a glance who paid the forty-five cents and who still owes for the past. You have a slim profit margin of ten cents. Son, you can't afford to lose track of those who were short on collection day."

His father advised him to buy an extra newspaper to carry. "You never know when someone along your route might want to start getting the paper. You can deliver on the spot and record a new customer." This strategy and Lou's dependability, promptness, and politeness helped build his base to one hundred customers. His profit was ten dollars a week. He deposited his profit in his college savings account in the bank. He spent his tips. Lou said, "My friend Paul and I always splurged on chocolate malts in the soda shop after walking our routes on collection day."

Lou followed Dad's pattern of sharing math skills with his son. "Here. I made you a spread sheet," Louis said to Marc. "Treat your paper delivery as the business it is. You can't find a way to make more money as a twelve-year-old. There's nothing like good old American enterprise. My dad and I were paperboys at your age."

The family tradition of passing the Old Newsboys' torch is the story behind the confusion of kindly Mr. Smith. Aged but enthusiastic, Mr. Smith, who lived on Smith

Street, tossed a baseball with Marc each week. When Marc arrived with his ledger to collect and record, Mrs. Smith would serve him cookies and milk while her husband got out his old mitt and ball. For the first year, he'd call his paperboy by his name. Shortly after, however, Marc became Louis to Mr. Smith. Memory loss meant that the years when Louis was their paper carrier were now his reality. After a while he called Marc by his grandfather's name of Art. Lou's father was the Smith's paper boy in his youth.

"Doesn't it feel odd when Mr. Smith calls you Art, honey?"

"Well, Mom, it was a little strange at first but it's okay. He can call me whatever name he remembers. He's still "Smith on Smith Street" to me. He and his wife are nice people. I like them a lot. It's great of him to help me practice my catch. And her cookies are delicious!"

And so, generations of young Rochon entrepreneurs learned the basics of bookkeeping, marketing, and consumer relations from the kindest of customers.

Louis' father, who was our children's only grandfather, became the world's best. Bless his heart.

Lou's loving family is a gift. His dad's heart and his mother's, however, are the root of Lou's legacy. The

Cardiac/Thoracic surgeon said when scheduling the operation, "Louis, your genetic link would always lead you to this diagnosis. Your father, and seven of his brothers—all dead from cardiac disease. Your mother and three of her siblings, one of your younger sisters and one of your younger brothers...all with major cardiac illness and multiple interventions."

Hours after operating, the meticulously groomed surgeon met with me, appearing to step off the cover of Gentleman's Quarterly. "Your husband's surgery...a *complete* success." The dark-haired, olive-skinned doctor with onyx-colored eyes smiled broadly.

There was peace in my heart that sunny September afternoon. There'd be lots of time ahead for the *What if?* and the gut gripping fear that question brings. With Lou's pillow propped to sleep in a lounge chair soon after his surgery, pain from his incisions declined. Alone in our bed, I'd fall deep into hell, jolted upright by my own screams. Night terrors put dead bodies beneath our bed in my sleep. In the following months, I'd grope in panic to feel Louis' heartbeat as he slept. But, for the moment, what I had was peace.

The deepest of my sleep had been interrupted. Grief-induced mania made my aunt wake me, announcing my dad's sudden death. Years later my late father returned and we celebrated my husband's survival. My sweetheart was alive! I was cushioned in comfort on a chaise in a garden when Dad and his grandmother's blessings awakened me. Backyard butterflies fluttered the air as I slept.

Chapter 49

Hello, Dad
06-25-17

For five months, I've had many nightmares with horrid scenes.

Thinking that I was tired because of the events surrounding Lou's emergency triple bypass surgery three months previous, I shrugged off my fatigue, dizziness, and weakness. Then I had a routine blood draw in my family doctor's office.

"Catch her quick," said Dr. Findy, as he and his nurse lowered me to the examining table.

I'd nearly fainted.

"Your blood pressure is routinely low. Today, however, it's extremely low," Dr. Findy said. "I'm referring you to a cardiologist."

By the time the cardiologist had an appointment open, I had other symptoms.

"Dr. Calf," I said. "Fatigue overwhelms me. When I walk I feel as if I'm slogging through a marshland. I'm dragging my legs. My heartbeat gets rapid."

It was such a strange sensation. I felt as though a stallion invaded my body. This huge horse bolted out of his stall and raced the track inside my chest. His hooves smashed against my innards. Just as suddenly, he was gone. But he kept thundering back again.

"Sleep disturbances are now routine," I said. "I wake time and time again because my heart is beating very fast. There's an overwhelming weight on my rib cage. My finger automatically rubs my chest to slow the beats. My hand presses on my heart. Rubbing and applying pressure helps lighten the weight that feels like bricks piled high on my chest. Even when I've slept all night I awaken exhausted and drenched in sweat. I feel an unseen steamroller moving across my upper body, crushing me in its wake. Sometimes it helps to change position."

"Hmmm," said Dr. Calf. "We'll start with some tests in the cardiology lab."

These progressed from a simple stress test to an echogram. Then they became invasive procedures in a hospital and required anesthesia. Staff scheduled me for an esophageal scope. Then they set up a heart catherization.

"You seem pretty calm about these tests," Louis said, pacing around the hospital waiting lounge. "I figured you'd be worried."

"You're right, honey. I'm kinda surprised myself. Maybe it has to do with my dreams."

"Your dreams?"

"Ya, for some reason, the nightmares are gone. Instead my dad keeps showing up. He wanders around in my head. Now, we're starting to have conversations."

"Conversations? Honey, your dad died an awful long time ago!"

"I know it sounds weird. But really, Lou, it's comforting."

Last night my father's appearance was a longed-for sweet dream.

"Welcome," I said. "I'm so glad you came."

His brown eyes met mine. His smile matched mine. Dad's mouth looks better because it's proportioned. I inherited the large mouth and big teeth but mine is a small face.

Father lifted one eyebrow as if in a tease. He smiled in his signature fashion, the left edge of his upper lips in a slight lift. His gaze didn't waver. He waited patiently until I finally saw what he meant.

What I'd said was just silly.

Dad hadn't just come. He'd been here all the while.

His voice took me back to Youngstown, Ohio and from there to Michigan where I saw our home next to his village barber shop. His words stilled my runaway heartbeat. "Don't worry, Bounce. It's all under control."

Pumping and pounding with beats slow, rapid, and finally steady, my heart responded to Father's message, "I'm here, Bounce. I'm here."

Whoa, I thought. It's been fifty-five years since I heard my nickname. Mom and Dad said I never walked, skipped, or ran. They thought I just bounced.

Maybe I was about to get my bounce back. That would be just great.

This was only our third conversation since Dad's death.

The first time my dead father and I talked was the morning after he had a massive heart attack in his sleep. I was praying to die too but Dad interrupted me. I saw no reason to live but Father disagreed.

"Just wait and see, honey. Your heart will heal. Tough times won't last forever."

"But you don't understand. I don't want to live without you."

"Oh, I'm always going to be with you. Your life will be long and full of joys you can't even imagine now."

"I sure hope you're right, Daddy."

Indeed, in the fifty-five years since my father's death I've had much more happiness than sorrow. I loved my university days and I enjoy my profession. I spent forty-eight years of my future with those Dad had never met. The sweet man I married, our children and theirs continue to fill my life with their love.

Our second conversation took place thirty-eight years after Dad's death.

"Dad, remember when Mom lay dying? You two had a brief marriage but an everlasting love. I knew you were with her, tenderly welcoming your sweetheart."

Father gave me his wide smile.

Because my sister Camille, husband, and I took shifts staying with Mom in the hospice center I was not with Mother when she died. I was on my way and phoned.

Camille said, "This is eerie. You called just as Mom died. The doctor is about to confirming her passing." "She opened her eyes. She had a faraway look, smiled, and soon she died."

Somehow, I knew she heard Dad whisper, "Come on home, darling. Come home with me." It was as though I eavesdropped as Mother waited to hear Father's welcome.

Anticipating tomorrow's heart catherization focused my attention on Dad's presence. The word "death" dominates the medical forms. I'll eagerly sign my permission, acknowledging that some don't survive the procedure ahead.

Dad certainly would have signed this form when his heart troubles began. He never could have imagined such a sophisticated test in 1962.

Surely, I'll awaken once they've filled me with dye, x-rayed my innards, located the problem, and, perhaps, inserted stents. But if I "die before I wake" as in my childhood rhyme, there's the gift of the mother of Jesus. In elementary school, I learned to request that she "pray for us sinners now and at the hour of our deaths."

Father's presence was a great comfort, a reminder that he's always been with me. By extension, that means that even if I should die during the heart catherization, I'll also be with my loved ones forever.

Of course, I immediately thought it was strange that unseen forces enabled my teenage conversation with my late father. But our talk was so soothing that I decided to just accept the gift. That reaction opened me to subsequent conversations with my continuously dead dad. Instead of trying to figure out how or why, I decided to simply trust what I experienced.

Nor are my personal conversations with my dead dad unique. Others related their own mysterious messages.

Chris, my lifelong friend, said, "My dad decided to donate his body upon his death. We had a Memorial Service. Two years later, the medical school completed their research and cremated his remains. They gave Mom the urn and she set the date to bury it in their cemetery plot. My brother and I told Mother we planned to fly in from our homes in North Carolina and New York respectively.

"Two days later our mother phoned each of us to tell us not to fly home. She told us that she dreamed of our dad and he said we shouldn't come.

"Good thing we listened and cancelled our flights. They were scheduled for 09-11-01."

These vital messages, magic moments, special forces, or cosmic connections might be mysticism.

Clients in therapy talk. I'm honored to quietly listen and help them reflect. Mary, a tall, middle-aged custodian, was a cancer survivor who struggled with unresolved grief.

"Why am I alive when so many I love haven't survived?" Mary asked.

There are no answers to this question, I thought as I sat in silence with Mary.

"My dead grandmother talks to me in my dreams," Mary said. "She told me, 'Now don't you worry, my darlin' girl. You're not about to die of the cancer.' She assured me that I'd die of old age in my sleep.

"I know you're thinking I'm talking crazy," said Mary.

"No. You're not talking crazy," I said.

"Well, another time she told me to get my two sisters together and go on a road trip. I told her that I was real busy but I'd think about it. Grannie said, 'Don't you be wasting time thinking. Just do it. And do it quick.'

"So, I had three tee-shirts made. For Mae, I had 'I'm the oldest and I'm the boss.' The shirt for me said 'I'm the middle and I'm the best.' On Jane's I had 'em print 'I'm the youngest and I don't care.' We put on our tee-shirts and piled into my car.

"We drove to our father's birthplace in Knoxville. Dad died of cancer years before. We had a great time. Two months later, Mae came down with cancer. She died within six months. Jane was killed in a car accident three months later."

"Wow!" I said.

"And that's not all. In another conversation, I told my gran that I was getting too tired, that I needed a desk job. I was sure that I couldn't keep up this working on my feet.

"'Don't you be worrying none, honey dear. You'll get the job you want.'

"'But, I'm not young, Gran. And the thing is, I don't have a college education.'

"'Don't worry, darlin'. You're about to get the right job.'

"Damn if my grannie wasn't right after all. I answered an ad. I got a job sewing all day. I never sewed before but the boss said I'd learn quick. And I did. I sit at the machine all day. And better yet, I make lots more money. How'd that happen?"

"Well," I said, "what do you think happened?"

"This is going to sound nuts but the thing is, I think my dead grandmother made it happen."

"It doesn't sound crazy to me."

As a psychiatric social worker I came to know crazy. Some patients with severe mental illness heard voices or saw people who weren't present. Clients with substance abuse might hear voices due to chemical influences. I see a subtle difference between symptoms and sensations.

When I provided emergency room psychiatric evaluations I reported to the psychiatrist on call. Patients and their families spoke their thoughts to me unreservedly. Something about a psychiatric crisis broke through barriers. I learned that unseen forces are everywhere.

A mother named Nancy drove her daughter to our hospital. During her psychiatric evaluation Claire described her suicide attempt the day before. The psychiatrist admitted Claire to the locked ward.

As I took leave of her there, Claire said to me, "Please tell my mom. I'm too ashamed."

"Of course, I'll do that. But major depression is a severe mental illness and nothing to be ashamed of, Claire. Specialists are here to help you. I'm so glad your mother brought you here."

Nancy said, "I just had a feeling something was wrong. I phoned her at the university last week. Claire said she was fine but very busy. I couldn't shake my premonition. Finally, apprehension made me drive the two hours to visit, just to reassure myself.

"She looked gaunt and exhausted. She said she couldn't keep food down. That's when my daughter told me that her boyfriend dumped her. She didn't argue when I suggested we come to the hospital."

"It's a good thing you acted on your intuition," I said.

Nancy's foreboding regarding her daughter, the message Chris' late father sent her mother, Mary's dream connections with her dead grandmother, and the mysterious moments I've shared with my late father are phenomenon. I've come to recognize these unseen forces as manifestations of love. Our lives are linked. Death is really the only way to live forever. Love connects us. Love is eternal.

Chapter 50

Heart. Broken.
05-28-17

"Madame Butterfly was dictated to me by God; I was merely instrumental in putting it on paper and communicating it to the public." —*Giacomo Puccini*

The cardiologist just told me that my heart is broken.

Shocked, I wanted to argue. My inner voice said, "I protest. What could be wrong with my loyal, hard-working heart? My healthy lifestyle and medical history guaranteed excellent health all the days of my life."

Oblivious to my confusion, denial, anger, and self-pity, my doctor said, "Your stress test went well but the echocardiogram shows an enlarged chamber and a hole. The heart monitor recorded irregular heartbeat. I'm concerned about the chest pressure you report. Schedule a transesophageal cardiogram so I can see your heart better through this tube down your throat."

"Yikes," said the little voice in my head. "This doesn't sound like fun."

Soon I wasn't just hearing voices, I was imagining an opera. After the transesophageal procedure, I lay in the recovery room. It was as if I'd entered an opera house. Had the dissonance of my heartbeat cried out for the mathematical precision of music? Did the drama of my dear Louis' emergency triple bypass surgery six months ago suddenly open to a second act? Was the spotlight on me instead of my supporting role of spouse on Lou's stage?

Turning my attention back to my doctor appointment, Dr. Calf gave me the great news that while my heartbeat is irregular, a chamber of my heart is indeed enlarged, and I have a leaky valve, I do not have a hole in my heart.

Having overdosed on anxiety, I sometimes slipped into irrationality and visualized an actual hole. Because I feel a large increase in heart pressure when rolling onto my side in sleep I dreamt of my heart, pitcher-shaped, pouring my life blood out of a spout hole. Whew! Glad to eliminate that recurring nightmare.

Then I noticed that Dr. Calf took on a troubled expression. He slipped on the other drama mask, the one signifying sadness. Soberly, he recommended that I schedule a catherization.

"Well, Dr. Calf," said Louis, "I have a request. Please don't take me into the 'little room' after Angela's heart catherization."

Louis and I smiled as we noted the confusion on our doctor's face.

"Little room? Little room?"

Louis and I nodded solemnly, stifling the smiles that tugged at our lips. "Yes," Louis said, "the conference room, family room, or consultation room. Whatever. Comfortable couches. Tasteful décor. It's the little room where the patient's family gets bad news privately."

"Yes," I said. "I should've noticed that all the other doctors in their scrubs walked into the surgical lounge, paused near the family members, and reassured them that the operations went well. But the receptionist ushered me into the 'little room' off the waiting lounge. You met me there. I should've been wary.

"You said, 'Your husband is a very lucky man. Look at this,' thrusting the results of your attempt at Lou's heart catherization into my hands. 'The dye traces the arteries. See the bulges? Any one of these, especially the big one we call 'the widow maker,' would soon have burst. When that happens, we can do nothing. Death occurs."

The memory of the moments that bound the three of us froze us in silence together.

Then Dr. Calf joined Louis and I in this macabre mischief. "Well," he said, "even worse than being ushered into the 'little room' was the following visit with the thoracic surgeon to prepare for Louis' bypass operation."

All of us laughed quietly. It cut the tension. Our no-nonsense doctor had a hint of the rascal in his deep, big, eyes. Nevertheless, the fact remains. Figuratively, when Lou's cardiologist explained that Lou was in danger of dying, I felt heartbroken. Now it was my heart that was broken, literally.

As if it were minutes ago, I recalled returning home with our oldest daughter momentarily after Lou's operation. Jen said, "Mom, we're getting some fresh clothes to bring back to the hospital for Dad. We could've been taking his clothes to the undertaker. We could be coming back home alone."

Confused, I said, "Alone?"

Then the severity of the trauma surfaced. Suddenly the kitchen we stood in looked very different. Why the change? The reminder that Louis might have died was enough to bleach my outlook. I saw our home in black and white. It became a shabby, old house. This momentary

413

visual hallucination signaled the intensity of our family's stress.

But heartbreak didn't start with me. Our family history was riddled with generations of tragedies. If our six-generation genogram had been written in living color, blood red would stain the pages, jet black would cloak the young widows' names. Loss marred my father's childhood. Born after his father was killed, Dad endured the killing of his stepfather when he was thirteen.

At thirty-two, Dad found and married his first love. My brave parents had the courage to conceive in wartime. Father was in the armed forces. Mom supported the World War II efforts in the factories. Algonac's VFW engraved local names on our park brick pavers, including the Rosie the Riveters.

Father and Mom welcomed the first pregnancy, praying Dad would survive the war. Miscarriage devastated them. Convinced he'd been too old to marry, sure that his sperm had lost its strength, uncertain of how to be a good father, Dad quickly plummeted to his signature state of sadness.

Twelve years younger than her husband and optimistic by nature, Mother knew that more babies would come. Hadn't she seen her own mother through nine births?

The oldest, she saw her immigrant parents bravely bear the loss of four of their babies.

Mom was right. Within months she was pregnant again. My parents reacted with caution and diligence. Suspecting that building their home may have been too strenuous during mother's first pregnancy, they sold that house. Dad hated it. They prayed devoutly for another pregnancy. Mom conscientiously ate the "greens" Dad swore would "build up her blood." Cooked Swiss Chard was to appear often on our menus in my childhood. To this day, I dread the texture, taste, and smell of this dish!

The first I heard about heartbreak was when I was in my mother's womb.

Mother researched the subjects of gestation and childbirth. Reading the works of the nascent science of psychology, Mom became convinced that both her physical condition and her general attitude were crucial. Consciously calming her mind, Mother pampered her body. She lay naked on a blanket on the floor, warmed by sunlight streaming in a window. Mindful of the developing person within her, Mom began early enrichment. She listened to opera.

In opera, heartbreak abounds. Thus, grandiose orchestras and exquisite voices joined to reach out to the "little me" during my pregnant mother's sun baths.

Not only was I born vigorous and whole, but my healthy sister was born four years later.

Opera continued to reverberate in my earliest years. I heard amazing voices sing of love, magic, suffering, joy, honor, passion, abandonment, death, and yearning in our home. When I was four, our family moved in with Mom's aunt and uncle and their four-year-old daughter, Stella. Aunt Leonardi played her record collection of 78s. Her songs of the forties and the early fifties sometimes brought tales of broken hearts. Uncle Antonino loved opera. Whenever possible, he switched to his own 78s. Opera continued to be my favorite background music.

Opera inspires. It offers something for all. It soothes the soul with instrumental music, elaborately costumed beauty, inspired stagecraft, performing artists who "sing their hearts out." Opera reassured my mother. Mom's gift in exposing me to opera in utero enriched me forever. Uncle Antonino filled his life with opera. When he and Aunt Leonardi shared their humble home with my parents and me, they opened their hearts to us. Their Stella and I became friends. We're lifelong close cousins.

Sixty years later, Stella phoned me late one night. "Dad asked for pasta e fagioli, his favorite. Mom cooked, pleased to see him enjoy a big dish. Then he relaxed in his favorite chair, listening to opera. He drifted off to sleep and quietly died of a heart attack."

Sobbing, I said, "Your father was my favorite uncle. I'll miss him. But it warms my heart to know his was a peaceful death."

Just after my seventeenth birthday, my father died in his sleep of a sudden heart attack. Fifty-four years later, my husband nearly did the same. He'd barely escaped death the year before from the anaphylaxis of a bee sting. A grey scrim slid over my stage, diluting the vibrant hues that dominated the scenes of my long and loving marriage. Is my cardiac condition simply random or did stress break my heart? Lou's near-death events forced me to consider my life without him. The sad fact is that someday one of us shall face the future alone.

The century old *Madame Butterfly* heart wrenching opera depicts a clash of cultures, one being Japanese. Coincidentally, in the 1990s it was Japanese medical research that identified Broken Heart Syndrome. Since then, sadly, this malady surfaced worldwide, arriving close to home as Sue's diagnosis.

"Sue," I said, calling my beloved friend, "tell me more about that terrible heart trouble you had ten years ago. I remember the trauma but not the details."

"Well," said Sue, "I had intense chest pain and shortness of breath. My family doctor diagnosed a heart attack and recommended surgery."

"Yes, yes," I said. "I recall the tense wait in the surgical lounge. It was strange. Soon after the incisions, the cardiac surgeon discontinued the operation. He came out in his scrubs to say, 'There's no evidence of blocked coronary arteries.' We were astounded."

Sue said, "Uh huh. He said I'd have a quick and complete recovery. He was right. He diagnosed Broken Heart Syndrome or tako tsubo cardiomyopathy."

"I'd forgotten the odd name."

"The heart is so weak that it assumes a bulging shape," she said. "Tako tsubo is the Japanese term for an octopus trap, whose shape resembles the bulging appearance of the heart."

"None of us realized that you had a cardiac disease," I said.

"Well, I never did before or since, and the Broken Heart Syndrome was over very quickly. I saw a cardiologist a few times. He couldn't tell me the cause but he said that stress is often a big factor. Thinking back, I remember being so worried about my husband's poor health, our granddaughter's elusive symptoms, and our son-in-law's terminal diagnosis."

After our phone conversation, I researched The National Institute of Health. It describes Broken Heart Syndrome as a condition in which extreme stress such as intense grief, anger, surprise or physical stress can lead to heart muscle failure. It's severe but often short-term. It's more prevalent among women. It often strikes widows. The heart cells are "stunned" by stress hormones but not killed. Some people die. But the "stunning" effects can reverse and the patient can return to health.

It would be so much better if I could think "stunning" only in terms of exquisite opera. But no. Suddenly, I am in an elaborate production. And I never even auditioned for the role.

Is my focus on Broken Heart Syndrome just another way my mind reassures me that my physical symptoms shall soon reverse and that I can reduce my stress appropriately? But I have neither shortness of breath nor intense pain. The months of pervasive exhaustion, the heart "flutters," and the heavy pressure on my heart continue. I do not have Broken Heart Syndrome. Nevertheless, I must

419

recognize that Louis' emergency admission and triple bypass surgery was stressful. Also, I need to try to relax and wait optimistically for the upcoming cardiac test.

Hope would help.

In the months of Lou's recovery, friends, family, and medical personnel reminded me to take care of myself. I did so. After all, I've given seminars on "Care for the Caregivers." I've worked with those in grief through hospice. I've tried to be a comfort to families while their loved ones were being admitted to inpatient psych floors. Clients in therapy got my full attention as their clinician. I applied what I had advised.

Prior to driving Louis to post-surgery and cardiac rehabilitation appointments, I packed healthy, tasty picnic lunches. I'd drive to beautiful parks. We'd take short walks near beaches if the weather allowed. We'd stroll nature trails. I took a cooking class where a chef taught heart healthy recipes. We ate them in class and I made the recipes at home. Louis and I enjoyed good meals. I scheduled visits with the ones we love. The company of family and friends was a welcome diversion from Lou's recovery and our attention to his medications and treatment. I filled our home with music. We attended operas.

Maybe my current health considerations would have come along anyway. Stress probably played a part. Opera inundated me in utero with the mind/body connection. Therefore, I know that what we think affects what we feel. Stress is dangerous. Who can say? In dealing with trauma, intellectualizing is not preventative. Yes, I have a brain, but I also have a heart.

And it is broken. And yet, like all the other broken hearts in my family, mine sings out a message of love and hope.

In mid-Spring, Louis and I celebrated his continuing recovery. We chose an afternoon at the opera, *Madame Butterfly*, to mark his perseverance, progress, and expert medical interventions. We also rejoiced in Dr. Calf's great news that my condition isn't life threatening.

When immersed in the grandeur of the opera house, bathed in sight and sound, in the company of my soulmate I felt profound joy. Vocal and instrumental talents described love, deep and eternal. Applause thundered. The audience rose repeatedly. The orchestra bowed frequently. Grateful for the lifetime we've shared, cherishing the moments we spent that day, I prayed for yet more time with Louis.

The opera provided me with prospective and peace. Madame Butterfly and I fell forever in love with our sweethearts. Then we experienced the wonder of motherhood. Yes, heartbreak forced us to face the potential loss of those we love and who had loved us. But we'd known love as powerful and unforgettable as magnificent music. She sings her final sentiments, "Under the great banner of heaven no woman is luckier than me."

I echo her words.

Chapter 51

Aftermath of a Mystery
08-31-17

Throughout my adult life, by focusing on the breathing and relaxation techniques in times of stress I've frequently found relief, but my current chest pressure eclipses mindfulness. Panic begins. My brain begins arguing.

"Stop worrying. Your cardiologist diagnosed Super Ventricular Tachycardia with very low blood pressure."

"Ya, but remember the lecture in Lou's cardiology care class last week?"

"I'm telling ya, get a grip."

"But it feels just like the heart attack symptoms listed on the handout."

"Forget that. Your specialist said this is not a dangerous condition. You might faint but you're not dying. Shape up. He gave you pills."

"Well they damn well aren't working. Maybe I should do exactly what they said in class. Call 911 and get right to the hospital."

"Stop it. Stop it. Stop it. Give the pills time to work. Get yourself together!"

Finally, exhaustion overtakes anxiety and I sleep. Within days, the prescription reduces my symptoms and I return to my full life.

Within months the cardiologist and I agreed to cut my dosage in half. Later I no longer need the prescription. I've learned to rest when my heart gives me that message.

Chapter 52

See You Someday, Sue

1969-2017

"To me, life after loss is an abrupt slideshow with an old-fashioned projector. Memories come unbidden, hitting us in the gut, as they try unsuccessfully to fill the hole."
—*Author and speaker, Laura Hedgecock*

The tiny, blue-eyed blonde bounced over to the tiny, brown-eyed brunette.

"Welcome to the family," said the blonde to the bride-to-be. "I can't wait to get to know you better. I knew you were special when my big brother brought you to see Chrissie, our newborn. Chuck and I knew right away that Louis loved you. When we saw the gentle way that you two held our precious baby, we figured you were meant for each other."

That was Sue. That was me. Hers was the welcome that never ended, the love that binds us forever.

Both Sue and I have lost a bit of our "bounce" in the time since I was a bride. Forty-eight years have that effect. The broken heart syndrome that struck her one day, the carotid veins that clogged up her system, and the COPD that made breathing hard work slowed Sue's life. And then there was the stroke that took half of her sight in each eye, wiping out her peripheral vision.

Louis told me that in her senior year, Bell's Palsy struck Sue. She screamed the morning she woke up for school and saw that her face had changed.

And then Sue sobbed.

"Ma," Sue said, "I'm never going back to high school!"

Lou heard their mother say, "Your dad and I want you to graduate but this is not about us. This decision is up to you."

Sue's girlfriends rang the doorbell. Mary popped her head in and said, "Come on. You're not even dressed for school yet."

Mary looked at Sue's tearstained face. She saw the change in Sue's frown. Mary acted immediately. She turned to the door and called their other two friends.

"Come in off the porch. Take off your snowy boots. Quick. We've got to help Susie."

The three classmates wrapped Sue in a group hug. Sue cried and so did they.

Mary snatched the tissues she carried in her little white purse. Soon Sue and her friends were blowing their noses and wiping their eyes. Mary stuffed the cellophane tissue packet back, next to the little, lace mantilla each girl also carried in an identical white purse. Lace would lay on their heads when they entered church. Their purses were part of their school uniform package along with knee length stockings.

"You look okay, Susie. You look even better now that you stopped crying. Finish getting dressed. We'll find your boots and your books. Unless we hurry, we'll be late to morning mass. Sister Mary Janis will glower." Mary said, "As it is, we'll have to run."

And the girls went out the door.

Watching the uniform-clad girls sprint by the school and into the church, Louis noticed the relief on his parents' faces.

Lou told me that Sue never looked back. Bell's Palsy did not ruin her signature optimism. She continued dating. She got a job and a car after high school graduation. Then she drove to Milwaukee where she found a better job. Sue smiled in a new way, but she always smiled.

Years after Sue's high school graduation, when we were dating, Louis told me about Sue's bout of Bell's Palsy.

Because I was teaching high school at the time I was especially impressed with Sue's reaction. Sue was shocked. Then she was devastated. Then she accepted the change in her facial expression. She went through the whole process of adjusting within hours of seeing the change in her smile.

Some of the senior girls in my classes fell to pieces if they had a "bad hair day." Others stopped smiling broadly when they were outfitted with braces. Their tight, thin smiles masked any happiness their smiles were supposed to convey.

Some of her muscles never recovered, splicing Sue's lips into a broad smile on the left and slightly slimmer smile on the right. Sue's crooked grin never left. Her unique beauty lay in the warmth of her obvious love for family, friends, and her insurance clients in an agency.

In the forty-eight years I was honored to know Sue, she continued to impress me with her positive response to setbacks. I never heard her complain. In fact, she found humor in situations I found awful. She mentioned that the biggest annoyance of being half blind was walking into walls or smacking into the sides of doorways. She followed those revelations with her silly laugh. Here's another incident Sue found funny.

At last year's annual reunion at the family farm, Sue surprised my youngest grandchild. She turned to me and said, "Aunt Sue just ate my cake."

The two of us looked at the picnic table where my granddaughter and Sue sat side by side, Sue quietly forking pieces from her dish and the plate that lay next to hers.

Sue heard my granddaughter and reacted first with surprise and then with a guffaw.

"I'm so sorry, honey." She was choking back more laughter when she said, "I just couldn't see where my plate ended and yours began."

All of us had a good laugh. My granddaughter grinned, got herself another piece of cake, and, eyes twinkling, moved across the table from Sue!

Last Thanksgiving, Sue smiled the whole day. Three of their four kids and their children surrounded Sue and Chuck. Their grown-up baby Chrissie, now called Chris, had just become a grandmother. Sue, the devoted great-grandmother, and Chris were radiant as they gazed at the newborn. Sue's joy permeated her dining room. Their formal living room wall featured the women who made up the freshly photographed four generations. I couldn't stop watching my wonderful sister-in-law. She was radiant, once again the young wife and mother who welcomed me to the Rochon family.

I was stunned into uncharacteristic silence by the return of Sue's vitality. Their oldest son was joking and teasing. Their second daughter, Denise, and her dad grinned at her fifteen-year-old daughter and sixteen-year-old son. He returned his mom's smile and described his favorite selections for his choir's upcoming Christmas Concert. Louis teased his kid sister, as delighted as I was to share her good day. Their youngest son phoned, detailing their kids' annual accomplishments. Chris left a bit earlier, to help settle her tiny granddaughter in her crib.

As Thanksgiving dinner wound down, I basked in the love at Sue and Chuck's table. My heart said, "Perfect holiday! I feel the peace. I know the joy." And, there was pumpkin pie.

This was the perfect pie. Yes, it tasted good, but it also represented fun. Feeling the need for a mini vacation, Sue and Chuck went to a casino the day before. They won a pie.

However, if I thought I knew joy, "I had another think coming" as my immigrant grandfather would say. Soon I was to witness a love scene that would etch itself forever on my soul.

Their fifteen-year-old granddaughter didn't want to go home. Like any teen, she didn't want the party to end. Also, like other teens, she is growing taller, stronger and clearer about what she does and does not want. There are many differences between this granddaughter and her same-aged cousins, however.

Denise gathered the diapers for her daughter, and the videos and ear phones she brings because her daughter sometimes needs a break from hearing people talk. Her brother leapt up to open the door for his mom. He carried the Thanksgiving leftovers his sister, their mom, and he would enjoy at home. He opened their van door to prepare the expensive, large-sized car seat specialized to accommodate his sister's erratic movements.

For many years, doctors diagnosed his sister as blind. It was always obvious that weak eye muscles caused her eyeballs to move unpredictably. Part of the misdiagnosis was her inability to give the specialists vocal feedback. Specialized ophthalmic and neurological testing eventually revealed some vision. Now she wears thick glasses but there is still no precise estimate of her vision. Nevertheless, she smiles constantly. She always seems happy and is most joyful when she swims or rides horses.

Sue, Chuck, and their kids consider her God's gift. Because of her, several other grandchildren are considering university studies in special education.

But this granddaughter cannot speak. And so, on Thanksgiving, Sue spoke for her.

Sue used her soothing voice. She knelt before the much taller and stronger teen. Sue wrapped her arms around her gangly darling. Sue covered her with kisses. Her precious granddaughter stropped thrashing as Sue stroked her gently.

"I love you," Sue said. "You know I will always love you, exactly how you are. You are more important to me than you'll ever know. You made my Thanksgiving wonderful. Now it's time to go. Everybody is going. Come on now. Your mother is taking you home."

Sue's granddaughter got up and followed her mom and her brother.

Two and a half weeks later, in the worst blizzard of 2017, Chuck called for the ambulance that carried Sue off into the night. Their granddaughter and her little family slowly drove Chuck, following the ambulance to the hospital, sliding over the icy highway. Denise met him there. Their oldest daughter, Christine, phoned our home long distance. She knew she could not get through the

432

blizzard if she attempted to drive to the hospital. I assured her that we would leave immediately to be with her family.

Louis and I slowly drove in stunned silence over the treacherous road to the hospital. There was no sense of danger, however. We were the only vehicle on the highway, save for the salt truck blazing a path in front of us. And we drove at a snail's pace. At one point, silence oppressed me.

Laying my hand on Lou's arm I said, "What are you thinking, honey?"

Softly, Louis said, "I doubt that there can be a good outcome from any of the possibilities tonight."

"Well," I said, "Chris told me that Chuck's voice was flat when he phoned to say that her mother was unresponsive at home. He told her that Sue didn't respond to the EMS attempts in the ambulance. Then Denise told me that her mom was unresponsive in the hospital and that the doctor was about to discontinue the aggressive stimulation of her chest."

"Yes," said Louis. "Maybe they are about to hook her up to a ventilator."

My heart went out to my beloved husband. It was clear to me that no one would suggest a ventilator. So many hours had passed. I was equally sure that I was not going to share my opinion with Louis. Mine would not be the words to break his heart.

As we walked into the hospital, Denise awaited us at the door.

"Do you have any recommendations for a good undertaker?" she said.

"Undertaker? Did you say undertaker? What!!!"

"Yes," Denise said. "She's gone, Uncle Louis."

Time sped up when the doctor signed the certificate. Despite Chuck's efforts, even though the EMS and then the hospital staff did their best, Sue was dead.

Chuck, Denise, Louis, and I stood together in the stark hospital hall. We were shocked. Tears became rivulets on our faces. By the time sobbing ceased racking our bodies, staff had somberly finished preparations. Then we could view Sue's remains.

Chuck smiled through his tears when he said, "She looks just as she did as my bride."

Sue looked peaceful and, as I said my goodbye, her peace came to me. The reality of seeing her dead body assaulted me but I sensed my continuing connection to my beloved sister-in-law.

Minutes later, a young nurse stepped up to Denise and me in the hallway. She told us that Sue's prior records showed that she was a donor. Pride passed between us. And then, the eerie silence in the hospital prompted me to speak.

"Well," I said, a broad smile spreading across my red-blotched face. "Just think what a gift Sue's donation will be. I remember mentioning that I donated my body many years ago to the University of Michigan Medical School. It was Thanksgiving night, after all you kids went home," I said to Denise.

"Your mom began talking about the family grave plots in our church cemetery. She said, 'Chuck and I planned to be cremated and then buried in the plots by our parents. But, maybe I should be a donor. Why should they just burn my body when it might do some good for somebody?' I agreed."

I told Denise that I said, "On my donation form the U of M medical school said they will harvest all they can and use the rest for surgical practice or research. They have a memorial service each year for all the donors. When they determine that there are no medical uses for whatever is left, they cremate the remains. They give the cremains to the family.

"Immediately, your Uncle Louis chimed in. He said, 'Well, maybe Angela and I shall already inhabit those two plots with our cremains.' Then we laughed with your parents.

"It seemed a bit strange for all of us to be joking and competing for burial rights. But somehow, the subject of death didn't seem a weird topic.

"Your dad said, 'I fully intend to die before you, Sue. I don't want to be the one left behind.'

"Your mom said, 'No. I want to die first.'

"Pretty soon, your uncle and I both said we wanted to die before our spouses. Me first! No, me first!

"Then I recalled my ninety-two-year-old friend's advice. I'd admired her for taking care of her ninety-six-year-old husband until he died last year. She said, 'I've long prayed for that honor. I hoped my presence was a comfort to him. I know his death spared him from the loneliness of living without a long-loved spouse.' Wow."

During Sue's funeral, the prevailing conversations I heard centered on "What about Chuck?"

He's been very ill a long time. But a strange sensation came as I saw Chuck stand tall, just as strong as he had always been at her side. I knew then his military service would help him battle with grief. I knew exactly what Chuck will do now.

Chuck will take care of his kids and their children. And they will take care of him. Chuck will help Louis and I take care of each other. Louis and I will help take care of Chuck. We are family. All of us married well in that we are family, blood or not.

Bone chilling grief sweeps over me like waves in a seaside storm. Glancing at my reflection as I pass windows or mirrors, my gait appears normal. But I don't associate myself with the person I see. My legs feel like logs with my feet in lead boots. I help with the work Sue's funeral requires. The person who looks just like me is in constant motion, grocery shopping, cooking, baking, packing food for Sue's mourners.

I hug my husband as he sits at the table writing Sue's eulogy. How can that be? It's the very table where Sue and Chuck just sat with us in our kitchen.

I'm also phoning stunned relatives with the bad news. I say what needs to be said, all the while hearing Sue's young voice.

"Come anytime, Angela. You never need to call."

"Well, I don't mean to bother you if you're busy."

"What're you talking about? I'm always busy. You too. But you're never a bother. Just drop in!"

The youthful mother inside me sits at Sue's dining table. Our combined children dart by. Hers is the house that's home to me too. Her first three children are almost same-aged as mine, cousins like siblings living eight miles apart. We share our patterns to sew our kids' clothes. We pass on the outfits our children outgrow.

"Come on," I say, "pick up all these toys."

"Don't worry about it. My kids will clean up before bedtime. What's the use of putting away things they'll pull out to play with later?"

"Ya but, this is a disaster zone. My children dumped everything out of the play box."

"And why not? Kids love to play. Have another cup of tea. I love having you here."

Oh Sue, I ache to have you here. My heart cries, can it be that you're dead?

Now I recall the two of us as even younger mothers. I remember our special conversation. Lou and Chuck had our little ones playing in our backyard. Newborn Marc slept in the family-heirloom blue crib next to Sue and me at my dining table.

"Here's some photos of the party Mom had in her home for your Julie's first birthday."

There were images of our toddler, Julie, and her twenty-seven-month-old big sister, along with Sue's tiny children. What a mess as they devoured birthday cake!

"Great pictures. Wish I could have been there."

Sue opened her mouth to reply. Then she paused to gaze lovingly at our curly haired newborn. Marc looked like an angel fast asleep. Sue sighed.

Then she spoke.

"Well, you'd given birth to Marc just five days before. You're having babies spaced too close. I don't care what our church rules about birth control."

"No. It's not the church at all. I want to have lots of children. I started late. I was almost twenty-four when I married. My cousins and most of my high school classmates married at eighteen."

Sue and I sat silently as we sipped our tea.

"Please think about this. You're going to wear yourself out."

Sue gave me the message everyone else avoided. She had pluck. I'll always appreciate that. In the end, however, it became a moot issue. I couldn't have more babies after all.

Mature mothers now, Sue sat with me in times of sadness. I cried when our oldest joined the Peace Corps.

She'd serve so far from us. Our second daughter married. She'd grown up. Marc moved on the day after he graduated high school, having found his dream job. I felt as though part of me was ripped away as each of our kids left home.

"They have to grow up," Sue softly said.

And, once again, my sweet sister-in-law was wise.

Snow blew in wild gusts, obliterating the tracks Lou made following Denise home from the hospital and driving Chuck to his house.

The unreality of the evening's sudden events made me doubt what I heard. My taciturn brother-in-law said, "You two are coming in, aren't you? I don't want to go into my empty house. I can't just go into our home alone." This was an assault on my sense of hearing. I couldn't recognize the tone or the message from the six-foot-seven, seemingly invincible Chuck.

Please God, I thought. Don't make me ever again witness grief so raw it takes a big man down. Chuck is a powerful force. Physical prowess and emotional strength sustained this big man throughout his demanding career running a steel fabricating factory and raising a family. But the death of his Sue was the biggest of blows. He'd just seen his beloved die.

Through the night at what is no longer Sue and Chuck's dining room table, we sat with him. We all said good-night in the wee hours. Soon after, ever stalwart, Louis drove seven miles to tell his brother that their sister died.

Louis told me, "Now there's one less place in the world for me. I can no longer drop in on Sue."

Hugging him in response, I was speechless. Indeed, there is one less place for my sweet Louis. A weird whoosh in time swiftly placed me back to 1962 and 1963 in the depths of my raw grief for my father. Revisiting my loss was not new. But this visit brought a long-delayed insight. This time I finally recognized that my aunts and uncles experienced the same anguish that engulfed my husband.

Concentrating solely on my loss of Dad's family when my father died, I failed to see that they were in deep grief. Their older half sibling served as their father figure. He took care of his mother all his life. Now they immediately had to take total responsibility for their mother, mad with grief, and their emotionally impaired sister for whom my parents' home had been a place of rest.

How I wish I had reacted with compassion for my father's family! Criticizing my relatives in my mind tainted the early happy family memories we shared. Grief blinded me when Dad suddenly died. My teenager egotism continued to this day. For years I blamed them for abandoning me. Neither of us reached out. Maybe it wasn't personal.

Like Louis, this sudden death in my father's family was the first time a sibling passed away. As in Lou's family, this sibling also held a parental role.

Lou, the first born, and Sue, born a year later, both figuratively stood in for their late parents. Sue held the Christmas party when it became an obvious burden to their gracious mother. Louis became the whimsical Santa his otherwise serious accountant father had been. Literally, they also took on parental roles. Sue took in a younger brother's daughter, giving her niece a new start. Lou prepared the annual taxes of his siblings and their offspring, adding a dose of financial planning upon request.

While consoling Louis, his cousin Tom pointed out that the death of a close sibling can be more grievous than the loss of a parent. This sibling often shares the same recollections of music, family outings, and local and national events. When that sibling dies they can no longer talk about the memories of their parents and extended family members during those snapshots in time. Tom and

Louis felt at home in their close aged sisters' houses. Both lost their second homes when their special sisters died.

Lou's cousin Roger said, "Sue was gutsy. You, Sue, my sister, Lori, and I played in Uncle Duke's fields. I swung over the creek on the rope swing. I lost my grip and fell into the muddy-mess up to my hip.

"I got scared and said, 'There'll be hell to pay when Mom sees me.'

"Sue laughed and jumped in the creek. You and Lori did too. Our parents just laughed at all of us."

In the months since the night she died Sue has invigorated us once again with her sweetness. Chuck found her love letter left for him next to her will.

Last weekend the family held Sue's memorial at the site of her parents' burial plots. The internment of Sue's cremains brought a certain sense of closure. This was an occasion of yet more kindness and love.

The eloquent young priest who had soothed us at Sue's funeral once again inspired us with his wise words. He and the church staff also patiently introduced us to the first time our family buried cremains instead of casket. Solemnly, quietly, and solicitously he asked Chuck and each of his children in turn, "Would you like to place the urn in the grave?" Each declined. Then the priest asked if anyone else wanted to do so. Chris turned to her Uncle Louis.

Louis swallowed hard and said, "It would be an honor."

Nearly blinded by my tears, I watched my sweet man kneel in the damp earth at Sue's grave opening.

"You are so strong, honey," I whispered as I gazed into his eyes, the azure blue color he shared with Sue.

Softly he replied, "I tucked my sister in."

I sobbed.

Moments later I noticed that Louis and Sue's oldest son were quietly chuckling. I was startled, even knowing that joking and laughing is often the family's way to deal with stress.

Lou soon cleared up the question. "As I bent over to lower the urn, the clip-on sunglasses I keep in the pocket of my dress shirt fell into the grave. I considered rooting around in the hole but decided that it might not be an appropriate time to 'play in the dirt.'

"But then, it might be for the best. This way, when Sue goes 'toward the light' she'll have sunglasses."

Silently, I sighed. "See you someday, Sue."

Chapter 53

My Cousin Called
2016

My cousin Michael's voice, formed in Youngstown, accented by strains of states where he's since lived, burst through the phone. From "Hello," I knew it was him.

"Hey! Good to hear from you," I said.

Michael said, "Our family reunion was cancelled. Carole and I, you and Louis were the only ones to accept the invitation. The date was inconvenient for everyone else."

They graciously invited Louis and me to their home instead, pointing out that the four of us already had the reunion date on our calendars.

"Let's make it a long weekend at least. We want to show you our city of Pittsburgh. We had a great time visiting you last year," Mike said. "We loved that Camille came, along with my brother and our cousin from Columbus and our cousin from Berlin Center, Ohio. We all got to see Algonac again, after all these years."

"So glad, Mike," I said. "I loved your visit too. In fact, I treasure each of the family reunions. It is always so good to be with you. When our cousin Pat organized our first gathering in fifty-plus years I was especially glad to talk to you. Do you remember what you told me about your early haircuts?"

"How could I forget?" Mike said. "I'd looked at our old family scrapbooks days before. Every photo showed my brother Tommie and me with the same hairstyle year after year. Your father taught all his brothers and sisters to cut their kids' hair and gave each family clippers and scissors. Our cousins' photos show the same haircut!"

Laughing, I told Mike that our scrapbooks show the same. I said, "Like yours, haircuts for my sister and me never changed."

Although warmed by his welcome, I declined their hospitality. Michael urged me to reconsider. Again, I demurred. Together on the phone he and his wife said, "You have an anytime invitation to visit. Always stay with us when you drive to your daughter's home."

"That's a great plan," I said.

"Whew," I said to myself as I hung up. We'd already scheduled road trips to our kids' homes in Georgia and New York City when the family reunion invitation arrived. With the gathering scratched, our lives had just become less hectic.

"Louis, the reunion's cancelled." I said, "We can spend more time with our kids and grandchildren now."

I'd accepted hectic because I couldn't turn down a big reunion with my cousins. Now that we were no longer splicing another lengthy drive between two major road trips, we were returning to the relaxation signature of our lives.

Relaxing might be what my once-lost cousins were doing too. Perhaps they also felt somewhat frenzied. We'd often gotten together in large or small numbers in the three years since cousin Sandy first phoned. Two cousins and their wives are coming to our home next month. Andino is coming for his cousin's graduation and my Andino cousins are especially keen to meet him.

Michael's call plunged me into a deep reflection pool.

"Louis," I said, "think of all that's happened since my Godfather's daughter Sandy called! She'd apologized for him! His dying wish. That letter I'd written Uncle Sam set him off years before. I wanted so much to reconcile with Dad's family. You remember his terse return letter and the horrid letter his sister sent to say I was no longer an Andino. Who can forget that? Marc said, 'I'll fix that!' And he did."

Naming his newborn Andino, our Marc made me joyous. He made sure there'd always be an Andino in our family.

For over fifty years I'd had no contact with my cousins. Fifty years ago, all of us were children. Sandy's apology made me whole. I've since celebrated every gathering of cousins.

"You know, Lou," I said. "I'm not only amazed that we cousins get together nowadays, but also that they never held reunions among themselves until now.

"Another surprise is that my cousins today are exactly who they were as kids. I'm not just talking about their looks, even though I instantly recognized our shared features. Strangers might take us for siblings. And it's not only their voices either, even though I'd pick them out in a crowd with my eyes closed.

"What I'm trying to say, honey, is that they act the same. Pat was always running around. He never stopped. He still doesn't. He had that silly grin, the one you noticed when all you guys played Bocce at the last reunion.

"Mike was the dominant twin. His brother was always quiet and bookish. They're the same now. Their sister was shy and sweet. She still is. I'd never met the people they married but I could've predicted their choices. It's been almost eerie getting to know their spouses."

Last year in our initial visit as grownups, I asked Michael about his siblings before I saw them again. I wondered if his sister married a highly intelligent man. "Yes," he said, "she did."

"Is her husband well educated, very thrifty, and dominant?" I continued.

"Yes," he said, "but how'd you know?"

"Figured she'd marry someone like your dad." I smiled. "It took a strong will, with you three monkeys getting into everything."

Later I said to Lou, "I'll have to ask them if I'm the same as when we were kids. They remember my dad, honey. I wonder if they could've guessed you'd be the guy I'd pick."

"That'd be interesting," said Louis. "You ought to ask them. Wish I'd met your father."

My sweet man! I had to turn my face. He mustn't see my pain, the ancient ache of knowing that Dad never met my husband, had never seen our children.

I changed the subject. "Our cousins organize reunions because they missed Camille and me."

"You're right, darling," Louis said.

"Maybe they even missed each other," I continued, "although most are nearly neighbors. We loved playing together as children. We want to be with each other. We do whatever it takes. Why else would my sister fly in?"

It would be wonderful if all my cousins came to all our reunions. But they do not. I witness conflict between cousins. Some are not speaking to others. Some are angry for reasons they don't reveal, not even to those with whom they are angry. The slights seem unimportant to me, but not surprising. Ours is a contentious family. Our history is rife with troubled times.

Phoning Camille, I said, "Looks like we've had enough togetherness for a while. We satisfied ourselves that all's well in each other's adult lives. When I wrote Uncle Sam years ago, I wanted to know what happened to our cousins. I'm very happy that they grew up to be good people. It certainly sounds like they raised good kids too."

Maybe the lapse between childhood and the present creates a gap too big to cross frequently. We'll see each other again, but probably not as often and maybe not in large gatherings.

Much came from my reaching out and their calling back. We catch up on each other's lives and get to know more of our shared history. Our grandmother and all our parents are dead. Through each other we learn more about our family and about ourselves. When we cousins come together, our late loved ones come along.

Cousins are my living link to my father. Dad and I did not share a long saga; instead we lived a short story together…a short story that never ends.

Afterword

Dear Jennie, Julie, Marc,

In 1962, I accepted that my father would not wake from sleep. I prayed to die after his death. I yearned for my father. But I was not immobilized by grief—stunted into a perpetually sad teen. Instead I have found happiness—great heaps of happiness—joy greater than I could ever have imagined—a pervasive contentment that defies the very definition of peace—all this despite my absolute certainty at the time that Dad's death ended any hope of pleasure for me.

In spirit my father is with me always, and yet I still ache for him—the person I created as I now remember him. How much of my loss is the death of Dad? Perhaps what I grieved was the loss of those I remember as my father and myself. With his death he ceased "fathering." I stopped being his child, becoming a fatherless teen instead. How did I change from the person I was before he died? How would he have differed had he lived longer?

What compelled me to drill deep into my psyche, my youth, Dad's childhood, the whole, messy, mad, joyful, horrendous, illusive past? Why did I write, not knowing, surprising myself with the detritus which surfaces? I wrote for myself. Dad can't gain from my efforts. Readers only glimpse. Sometimes writing brought my father back. Those moments were worth the effort, pain, confusion. I have resolved my grief, coming to understand those who offended me and those whom I have hurt, forgiving and accepting them and myself with all our imperfections.

May you and your children pass on your strength and kindliness and that of your father, his father, and my father to all the generations to follow. This is my wish with all my love.

Resources:

A Remarkable Mother. Jimmie Carter, Simon & Shuster, 2008

All Rivers Run to the Sea, Elie Wiesel Memoirs, Alfred A. Knopf NY, 1995

A triangular theory of love, Psychological Review-93 (2), 119-135. R. J. Sternberg 1986: three kinds of love

Angela's Ashes. Frank McCourt, Scribner, 1996

Annie's Ghosts, A Journey Into a Family Secret, Steve Luxenberg, Hyperion, New York, 2009

Before I Forget, Love, Hope, Help, and Acceptance in Our Fight Against Alzheimer's, Biography, B. Smith & Dan Gasby, Harmony Books, a division of Penguin Random House, 2016

Big Russ &Me, Father and Son: Lessons on Life. Tim Russert, Hyperion, 2004

Detroit Working Writers

DjHendrickson, Editing

Dr. Elizabeth Harper Neeld, Professor/psychiatrist Dr. Pietro Castelnuovo-Tedesco

Encyclopedia Britannica www.britannica.com (referencing Calabria and Abrussi)

Expecting Adam: A True Story of Birth, Rebirth, and Everyday Magic. Martha N. Beck Ph.D., Berkley Publishing Group, a division of Penguin Putnam Inc., 1999

Family photos, music, scents, tastes, & textures

Goleman Daniel: Emotional Intelligence. Bantam Books, 1995

Growing Up, Russell Baker, St. Martin's Press, 1982

FatherLoss, How Sons of All Ages Come to Terms with the Deaths of Their Dads. Neil Chethik, Hyperion, 2001

Friends/family who read/share insight into author's work & families of author's parents who shared their stories

Halfway Home, My Life 'til Now. Ronan Tynan, Scribner under license of Simon & Schuster, 2002

https://www.tidyform.com/genogram-template.html Genogram Template 2 file type: DOC/PDF, 1 page 38 KB 28KB

Inventing the Truth, The Art and Craft of Memoir, edited by William Zinsser, Mariner Books/Houghton Mifflin Company, 1998

Legacy.com

Losing Mum and Pup, a memoir. Christopher Buckley, Twelve, Hachette Group, Grand Central Publishing, 2009

Lucky Man, a memoir. Michael J. Fox, Hyperion, 2002

Mommie Dearest. Christina Crawford, William Morrow, 1978

McGoldrick, M. & Gerson, R., Genograms in Family Assessment. New York: W. W. Norton, 1985

McGoldrick, M., Gerson, R. & Shellenberger, S., Genograms: Assessment and Intervention. New York: W. W. Norton, 1999

McGoldrick, M., Gerson, R. & Petry, S., Genograms: Assessment and Intervention. New York: W. W. Norton, 2008

McGoldrick, M., The Genogram Journey: Reconnecting with your family. New York: W. W. Norton, 2011

On Writing Stephen King, 2000

The National Institute of Health www.nih.gov (referencing Broken Heart Syndrome)

Seconds Away, Harlan Coben, Young Adult category, Penguin Random House 2012, p. 102 "I climbed into bed, thinking about the fact that both Rachel and I had lost a parent. It made you feel like you were always standing on shaky ground, like the earth could give way at any time and that you could fall, and no one would be able to grab you."

Sex, love, and romance in the mass media: Analysis and criticism of unrealistic portrayals and their influence. Mahwah, NJ. Lawrence Erlbaum Associates. Mary-Lou Galician 2004. Dr. Mary-Lou Galician said, "There is no such thing as love at first sight."

StoryCorps.org, StoryCorps Commemorate Toolkit

The Legacy Guide: Capturing the Facts, Memories, and Meanings of Your Life, Carol Franco, Kent Lineback,Tarcher/Perigree division of Penguin, 2006

The Road from Coorain, Recollections of a harsh and beautiful journey into adulthood. Jill Kerr Conway, G. K. Hall & Co, with Alfred A. Knopf, Inc., 1991

Thinking About Memoir, Abigail Thomas, AARP, 2008

10 Rules of Writing, Elmore Leonard, Reader's Digest an imprint of Trusted Media Brands Inc., 2007

41, A Portrait of My Father. George W. Bush, Crown, Random House LLC, 2014

FAMILY & FRIENDS SHOWN

Author's birth family: Angelo Luigi Marcheoma Andino, Venera Polito Andino Roggeman, Camille Andino, Angela M Andino Rochon

Author's Father's birth family: Angelo Marcheoma, Guilianna (Julia) Bartolomeo Marcheoma, Luigi Marcheoma, Angelo Luigi Marcheoma Andino

Father's Mother's second family: Pasquale Andino, Guilianna Bartolomeo Marcheoma Andino, San, Dom, Lizzie, Helen, Maria, brother-in-law called "Vito" Andino

Author's Mother's family: Giuseppe Polito, Giovanna (Jennie) Guarella Polito, Venera Polito Andino Roggeman, Sarifina ('Fina) Polito Ippolito, Agata Polito Rockwood Basinski, Ninfa Polito George, Calogero Polito

Author's Father's grandparent's family: Grandfather and 'Mamouche' Bartolomeo, Ralph Bartolomeo, Antonio Bartolomeo, Guilianna Bartolomeo Marcheoma Andino

Author's Mother's grandparent's family: Salvatore and Sarafina Guarella, Giovanna, Leonardi, Ninfa, Giuseppe, Edoardo

Author's cousins: Patrick, Sandy and Patsy and their sister, Patrick, Michael and their wives Denise and Carol

Author and spouse and children: Angela M Andino Rochon, Louis Rochon, Jennie Rochon, Julie Rochon Brockley, Marc Arthur Rochon

Children & spouses & grandchildren: Julie & Mike Brockley's Jessica & Melissa, Jennie Rochon & Josh Goldberg's Paley & Louis Goldberg, Marc & Mindy Rochon's Andino & Anthony

FRIENDS SHOWN

Angelo & Vera's friends: Freddie, Bill & Jeanne & daughter Mary, Carl, those called Mrs. Tega, those called Sal & Vicenza & son Sallie & daughter Dannielle, those called the Magdalenas, Mr. Lake, Dr. Wick, Angela's friends Dorine, Mary, Marge, Kelly

459

TRAUMA DETAILS

See genograms

Early deaths: Luigi Marcheoma, Angelo Marcheoma, Pasquale Andino, Giovanna Guarella Polito, drunk driver murdered by Vito Andino, Sal & son Sallie, Albert L. Rockwood, L Ippolito, Ninfa Polito George. Widowed: Giuseppe Polito, Guilianna Bartolomeo Marcheoma Andino (twice), Venera Polito Andino Roggeman (twice), Agata Polito Rockwood Basinski, Robert George.

Inventing the Actual

Fifteen Suggestions for Writing Your Memoir

1. Start with one of your memories. Write everything about it that comes to mind, creating a scene with characters, plot, and actual or realistic dialogue. Later discard or embellish, editing your work. Examples from my memoir, *Fatherless*, include the chapters entitled "Call Your Cousin," "Children of the Lord," and "Two Dollar Haircuts."

2. Conclude your memoir with the end of your opening essay or a reflection on that introductory tale. Some good endings give a surprise. Others provide helpful advice. Sometimes there's a description of unresolved feelings. Reward readers for staying with you to the last page.

3. The richer your beginning, the more motivation you give your reader to continue. The better your ending, the more satisfaction you provide. You've completed the goal every author seeks. You've built the longed-for bridge connecting writer and reader. She became a welcome guest in your world and you became the perfect host. Keep your reader in mind. Without him, have you communicated?

4. Fill in the middle using my fifteen suggestions.

5. It's easier to fill in the middle if you write often.

6. Create family genograms. This takes skill, hard work and a great deal of time. The effort is well worth it both to the writer and the reader. Genograms of my people in *Fatherless* placed them in relation to each other, prompting many memories and giving my reader concise visuals. *Fatherless* described our family's signature feature of sudden deaths of loved ones at early ages and coupled that narrative with graphics. Expansive genograms graphed the generational effects of tragedies, repercussions, and joys. A genogram might focus on medical, genetic, or emotional relationships or all these plus ancestries. Genograms use standardized symbols. Resources on constructing genograms appear at the end of *Fatherless*. Ancestry websites are widely available but Aunt Agata researched our ancestry at Ellis Island, sharing the data with all our family. Years later I visited Ellis Island archives and discussed details with her. Our memory mining conversations became her gifts to me. Mine were her brief diversions from her deteriorating health. The Statue

of Liberty is special to our family. A six-year-old grandchild called it *The Statue of Liberally.* It is my *Statue of Literally.* All my genes literally are from immigrants to New York City.

7. Calling on taste, smell, hearing, touch, and vision helps. Immerse yourself with memory recall prompts. I enjoyed the foods of my childhood and those of my parents and grandparents. The *Fatherless* chapter, "Good Like Bread," is the direct result. With the songs popular during the time periods of my parents' youth and mine playing in the background I surrounded myself with family photos. Classic movies set in these times further stimulated my senses. A prop, wardrobe item, or automobile model brought family scenes to my mind. Sometimes I could recall verbatim dialog. Other times required that I invent the conversation's residue from my dreams peppered with phrases like "soldier boy," "She's swell," "My trousseau," or "You're my cookie!" In childhood I frequently heard snatches of Sicilian, therefore I watched foreign movies to recall the lilt of the dialect. In 1967, Mother, my sister and I visited my grandfather in his boyhood home in Palermo. The

sights, smells, tastes, sounds, and textures remain within me.

8. Imagine and describe your characters' feelings in the circumstances you reconstruct. Put your reader in situations so she'll feel those emotions and he'll connect with your words.

9. What is memoir but the unique story only you can remember? We must acknowledge, at least to ourselves, that others may remember the same events differently. Encourage them to write from their points of view. One of the benefits from *Fatherless* came while I was still writing it. In attempting to put my family members in the context of their times I became a little more sensitive to their circumstances. I forgave them their failings and apologized for my own (sometimes posthumously) and gloried in their resilience and our long overdue reunion and reconciliation.

10. Talk to your reader by writing in your own voice. Read what you wrote aloud. Does your tale ring true? As humans we link by sharing the stories of our lives. Do our written words reflect us?

11. There is no right way to tell our stories, other than to avoid misspellings and grammar errors because

they distract our readers. Some travel through life from point A to point B, avoiding eye contact. They might tend to present events sequentially. I meander, making friends with strangers. I write what one memory leads to another. Remember that "All comparisons are odious." Proust could not have written my story authentically.

12. Read many memoirs. At the very least, it will convince you that there are infinite ways to tell individual stories. Explore various writing techniques. Other authors might excel at employing flash backs, building suspense, or showcasing smooth dialogue. Some might write about similar lives but in different circumstances and with distinct responses.

13. Regarding facts, it is enough to do the best you can. There might be some slight inaccuracies. This is especially true if your sources include immigration documents. Perhaps you'll change some names or personal descriptions for privacy

14. Join a critique group or form one. Writers help others write.

15. Some say, "Nothing interesting ever happened in my family." I respond, "Everybody has a story. Please tell me yours."

About *FATHERLESS*

Angelo's family is joyful, hard-working, devout, and kindhearted …except for the murderer among them.

Sicilian immigrants in squalid steel city Youngstown, Ohio cherished Angelo, who was a kind boy. Born to a widow who was widowed again, he helped raise his half siblings. World War II brought Angelo to Algonac, Michigan, as a leader of men. Hope and love were his signature features. The village embraced him, commending his kindness. Wealthy by now, haunted by the memory of hunger, he built a church and treasured his family, who soon became fatherless. Spanning two centuries, describing Ellis Island immigration, world wars, the Great Depression, national prosperity, and recessions, *FATHERLESS* hails reconciliation after a fifty-year feud. It features Italian customs, cooking, and celebrations. Six generation genograms display resilience.

Connect with the Author

A.M. Andino Rochon M. A., MSW, had a succession of professions in education, psychiatric therapy, and management. They led to teaching memoir writing and guiding reminiscence groups and grief support. The author, a member of Detroit Working Writers, was published in newspaper columns, academic journals, and award-winning poetry, and earned the Toastmasters International DTM.

If you're glad you read *Fatherless,* please tell a friend and post positive thoughts on Amazon and CreateSpace. Consider writing your memoir even if it's for your eyes only. It's an eye-opening experience. Contact A. M. Andino Rochon at a.m.rochon@aol.com with your comments or to schedule a Mining Memories or Introduction to Genograms event.

Bartolomeo-Guarrella-Marcheoma-Polito-Andino
Completed: A M Andino Rochon 07-04-18

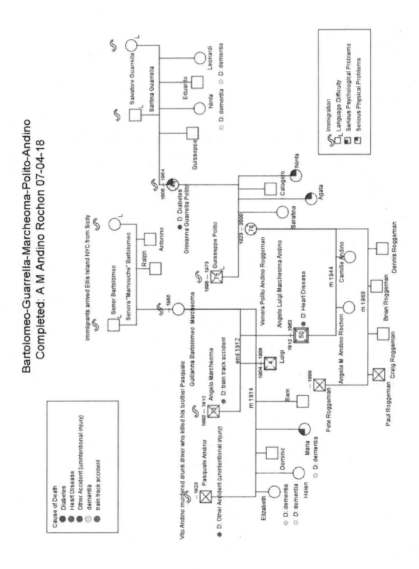

Marcheoma-Andino-Polito-Rochon
Completed: A M Andino Rochon 07-04-2018

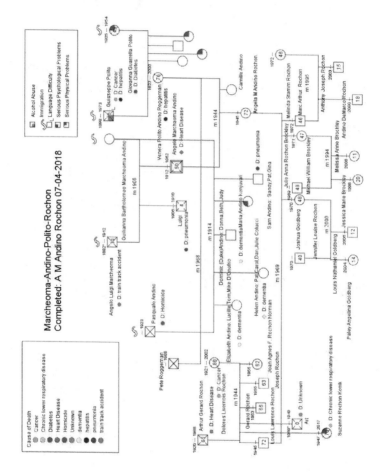

Made in the USA
Lexington, KY
07 January 2019